Britain 1780-1850:
A Simple Guide

Richard Brown

Published by Authoring History

http://richardjohnbr1066.wordpress.com/
https://sites.google.com/site/lookingathistory/

© Richard Brown, 2017

All rights reserved. No part of this publication may be reproduced in any form, stored in or re-introduced into a retrieval system, or transmitted, in any form or by any means, electronic, mechanical, photocopying, recording or otherwise without the prior consent of the author.

The moral right of Richard Brown to be identified as the author of this work has been asserted in accordance with the Copyright, Designs and Patents Act 1988.

ISBN-13: 978-1546365945

ISBN-10: 154636594X

Cover: Portrait of George III by Sir William Beechey, 1799-1800

In memory of my beloved Margaret

Contents

Preface	iv
1 Britain in the 1780s	**1**
In what ways was Britain a country of economic diversity?	2
How was British society structured?	6
How did Britain's political system work?	10
2 William Pitt 1783-1806	**14**
Pitt in power 1783-1793	15
Realigning the Tories and Whigs to 1812	18
Why did Pitt dominate politics between 1783 and 1793?	22
How did Pitt face the French Revolution between 1789 and 1801?	27
3 Tory dominance and decline 1815-1830	**34**
How did Lord Liverpool's economic policy develop 1812-1822?	36
How did the government react to demands for political reform?	43
How 'liberal' were the Tory governments of 1822-1830?	47
4 The Whig reforms 1830-1841	**53**
Constitutional reform	53
Whig reforms 1832-1841	58
Problems for the Whigs	60
5 Redefining Toryism	**63**
How effective was Peel as a party leader in the 1830s?	64
Why is Peel's ministry of 1841-1846 considered so successful?	68
Why did Corn Law repeal lead to the end of Peel's government?	72
6 Pitt, Peel and Ireland 1789-1846	**76**
Why was Ireland a problem for William Pitt?	76
Why was Catholic Emancipation such a contentious issue?	80
Why was Ireland so important in Peel's career?	83
What were the social and economic effects of the Famine?	87
7 Britain at War 1793-1815	**90**
What were British interests between 1793 and 1841?	90
Why did Britain not win the war with France 1793 and 1802?	93
Amiens to Waterloo 1802-1815	99
8 Foreign Policy 1815-1841	**104**

Did Castlereagh secure an effective peace 1814-1822?	104
How did Canning secure British interests 1822-1830?	109
How did Palmerston secure British interests 1830-1841?	112

9 The First Industrial Nation. — 123

How did industrialisation occur in Britain 1780-1850?	123
What was the nature and extent of change?	130
An industrial revolution or not?	136

10 Responding to economic change. — 137

How did the rural economy change between 1780 and 1850?	137
A chronology of change	142
Why were there so many problems in the countryside?	143
How did the working-class develop between 1780 and 1846?	146
How did working people respond to economic change?	149

11 The Condition of England 1832-1853 — 157

A context in ideas	157
A 'revolution in government'?	159
What had and had not been achieved by 1850?	162

12 Children, work and education 1833-1853 — 164

Children, factories and reform 1830-1853	164
Elementary education and children	173
The state and working-class education 1833-1850	175

13 Speenhamland to the New Poor Law 1830-1847 — 178

The Old Poor Law	179
The 1834 Poor Law Amendment Act	183
Operation 1834-1847	188

14 Chadwick and public health 1830-1854 — 195

Why was the urban population vulnerable to epidemic diseases?	195
What were the major constraints on public health reform?	198
How was public health reformed?	201

15 Chartism and the Anti-Corn Law League — 208

Chartism	208
The Anti-Corn Law League	219
Further Reading	222
Index	226

About the Author 233

Preface

Since the late 1980s, I have published a series of books that consider the economic, social and political development of Britain during the 'long' nineteenth century, the decades between the 1780s and the conclusion of the First World War and its various settlements by 1922. This book draws together much of that work into a guide to Britain between 1780 and the Great Exhibition of 1851, traditionally regarded as the apex of Britain's global economic dominance. It is deliberately written as a simple guide covering the key developments in Britain during these decades with footnotes that provide explanations of key terms and short biographies of key figures and a short reading list.

After an introductory chapter examining what Britain was like in the 1780s, there are five chapters that look at political developments chronologically--William Pitt, Lord Liverpool, the Whigs in the 1830s, Sir Robert Peel in the 1830s and as Prime Minister and a chapter on Ireland. This is followed by two chapters on foreign policy examining Britain and the French Wars between 1793 and 1815 and foreign policy under Castlereagh, Canning and Palmerston between 1812 and 1841. The second part of the book discusses thematically the 'industrial revolution' and the ways in which society and government responded to change. With the dramatic growth of population and people living in towns, the shift from small-scale to factory-based manufacture and growing criticism of the cost and effectiveness of working-class schooling and of provision for the poor, the state took an increasingly important role in social control through local and national action.

1 Britain in the 1780s

From the 1780s, writers tried to make sense of a Britain of increasing contrasts. Thomas Carlyle[1] stated in *Signs of the Times* in 1829 that:

'Were we required to characterise this age of ours by any single epithet, we should be tempted to call it, not an Heroical, Devotional, Philosophical, or Moral Age, but, above all others, the Mechanical Age. It is the Age of Machinery...Nothing is now done directly, or by hand...Our old modes of exertion are all discredited and thrown aside'.

Ten years earlier, the poet John Clare[2] saw things differently:

'My hopes of bettering my station with the world was agen and I started for Wisbeach [in Cambridgeshire] with a timid sort of pleasure and when I got to Glinton turnpike I turnd back to look on the old church as if I was going in to another contry. Wisbeach was a foreign land to me for I had never been above 8 miles from home in my life and I coud not fancy england much larger then the part I knew...In these journeys I had haunted spots to pass as the often heard tales of ghosts and hobgoblins had made me very fearful to pass such places at night it being often dark ere I got there.'

England in the 1780s was in some respects very 'modern'. It was a country of rapid industrial change where a growing population was being drawn to the expanding towns and cities of the north and midlands. It was a land of canals and newly surfaced roads feeding economic growth. It was also an old country. In the 1780s, the tensions between change and continuity were unresolved and in some ways, they remained unresolved in 1846. For many contemporaries, Britain was a country of opposing poles: improvement and resistance, modernity and tradition, change and continuity, Englishness and cultural and linguistic nationalism, north and south, rich and poor. As is always the case, reality was far less clear-cut and far more complex than the rhetoric suggested.

---

[1] Thomas Carlyle (1795-1881) was one of the leading critics of the impact of industrialisation on England.
[2] John Clare (1793-1864) was the son of a farm worker from Northamptonshire. His poems mourn the passing of the old way of life in the countryside. He was in an asylum for the last twenty-five years of his life.

In what ways was Britain a country of economic diversity?

Population had been growing since the first half of the eighteenth century. By the first national census[3] in 1801 it had reached 15.7 million and by 1831 some 24.1 million. The reasons for this were straightforward. The birth rate[4] increased and the death rate[5] fell after the 1750s. Women married younger at just below twenty-five years so increasing childbearing years.[6] Historians disagree about the reasons behind these trends. Decline in 'killer' diseases like smallpox, improving living conditions, economic prosperity encouraging early marriage and higher life expectancy are suggested causes of growth. Whether there was a single cause or whether as is more likely there were several, growth was far from even. In England and Wales between 1750 and 1800, the annual average population increase was 0.7 per cent compared to 1.8 per cent for the following fifty years. For Scotland and Ireland, the figures respectively were 0.5 and 1.6 per cent and 1.1 and 0.6 per cent.

Population growth stimulated demand for raw materials, manufactured goods, food and services that could be produced by the growing reservoir of available labour. Manufacturing industries, whether in the areas of dynamic growth like cotton textiles or in traditional artisan-based trades, expanded. The service sector saw growth with increased demand for domestic, medical and legal services and the creation of new professions to support expanding industries, towns and agriculture. Population growth stimulated urban growth with internal migration especially to the newer urban centres of production and to London. Urban growth too was far from even. Urban growth had its costs as well as benefits. It heightened squalor with many migrants finding they had exchanged rural for urban slums. There were higher levels of mortality especially among the labouring population, increasing exploitation in the workplace and a growing gulf between rich and poor.

An Agricultural Revolution

Farming dominated the British economy in the 1780s.[7] The previous

---

[3] A census is a count of the population. Census data is a valuable source for historians.
[4] Birth rate is measured as births per year per thousand of the population
[5] Death rate. The number of people who die each year per thousand of the population
[6] The age of marriage fell in the eighteenth century from around 28 years to 26 years for women. This increased the childbearing period.
[7] Agricultural Revolution. The sweeping changes that took place in British agriculture over the period 1750-1850 in response to the increased demand for food from a rapidly expanding population. Recent research has shown these

century had seen major changes particularly in the use of arable land. Turnips and crops like clover ended the need for fallow land. Cheaper iron making led to major developments in ploughs though it was not until after 1850 that machines were widely used. Selective breeding increased the quality and quantity of meat and dairy produce. Enclosure of the lighter arable land led to better use of land.[8] This transformed the rural landscape. A pattern of field, stonewall and hedgerow already existed in northern and western England and in Wales and in much of eastern England which had already been enclosed. For central England, the open fields remained. Here the modern chequer-board pattern of small fields replaced the open landscape in a generation. Enclosure may have led to the dominance of large farms in southern England but most farming was on a much smaller scale. In Yorkshire, for instance, seventy per cent of farms were less than one hundred acres and across the Pennines in Lancashire and Cheshire the figure was ninety per cent.

The growing needs of population, as well as the increased profitability of farming during the French Wars, pushed back the margins of arable land as never before. By 1820, twenty-five million quarters of corn were produced annually compared to fifteen million in 1760. This was not enough. From the 1760s, Britain relied on imports of wheat to feed its growing population. Urban growth could not have been sustained without this. The French Wars marked a high point in British farming.[9] Farmers invested heavily in improving their land, borrowing funded from high grain prices. Falling prices, a collapse from 127 shillings a quarter in 1812 to 74 shillings within two years, and cheaper continental imports after 1815 brought problems for arable tenant farmers.[10] It led to successful demands for protection. The Corn Laws were passed in 1815.[11] Urban and industrial Britain saw the Corn Laws as a means of keeping food prices artificially high and of supporting farming at the expense of

---

changes to be only part of a much larger, ongoing process of development. Changes of the latter half of the eighteenth century included the enclosure of open fields, the introduction of four-course rotation together with new fodder crops such as turnip, and the development of improved breeds of livestock. Many of the changes were in fact underway before 1750 and other breakthroughs, such as farm mechanisation, did not occur until after 1850

[8] Enclosure turned the large open or strip fields into smaller fields with hedges or fences. In England and Wales, land was enclosed for arable farming. In Scotland, land was 'cleared' of people to make way for sheep.

[9] The French Wars lasted, on and off from 1793 to 1815. First, Britain fought against revolutionary France and then against Napoleon Bonaparte.

[10] Tenant farmers rented land.

[11] The Corn Laws 1815 provided protection for farmers by banning the import of foreign wheat until English prices reached certain figures. It proved to be a very unpopular law for many living in towns.

manufacturing industry.[12] The advantage farmers thought they would gain was far outweighed by the propaganda advantage gained by its opponents. High costs certainly made wheat farming difficult when prices were low. Many farmers complained of 'depression' after 1815 through to the mid-1830s. Those who survived did so by reducing labour costs significantly. This was paid for through the 'distress' of agricultural labourers especially in southern England where little alternative employment was available.

The role of agriculture in the English economy was showing signs of declining national importance by the 1820s. This was less so in Wales, Scotland and Ireland where farming remained important. In Wales in the 1780s, around seventy per cent of the working population worked in self-contained farming communities. Demand for farm tenancies remained high but land hunger and the ignorance of new techniques limited improvement. Similar problems existed in Ireland where sub-division of land meant that almost two-thirds of all holdings were below fifteen acres. Ireland was also an important exporter of grain and livestock to England. There was, however, a trend away from arable to pasture and livestock prices fell less dramatically than grain. Perceptive landlords soon recognised that urban growth meant markets for Irish meat. In 1825 47,000 Irish cattle were exported rising to 98,000 ten years later. In Scotland, there was a clear difference between the improving farming of the Lowlands and the more traditional methods used in the Highlands. Scottish pioneers developed the threshing machine in 1786 and the horse-drawn reaper in 1826 and, more importantly, new methods of field drainage that allowed a revolution on Britain's heavy clay soils after 1840.

An 'Industrial Revolution'.

Between 1750 and 1850 the British economy experienced a very rapid and, by international standards, pronounced growth in manufacturing.[13] The proportion of the labour force[14] employed in industry, whether in the

---

[12] Protection. Support for the imposition of tariffs on overseas imports to limit, or prohibit, the entry of such imports into the home market, thus protection home producers from competition. The opposite of free trade. The Corn Laws were the most controversial form of protection in this period. After they were repealed in 1846 the Conservative Party split into Peelite Conservatives and Protectionist Tories led by Lord Derby and Benjamin Disraeli.

[13] Industrial Revolution. The sudden acceleration of technical and economic development that began in Britain in the second half of the 18th century. The traditional agrarian economy was replaced by one dominated by machinery and manufacturing, made possible through technical advances such as the steam engine.

[14] Labour means the available workforce. This consisted of skilled workers or artisans as well as semi-skilled and unskilled manual workers.

manufacturing or service sectors increased, and the proportion employed in farming fell. The textile, iron and coal industries underwent dramatic change as new technologies and new markets stimulated growth on an unprecedented scale. This traditional view of an 'industrial revolution' provides only part of the picture. The experience of cotton textiles was not typical of manufacturing industries. There was no general triumph of steam power or the factory system by 1850. Growth was modest. There was no great leap forward for the economy despite the experience of cotton production. Change took place on a far broader canvas. There was growth of a far less dynamic nature in a whole range of traditional industries. Most employment in manufacturing industries remained small-scale, handicraft activities producing for local and regional markets. These trades were hardly affected by new technology. It was the wider use and division of labour[15] that allowed output to grow. Economic transition was the result of the combination of old and new processes. Steam power did not replace waterpower at a stroke. Work organisation was varied and factories coexisted with domestic production,[16] artisan workshops and large-scale mining and metal producing industries. Change varied across industries and regions. Lancashire may have seen vigorous industrial development but in Norfolk and Suffolk, the woollen textile industry declined in the face of competition from the more advanced and mechanised production of Yorkshire.

The industrial landscape changed under the impact of the 'industrial revolution'. Industrialisation in the eighteenth century occurred largely in the countryside and rural industry was domestic often in conjunction with farming. This industry was capable of mass production and of supplying regional, national and international markets. The move of some industries to factories did not lead to the emergence of the modern industrial landscape. Waterpower did not create smoke or dirt. Only when coal and steam were used directly did towns become blackened and their air and water polluted. Steam power led to larger concentrations of industries, often near canals or navigable rivers, and of the labourers needed to work in them. The move from the rural cottage industry to the urban factory is over-exaggerated. As late as 1851, most people employed in Britain worked in the unmechanised sectors of the economy.

The market, local, regional, national or international, was at the heart of the economy in the 1780s. The transport of bulky good, and a reduction in the cost of carriage, was made easier by the development of the canal network in the second half of the eighteenth century and by

---

[15] Division of labour. Instead of one person making an item, the process is divided up and undertaken by different people speeding up production

[16] Domestic production is sometimes called outworking or cottage industry and largely took place in the home.

railways after 1830. Coastal and river transport became increasingly important but Britain remained predominantly a horse-drawn society until the late nineteenth century. The last half of the eighteenth century saw growing demands for consumer goods. London, for instance, used over three million tons of coal each year and thousands of cattle, sheep and fowl were driven to the London food markets from Wales, Scotland and Ireland. The experience of London was paralleled in the growing cities of the Midlands and the North. Population growth stimulated home demand for cloth, leather for shoes, bricks, pottery, iron pots and pans. Growing consumption influenced, and was in turn influenced by, trade and economic growth.

How was British society structured?

All societies are, to some degree, stratified or divided into different social groups. These groups may be in competition with each other for social control or wealth. They may be functional, defined by their contribution to society. They may share common 'values', have a common 'national identity' or they may form part of a society in which different 'values' coexist with varying degrees of success or conflict. What was British society like in 1780?

The working population

The labouring population made up the bulk of society consisting of those who earned their wages largely through manual work. There were, however, important differences within the working population. People worked in rural or urban environments. Their employment was agricultural, manufacturing or in the growing service sector. Some were skilled, others semi-skilled or unskilled. They were male or female. Agricultural labourers formed a major part of the workforce in rural Britain. There was, however, a distinction between the low waged southern English counties where little alternative employment was available and the higher waged northern counties where farmers had to compete for labour with expanding urban manufacturing industries. Within rural communities there was an important hierarchy based upon levels of skills that paralleled levels of income. Bird-scarers, generally children, were at the base of the hierarchy while ploughmen were at the top. Only the better-educated shepherds had greater status.

The same hierarchy of skill existed in industrial Britain and the distinction between skilled and unskilled or general labourers was one of enduring importance. Artisans formed the 'aristocracy of labour', highly paid and relatively secure in traditional trades largely unchanged by the industrial revolution. They guarded their skills, developed through the process of apprenticeship, against 'dilution' by semi-skilled workers who were paid less. Skilled factory workers, like the fine-cotton spinners and weavers of Lancashire, benefited from new technology. Others like handloom weavers and framework knitters became redundant. The creation of new skills during the industrial revolution led to the gradual creation of new skilled elites: foremen, overseers, mechanics and technicians as well as managers. Semi-skilled and unskilled manual labour was more vulnerable to economic fluctuations and to unemployment or under-employment. Men were generally able to push women to the lower-paid margins of manufacturing. In the textile industries, for instance, men dominated new technology like the self-acting spinning 'mule' perfected in the early 1820s.[17] The 'sweated trades' or the growing demands for domestic servants, low skill, low pay, long hours, was the destination for many women.

The diversity of experience is at its starkest in the debate over whether working-class standards of living rose or fell between the 1780s and 1840s. Some workers, like navvies, experienced rising wages while others, for example handloom weavers, saw their income decline. This should not be surprising. There were always winners and losers of economic change especially when new technology made skills redundant. Even within the same occupation wages varied. In the 1810s printers earned 12-19 shillings in Scotland, 18-22 shillings in northern England, 18-24 shillings in the south east and as much as 25 shillings in London. The difference between the skilled London artisan and a Scottish crofter was, in many respects, as great as that between a member of the aristocracy and a prosperous shopkeeper. Yet, both often shared a common sense of resentment and disillusion at the inequalities in society.

The middle-classes

The middle-classes were increasingly defined as a 'class' in the late-eighteenth century. They were distinguished from the aristocratic elite by the need to earn a living and from the labouring population by their property, however small, represented by stock in trade and tools or by educational investment in skills or expertise. As a class, they benefited from the changes in the economy and, though not exclusively urban, were increasingly found in the growing provincial towns. Their homogeneity as a class came from their growing acceptance of a common social and

---

[17] Samuel Crompton developed the mule in the later 1770s. It took forty years to turn it into a major force in cotton production.

political ideology. This had three strands. First, evangelicalism[18], whether Anglican or Nonconformist, provided a firm religious foundation grounded in a 'call to seriousness'.[19] This contrasted with the immoral behaviour of the aristocracy. It emphasised the virtues of hard work, plain and moral living, respectable family life and above all conscience. This converted middle-class occupations like the law, medicine, the Church and the armed forces into 'callings' or vocations. The ideas of Jeremy Bentham[20] also allowed attacks on the inefficiency of the aristocratic conception of society. Tradition, restriction and 'influence', the values of landed society, were compared, generally unfavourably, with the middle-class virtues of order, discipline, merit and application. Finally, Political Economy provided an economic justification for their growing power with its focus on the freedom of the market and the virtue of individual enterprise. The middle-classes promoted their ideology with missionary zeal.

In the 1780s the middle-classes embraced at one end city bankers and large industrialists with incomes from investment and profits of over £500 per year and at the other extreme small shopkeepers and clerks with annual earnings of only £50. The provincial elites were a small group of men and families who controlled growing industrial complexes. In London, there were the merchant bankers. This elite, on familiar and sometimes marrying terms with the aristocracy, was not representative of the middle-classes as a whole. The lower middle-class was composed of smaller manufacturers, shopkeepers, milliners, tailors, local brewers as well as the rapidly growing number of clerks in both business and government, schoolteachers, an emerging managerial class, accountants, pharmacists and engineers. Aware of their status they maintained an important distinction between themselves as salaried or fee-earning employees and wage-earning manual workers.

The landed classes

In the 1780s, economic and political power lay in the possession and exploitation of land. Landowners did not simply farm their own land or rent it out to tenant farmers. They exploited mineral deposits on their

---

[18] Evangelicalism brought a sense of religious commitment to existing religious groupings. It was based on moral earnestness and believed in salvation through conversion and faith.

[19] Nonconformists or Dissenters were people who did not conform to the Church of England or dissented from its beliefs.

[20] Jeremy Bentham (1748-1832) was a philosopher who believed in 'the greatest happiness for the greatest number' and used this to make judgements about how society and its institutions should work.

estates providing stone, slate, sand, brick-clay, timber and coal for growing industries. They rented their urban properties in response to a growing housing shortage. They invested in government stocks, the Bank of England, in industry and transport. The Duke of Bridgewater funded the first canal in the 1760s. Landowners benefited from the profits of political office since they monopolised the offices of state, their patronage and revenues. They were adaptable, if conservative, in outlook. A peerage[21] of three hundred wealthy families dominated the landed classes. The estate and the country house were at the heart of their power providing authority and status. They controlled patronage rewarding the loyalty of friends, family and clients openly and without moral scruple to maintain their political power. Beneath of great landowners were the gentry who dominated the counties as squires, Justices of the Peace, Poor Law officials, churchwardens and backbench MPs.[22] Below the gentry, landed society forked. There was a hierarchy of owner-occupiers or freeholders with incomes ranging from £700 down to as little as £30 per year; and tenant farmers who after 1815 found their profits threatened by falling food prices and were the most vocal proponents of the Corn Laws.

The basis of landed society was mutual obligations within a hierarchical framework. Deferential attitudes were due to those above and paternalistic attitudes to those below.[23] This was acceptable to most people in rural England and Scotland where the landlord was normally of the same nationality and culture. This was less the case in Wales and Ireland where landlords were often both from an alien culture and religion. However, the 'bond of dependency' between landlord, tenant farmer and labourer was beginning to break down by the 1780s. There had always be popular disturbances like food riots when people reminded those with power of their responsibilities and of the need for 'just wages' and 'just prices'. Food riots in the 1790s, the rural slump after 1815, the riots in the Fens in 1816, in Norfolk and Suffolk in 1822, and particularly the 'Swing' riots across southern England in 1830 challenged established values. Each was unsuccessful and harshly repressed. This indicated of a breakdown in the dependency system, what Carlyle called 'the abdication on the part of the governors' with the dismantling of the legislative and cultural basis of a 'moral economy'. The market, not appeals to custom

---

[21] A peerage meant that an individual had a seat in the House of Lords.
[22] Backbench MPs were those members of Parliament without a government office
[23] Paternalism (from the Latin pater meaning father) is a difficult concept to define. On one level, it meant being supportive to those with less wealth. At another level, it meant acting as a father disciplining people as if they were badly behaved children

and established practice, increasingly determined the social behaviour of the landed classes.

A diverse society

Society in the 1780s was multifaceted.[24] Attitudes were a result of circumstances, opportunities and fears created by an economy in which there were elements of continuity as well as change. Social attitudes, behaviour and work patterns were closely linked to support for the social hierarchy. Power was converted into moral authority and ensured the stability of a social hierarchy threatened by change. Deference, whether in urban or rural settings, remained strong because family, work patterns and communities did much to promote it. No one criterion, whether class or paternalism or dependency, can explain the complexities of society in the 1780s.

How did Britain's political system work?

The United Kingdom, based on a single Parliament at Westminster, was quite new in the 1780s. Wales had been united with England by legislation since 1536 and 1542. The Act of Union with Scotland was in 1707. However, Ireland did not lose its legislative independence in 1801. The mixed British Constitution of Monarchy, House of Commons and House of Lords was held up, particularly by continental writers, as a model of how a country should be run. The American War of Independence (1775-1783) and the outbreak of revolution in France in 1789 led to increasingly radical demands for reform of the system.

The electorate

In the 1780s about 435,000 people in England and Wales could vote out of a population of nine million, or just over five per cent. In Scotland and Ireland, it was less than one per cent of the total population of ten million.[25] The House of Commons was made up of MPs from the boroughs or towns and the counties or shires. Both counties and boroughs sent two MPs each to Parliament. In the counties, all forty-

---

[24] Broadly, England was divided into London (the Metropolis) and those areas outside London (the 'provinces').

[25] The Septennial Act 1715 established seven-year Parliaments though General Elections were also held on the death. of the monarch, a practice finally ended in 1867. This meant that there were General Elections in 1820, 1830 and 1837. Until 1926, a by-election was triggered by the appointment of a sitting MP as a minister in the Cabinet.

shilling freeholders were entitled to vote and some of the counties had a considerable number of voters. Yorkshire, for instance, had about 20,000 in the 1780s. Bedfordshire had nearly 4,000 just before the Reform Act, an average for English counties. In the boroughs, the situation was much more confused. In some towns, the vote was given to the corporation or town council. In others, it was restricted to 'freemen' or to all who owned or occupied certain types of property, who paid local taxes ['scot and lot'] or who were not getting alms or charity ['potwallopers'].[26]

Counties were more democratic than boroughs because the size of the electorate was important in determining the level of corruption. There were 'rotten boroughs', like Dunwich in Suffolk where thirty-two electors chose the two MPs. Where there were a small number of voters, elections allowed them to sell their votes. When William Cobbett stood, unsuccessfully, for Parliament in 1806 on a non-corruption ticket he was accused of talking the bread from the mouths of voters. The price varied. Some electors accepted straightforward bribes. Others preferred to negotiate benefits for their town or corporation. Successful candidates were expected to show their gratitude and 'treating' was widespread. An elector had two votes, but could give both their votes or 'plump' for one candidate. When it is recalled that more than 40 per cent of the English boroughs had electorates of less than 100 and that two-thirds had electorates below 500, the importance of influence through corruption or 'management' is more understandable. Some boroughs were under the control of a particular family or patron: they were known as 'pocket boroughs' or 'nomination boroughs'. Although control by patrons was accepted, it could not be taken for granted and once achieved it had to be cultivated carefully. Since elections were expensive great efforts were made to avoid a contest whenever possible. Local Whigs and Tories might agree to share the representation rather than incur the cost of disputing it. When the ambitions of two families clashed, it was cheaper for them to take with one seat each rather than embark on the costly and uncertain procedures necessary to win both.

Elections

Eighteenth and early-nineteenth century elections were noisy, rough and held in public. Drunkenness and rioting were normal events and through the days on which polling took place, the mob revelled in the exhilarating diversions that accompanied the poll. Voting took place on an open husting and unpopular preferences were greeted with catcalls, whistles or

---

[26] Burgage boroughs attached voting rights to those who owned or rented property.

over-ripe fruit.[27] Opponents were lured into taverns where they were got drunk and locked up until voting was completed. A memorial tablet in Leeds Parish Church reads 'Roger Holt Leigh severely injured by an excited populace when engaged in the exercise of his franchise as Burgess of Wigan that he subsequently died.' Since there was no voting register documents were often forged to give people the vote that did not have it. Dead men were impersonated, votes were cast twice and the returning officer often embarrassed his opponents by transferring the hustings to some inaccessible and unadvertised spot. Known enemies were disqualified on trumped up charges. Once all the votes had been cast, there could still be disputes over whether individuals had the right to vote.

Parties

Before 1832, working out election results was complicated by the vagueness of party lines, the number of uncontested elections and the presence of 'independent' candidates. National political parties, like those we have today, offering distinctive political programmes and with an organised national and local party machine, did not begin to emerge until after the 1832 Reform Act. However, from the 1780s the number of MPs consistently supporting Tory[28] or Whig[29] positions in divisions in the House of Commons did increase. To talk about the 'Whig' and 'Tory' parties is deceptive. In neither case did the term mean a tightly knit political group, although they both came from the aristocratic landed elite, and it is necessary to give both words a very loose meaning. Lord Liverpool led a broadly Tory government between 1812 and 1827 but his cabinet was not united on fundamental issues. Liverpool remained in office not because he had a united and disciplined party behind him but because he could manage a majority in the Commons and Lords, on most occasions, and because he had the support of George, as Regent before 1820 and then as king. His long period in office demonstrated two particular things. As Prime Minister, he had at his disposal large amounts of political patronage, which he used to maintain his authority and 'manage' Parliament. In addition, the pursuit of planned policies was

---

[27] The electors voted in public on a stage or hustings. Elections took place over several days.

[28] The term Tory was applied to those who upheld the rights of the Crown resisted the removal of disabilities from Roman Catholics and Dissenters and opposed parliamentary reform. George Canning revived the name 'Tory' in the early-nineteenth century for the natural party of government that was opposed by the Whigs. Under Sir Robert Peel, the term Conservative replaced Tory.

[29] The Whigs were defenders of parliamentary government and accountability of ministers to Parliament. They were in favour of religious toleration and became supporters of moderate parliamentary reform in the 1820s.

difficult and through the period successive Prime Ministers tended to react to situations rather than determine them. Changes in direction were only possible when they had widespread support across the political establishment or if the policies were uncontroversial.

Religion

Organised religion in the 1780s played a dominant role in people's lives. Christian principles formed the bedrock of society and its system of morality. Baptism, marriage and burial were key events for individuals. The pulpit was an important means of communication. The churches provided education, especially for the poor, in the form of day and Sunday schools.[30] People often learned to read from the Bible. The language, images and messages of religious belief permeated throughout society.

The fundamental religious division was between Roman Catholicism and Protestantism, the religion of the state throughout Great Britain. The Church of England or Anglican Church was the Established Church except in Scotland where the Presbyterian Church had the same role. It was created by Parliament in the sixteenth and seventeenth centuries and its archbishops and bishops, a conservative body largely unwilling to contemplate reform, sat in the House of Lords. The strength of the Church of England lay in rural England and was based on the bond between the squire and the parson. By the 1780s, this cosy relationship was threatened by a weakening of social ties and widespread criticisms of clerical abuses. It was, however, weak in the growing towns. It failed to accommodate growing congregations leaving a religious vacuum among the working population that Nonconformity or Dissent filled from the 1760s and 1770s. Anti-Popery ran deep in British society and Roman Catholics were, until 1829, denied the same civil rights as Protestants. Catholicism in Ireland, the religion of the majority, was seen as a means of expressing nationalist aspirations and consequently as subversive. In Wales, Calvinist Methodism increasingly took a similar stance. Chapel and Church were at the heart of many communities providing a focus for spiritual and practical support and political identity.

---

[30] Sunday schools had begun in the 1780s. They were designed to keep working-class children off the streets and provided a limited education.

2 William Pitt 1783-1806

The years between 1760 and 1783 were ones of varied political success. Between 1760 and 1770, there was widespread instability as George III sought a minister acceptable to himself and Parliament. This was followed by political stability until 1782 under the administration of Lord North. Plagued by the American crisis,[1] which turned into war after 1775, North survived until early 1782. Short-lived Whig administrations led first by Rockingham, Shelburne and by Fox and North led to a period of political instability that ended with the dismissal of the Fox-North coalition in December 1783. The events of 1783 and 1784 showed that the support of the monarch was essential if a government was to survive and that the 'influence' of the Crown was still considerable.[2]

Lord North[3] resigned in March 1782. This led to a political and constitutional crisis not resolved until the General Election a year later. Successive governments did not have the king's support and had difficulties in forging reliable majorities in the Commons. Whig governments, led by Rockingham[4] and, after his death in July 1782 by Shelburne[5] worked with a monarch resentful at losing Lord North. Effective government proved difficult though 'economical reform'[6] was pushed forward and a peace agreed with America. In early 1783, North

---

[1] The American crisis. The relationship between the thirteen American colonies and Britain was of growing concern in the years after 1763. Neither the king nor successive governments understood the depth of feeling in the colonies. The result was war in 1775 and the declaration of American independence the following year. Britain was defeated by a combination of political and military mismanagement and French support for the colonists. The Treaty of Versailles 1783 recognised American independence though George III never got over it.

[2] The 'influence' of the Crown was the patronage at the disposal of the Crown to support the King's government

[3] Frederick, Lord North (1732-1792) was Prime Minister between 1770 and 1782. An able domestic politician, his mishandling of the American crisis and conduct of the war led to his downfall. He was secretary of state for colonial affairs in the Fox-North coalition, April-December 1783

[4] Charles, Marquess of Rockingham (1730-1782) was Prime Minister of Whig governments in 1765-1766 and from March 1782 until his death in July.

[5] William, Earl of Shelburne (1737-1805) was a minister in the 1760s, Home Secretary under Rockingham in 1782 and briefly succeeded him as Prime Minister.

[6] 'Economical reform' was a late-eighteenth century movement aiming to reduce the patronage (in the form of sinecures and placemen) at the disposal of the government in Parliament. Sinecures were well-paid jobs where a person was paid for doing little or nothing. Placemen owed their jobs to the government or Crown. In both cases, they were expected to support the government of the day.

formed a government with the Whigs now led by Charles James Fox.[7] George III had little choice but resentfully to accept the coalition. Faced with an East India Bill attacking the rights of the East India Company[8] and royal patronage, the King and William Pitt[9] managed its defeat in the House of Lords. Under sustained pressure--the king let it be known that those who voted for the bill would be regarded as 'his enemies'--the coalition was defeated twice in two days and in mid-December 1783 was summarily dismissed.

Pitt in power 1783-1793

Pitt formed the new government. The king's intervention was controversial but he argued his actions were justifiable because of the conduct of the coalition politicians. He had considerable popular support and many people believed that a threat to the constitution had been averted. Yet a Whig hostess quipped, 'it will be a mince pie administration', over by the end of the Christmas festivities. In the Commons in late 1783, the Fox-North coalition had 231 votes in the House of Commons while Pitt could only muster 149. With independent support of 74 for Fox and 104 for Pitt, the opposition could rally 305 MPs. Pitt could only count on 253 and initially faced persistent defeats in the Commons. But Fox and North underestimated Pitt's political skills. He had the support of the King who refused calls to dismiss his government. Pitt became increasingly confident, winning the votes of many independent members and majorities against him began to fall. Fox and North also under-estimated the support Pitt had outside Parliament. He

---

[7] Charles James Fox (1749-1806) entered Parliament in 1768 but apart from two short periods in office (Foreign Secretary in the Fox-North coalition in 1783 and briefly in the Ministry of All the Talents in 1806) he remained in opposition. He opposed the government's American policy in the 1770s, welcomed the French Revolution and opposed the war with revolutionary France. During the 1790s, he emerged as the champion of English liberties in the face of Pitt's repressive measures

[8] The East India Company had a monopoly, and therefore considerable power in India. Until 1773, it ruled large tracts of India as a private company. The Whigs wanted to see its power brought under the supervision of Parliament and Fox and North tried and failed to do so in their India Bill in 1783. Pitt took a less drastic approach and in 1785 his India Act set up a Board of Control in London to determine Britain's policy to India. The Company was allowed to continue ruling its conquered territories as well as conducting commercial operations.

[9] William Pitt (1759-1806) 'the Younger' was the son of William Pitt 'the Elder' (1708-1778), Prime Minister between 1766 and 1768. Pitt entered Parliament in 1781, was Chancellor of the Exchequer 1782-1783 and Prime Minister 1783-1801 and 1804-1806. He is Britain's youngest ever Prime Minister.

had a reputation as a reformer and as an individual 'above Party'. In March 1784, when the opposition's majority had dwindled to one, George III dissolved Parliament and called a General Election. His action in 1783-1784 was unconstitutional and he infringed the independence of Parliament to make decisions.

The 1784 election

The General Election was highly successful for Pitt. Coalition supporters were routed both in the larger constituencies, where popular support for Pitt was strong and in many of the smaller ones where he manipulated royal influence. Two things are, however, quite clear. First, Pitt now had the majority necessary for effective government and had restored the principle of a minister governing with the support of King and Commons. Despite the loss of party members and sympathetic independent MPs--the so-called 'Fox's Martyrs'--the Whigs had weathered the storm quite successfully. They had not been destroyed as a political force. By the end of the 1780s, the term 'Leader of the Opposition' was coming into use. It applied to Charles James Fox in the Commons rather than Portland, the nominal leader of the Whigs, who sat in the Lords. Public perceptions of notions of 'government' versus 'opposition' were heightened by the personal rivalry between Pitt and Fox and throughout the 1780s the opposition Whigs more or less maintained their voting strength.

By 1788, Pitt firmly controlled both Commons and Lords. One estimate of government support gave Pitt 280 MPs, 185 of whom owed their primary loyalty to the King, 50 or so who attached themselves to Pitt and just over 40 whose allegiance came through family or patronage to other ministers, principally those Scottish MPs controlled by Henry Dundas.[10] The opposition Whigs had about 155 MPs with independent members making up the remaining 122 MPs. Pitt extended his control over the Lords through George III's readiness to create peers, something he had not done for other ministers. Almost half of the peers created while Pitt was Prime Minister were ennobled between 1784 and 1790.

Pitt may have won in 1784 but this did not mean that the following decade was without political tensions. Between 1784 and 1786, Pitt was defeated on four substantial issues including defence, parliamentary reform and economic union with the United States and Ireland. His support came from those who believed in strong, stable government, and it was consequently looser and more heterogeneous. To these supporters improving administrative structures was more acceptable than legislative

---

[10] Henry Dundas (1742-1813) was a close political ally of Pitt. He was Treasurer of the Navy 1783-1791, Home Secretary 1791-1794 and Minister for War and Colonies 1794-1801. He was unsuccessfully impeached for corruption in 1806.

programmes particularly if it produced more efficient and cheaper government. Pitt was content to work within this system and never attempted to fashion popularity in any way independent to that of the king. His achievement was to reduce the temperature of political debate in the Commons, just as the opposition preserved the essentials of party identity under adverse conditions. Pitt was always willing to serve, just as Fox was always willing to oppose, and this, rather than any desire to be popular, was the key to his political career.

The Regency crisis 1788-1789

The most serious threat to Pitt was the Regency crisis of 1788-1789. When George III was stricken by an attack of apparent madness[11] in late 1788 the Whigs were in a state of disarray. The Fox-Portland group had been associated with the reversionary interest[12] round George, Prince of Wales, for six years--an alliance of convenience. The Whigs saw the succession of the Prince as their route to office. The Prince was happy to use the Whigs to embarrass his father and this proved a two-edged sword for them. The application to Parliament for additional money to clear the Prince's unpopular debts was necessary while the admission that he had married the Catholic Maria Fitzherbert secretly in 1785 alienated Portland and other aristocratic leaders.[13] These stresses within the Whigs surfaced in 1788 shortly before the king's illness made clear the dependence of the Whigs on the Prince if they were to achieve power. Fox relied on the future king for power highlighting the hypocrisy of his attacks on Pitt who owed his position to the existing king.

Pitt and his supporters framed a Regency Bill closely limiting the power of the Regent. Unwisely, the Whigs delayed the passage of the bill arguing that the limitations placed on his powers, especially his right to make new peers was an unfair restriction on the power of the Crown. They argued unconvincingly in favour of the unlimited power of the Prince without the need for parliamentary approval. This played straight into Pitt's hands, and he pointed to Fox's reversal as the champion of parliamentary

---

[11] The symptoms of the 1788-1789 attacks suggested madness to the King's doctors. Research suggesting that porphyria, a hereditary genetic condition caused by blood deficiencies, was the cause have recently been questioned. Its conclusion is that George III did suffer from mental illness, possibly a bipolar disorder, after all.

[12] Reversionary interest was the name given to politicians who clustered about the Prince of Wales in the eighteenth and early nineteenth centuries

[13] A secret marriage with the Catholic Maria Fitzherbert. The Royal Marriages Act 1772 made it illegal for a member of the royal family to marry without the permission of the monarch. The Act of Succession 1701 forbade marriage to a Roman Catholic

authority. Pitt's majority held and he could push his bill through Parliament. By mid-February, the bill was reaching its final stage in the Lords but the process was ended with the rapid recovery of the king. The opposition had been defeated. Pitt had preserved his ministry and won the thanks of the king and large sections of public opinion.

During the Regency crisis, the Whigs had made some important blunders, and disagreements between Fox and Portland threatened the cohesion of the party. Fox came across as opportunistic rather than principled and reluctant to control the younger Whigs like Richard Sheridan[14] and Charles Grey.[15] Nevertheless, the Whigs entered the 1790 General Election in reasonable shape thanks to the electoral management of William Adams. Between 1783 and 1790, the Whig coalition had consolidated into a party of 130-140 MPs.

Realigning the Tories and Whigs to 1812

The French Revolution transformed British political life. Between 1790 and 1794, tensions within the opposition Whigs led to division and gradually Pitt remodelled his government. The first split was provoked by the publication in November 1790 of Edmund Burke's *Reflections on the Revolution* in France.[16] He challenged the notion of equal natural rights, maintaining that government did not derive its authority from the consent of the governed but from custom, practice and experience. However, Burke was no reactionary, arguing that any state that did not embrace change had lost the means of conserving itself. He laid down principles subsequently identified as central to the ideology not of the Whigs but of Conservatism.

Fox under pressure

In May 1791, Fox who enthusiastically supported the Revolution, and Burke parted company. Burke only took a few supporters with him but the rift within the party widened during the following year. Fox sponsored a Libel Act. In April 1792, a group of radical Whigs formed the Friends of the People to try and commit the party to parliamentary reform. The Whigs had to make an uncomfortable choice. Burke had emphasised the dangers of well-meaning reforms leading to revolution and increasingly the

---

[14] Richard Sheridan, Irish playwright and friend of Fox and the Prince of Wales
[15] Charles Grey was a future Whig Prime Minister between 1830 and 1834
[16] Edmund Burke (1729-1797) was an Irish lawyer who came to England in 1750 to advance his fortune. He became private secretary to Rockingham and entered Parliament in 1766. He opposed the American war but drifted away from a central position in the Whig opposition from the mid-1780s.

debate within the Whig party polarised over whether it should emphasise reform and liberty or order and public security.[17]

Fox did not join the Friends of the People though he sympathised with its aims. He became increasingly convinced that Pitt intended to undermine English liberties and in December 1792, he was driven to a defence of both the French Revolution and parliamentary reform. Fox believed that Britain had more to fear from the influence of George III than from the French Revolution. As a result, thirty conservative Whigs distanced themselves from Fox and Portland and declared their support for the government. The execution of Louis XVI in January 1793 and the outbreak of war with France the following month aggravated Whig problems. Fox opposed the outbreak of the war. Portland regarded it as a regrettable necessity. Fox supported Grey's motion for parliamentary reform in the Commons in May 1793. Portland opposed it. Neither Burke nor Portland still wished to safeguard the Whig constitution, but what separated them from Fox was how this could be done. Fox found it impossible to keep the Whig party together. By late 1793, the conservative Whigs had separated from the party. Portland[18] formed a coalition with Pitt in July 1794, when Portland became Home Secretary and four other conservative Whigs, Fitzwilliam Mansfield, Spencer and William Windham,[19] entered the cabinet, marked a realignment of political forces.

A restructured coalition 1794-1801

The 1784, 1790 and 1796 General Elections confirmed Pitt's dominance. This is, however, misleading. His control of the Commons came from the support of the 200 MPs in the court and administration group. In the House of Lords, about half the peers were open to royal influence. Pitt's personal following was only 50 MPs. His cabinet until 1794 was, with the notable exceptions of Henry Dundas and Lord Grenville lightweight.[20] It

---

[17] The Libel Act 1791 gave juries rather than judges the responsibility of determining whether a libel had been committed. Fox believed that the power of the executive had been significantly reduced by this measure

[18] William, Lord Portland (1738-1809): Prime Minister 1783 and again 1807-1809; Home Secretary 1794-1801 and Lord President of the Council 1801-1805; leading conservative Whig.

[19] William Windham (1750-1810), a friend of Edmund Burke and MP for Norwich 1784-1802. He was a conservative Whig who sided with Burke against Fox in 1792-1793 and was Secretary at War 1794-1801.

[20] William Wyndham, Lord Grenville (1759-1834) was Speaker of the House of Commons 1789, Home Secretary 1789-1794 and Foreign Secretary 1794-1801; leader of the war party in the government and its leading spokesman in the House of Lords.

was his talents and the support of the king that kept him in office. In addition, the only alternative to Pitt was Fox supported by the Prince of Wales, something George III found unthinkable.

Did the formation of the coalition in 1794 mark the birth of the Tory party? Pitt certainly did not see himself as a Tory, considering himself an independent Whig. Portland and the conservative Whigs did not abandon Whig beliefs nor did they lose their long-standing distrust of Pitt. Between 1794 and 1797, Pitt could count on the support of over 500 MPs, consisting of 426 Pittites and 80 Portland Whigs. The Foxite Whigs, numbering about 60MPs stood apart. Between 1794 and 1797, they demonstrated a commitment to peace and reform calling for an end to the war, religious freedom and parliamentary reform. In 1797, Charles Grey's reform motion was defeated in the Commons and the Foxite Whigs renounced regular parliamentary attendance though secession was never complete. Pitt's resignation in 1801 brought them flooding back to Parliament.

The fall of Pitt in 1801 was a matter of conflicting constitutional principles. Pitt saw Catholic Emancipation as a necessary part of the Union with Ireland. George III could not accept this. Pitt, though he promised not to raise the question while the king lived, felt obliged to resign. He had been in power for nearly eighteen years and had fought a hardly successful war for eight. He was physically and mentally exhausted. His management of the cabinet had, since the mid-1790s become increasingly high-handed and he had taken the king's consent for granted. The king's refusal to accept Emancipation may have been his way of re-establishing royal influence and the ministerial crisis of 1801 clearly showed the continuing importance of the monarch in politics. It is also important that the king's attitude reflected the anti-Catholicism of public opinion.

An unstable interlude 1801-1812

Between 1801 and 1812, five weak ministries ruled Britain, none lasting more than 3¼ years. The Pittites were transformed into Tories and the Whigs re-emerged as a credible opposition. Pitt's large governing coalition was split by his resignation into groupings of Pittites (60), Addingtonians (30-40), Grenvilles (20-30) and Canningites (10-15). Stable government needed the alliance of at least two parts of the old Pittite coalition to lead the Court and Treasury grouping. It took eleven years before three of these groups reunited under Lord Liverpool.

Addington 1801-1804

Henry Addington formed his administration in 1801. Pitt had readily agreed not to oppose the ministry as Addington's condition for accepting office. Canning refused to serve and, although Portland remained in office, Windham and Spencer left. In 1802, Grenville went into opposition against the Treaty of Amiens and, with Windham, formed a separate war party of about thirty MPs. Despite Pitt's neutrality, Addington's ineffectiveness and the renewal of war in 1803 could not delay the inevitable. In April 1804, he resigned and Pitt returned for a second time.

Pitt returns 1804-1806

Pitt could not reunite his old supporters between 1804 and his death in January 1806. The Fox-Grenville group deprived him of support and he did not enjoy assistance from Addington. His ministry was unstable and narrow. However, initially the opposition was disunited. The Grenvilles did not understand the personal animosity between Pitt and Fox and the two opposition groups took time to work together effectively. By late 1805, however, the opposition coalition was performing well and there was little doubt that an effective opposition existed for the first time since 1791.

'All the Talents' 1806-1807

George III had no alternative after Pitt's death but to turn to Grenville and, with reluctance, Fox. The 'Ministry of All the Talents', as it was widely dubbed, was led by Grenville, with Fox as Foreign Secretary and, though Whig-dominated, was a coalition of politicians including the group round Addington, who became Viscount Sidmouth in 1805. No action was taken on religious concessions to Ireland or parliamentary reform, both of which were unacceptable to the Addington. Fox's death in September removed the ministry's most talented member and the 1806 General Election added little to its popular support. The war was going badly, the king was lukewarm in his support and the ministry lingered until dismissed in March 1807.

Portland 1807-1809

Grenville's refusal to give the king a written promise that he would not raise the Catholic question was the cause of the dismissal of the Talents. Many people believed that the king had acted in an unconstitutional way but as in 1783-1784, reactions to his actions in the form of petitions and the result of the 1807 General Election showed that his intervention was generally approved. Public opinion was vehemently anti-Catholic. The electorate was given a clear choice between Whigs and Tories, denoting opposition or support for the king's position on religion. The 1807 election was a clear victory for the Tories. Portland could count on the support of about 370 MPs while the opposition could only muster about 290. The Whigs did not to hold office again until 1830.

Perceval 1809-1812

The development of Toryism between 1807 and 1812 was far from smooth. Personal rivalries, which went so far as a duel between Castlereagh and Canning in 1809, and the final mental collapse of the king with the establishment of the Regency in 1810-1811, were obstacles to stable government. So too was the erratic progress of the war, resulting in increased taxation, commercial disruption and the revival of extra-Parliamentary radicalism. Portland retired in 1809 and his successor, Spencer Perceval, could not hold the Pittites together. Canning refused to serve and Perceval was unable to gain the support of the Whig opposition, which believed that the advent of the Regency would enable them to take office independently. Whigs divisions in September 1809, early in 1811 and February 1812 allowed Perceval to remain in power. His government was not secure until March 1812 with the return to Sidmouth and Castlereagh to strengthen its anti-reformist base. After his assassination in May 1812, the appointment of Lord Liverpool, despite the eventual length of his administration, was neither immediate nor inevitable.

Why did Pitt dominate politics between 1783 and 1793?

Pitt was a cautious reformer. In 1785, he unsuccessfully attempted to abolish thirty-six rotten boroughs and transfer their seats to London and the counties, failed to achieve economic union with Ireland and dropped the idea of economic union with America. These failures confirmed Pitt's inability to lead the country in his own reforming terms because of the extent of opposition. Parliamentary reform was lost in the Commons by 248 votes to 174 and he abandoned economic union following opposition from British manufacturing and commercial interests. The framework of government within which Pitt operated was 'administrative', reacting to problems when they arose rather than initiating programmes of a fundamental reforming nature. He was primarily an administrative reformer responsible for a 'national revival' between 1783 and the early 1790s.

Restoring national finances

In 1783, government expenditure exceeded income by £10.8 million, largely because of the cost of the American War and inefficiency in collecting excise duties. Government had difficulty in raising loans and confidence in a recovery of national finances was low. Between 1783 and 1791, annual governmental revenue increased by almost £4 million of which half came from new taxes, reducing smuggling and fraud and by increasing the efficiency of collection. Pitt's initial priority was to raise revenue and his first target was smuggling. It is difficult to estimate the effect smuggling had on national finances but perhaps a fifth of all imports was contraband. The finances of the East India Company were undermined by smuggled tea, which in the early 1780s amounted to between 3 and 4.5 million tons per year.

Pitt adopted a two-pronged approach. He introduced restrictive legislation to reduce the attractiveness of smuggling and extended the rights of search over suspect cargoes. An extended 'Hovering Act', for instance, allowed confiscation of certain types of vessel carrying contraband goods found at anchor or 'hovering' within four miles of the coast. Parallel to this was a massive reduction of duties. The 1784 Commutation Act reduced the duty on tea from 119 to a uniform 25 per cent and this was followed by reductions on wines, spirits and tobacco. The tightening up on revenue agencies and the transfer of more business to the excise department led to increased yields: 29 per cent on spirits, 63 per cent on wines and 39 per cent on tobacco by 1790. Pitt did not extinguish smuggling but he made it a far less profitable and far more risky activity.

The loss of revenue through reducing duties was recovered by the increased efficiency with which taxes were collected. Pitt was one of the most efficient tax-gatherers ever to govern England. His taxation policy was based on the prevailing view that all should bear a share but that the poor should not be overburdened. Luxury goods were consequently the major taxable items: horses, hackney carriages, gloves, hats, ribbons, candles, servants and hair powder plus a graduated increase in the tax on windows. Pitt's taxation policy was sensible but could be both unpopular and misguided. The window tax may have held back the development of the glass industry. A projected tax on coal was withdrawn because of opposition and taxes on linen and cotton in 1784 had serious economic implications and were withdrawn. Pitt's only real innovation was a tax on shops, introduced in 1785, but withdrawn in 1789 after widespread opposition and public disturbances in London.

In 1783, the National Debt stood at £238 million with interest charges amounting to about a quarter of government spending. Pitt wanted to reduce this by extending the 'sinking fund', a device where annual sums were set aside to pay off or reduce the National Debt. It had existed since 1716 but its value had been reduced by ministers raiding it for other purposes. Richard Price had argued in 1772 for a regularly supported fund and, as in many other areas of policy, Pitt was willing to use other people's ideas and the reform of the sinking fund in 1786 was perhaps more important in restoring national confidence than in producing financial improvement. It was placed under the control of a board of six commissioners. The scheme worked well until the outbreak of war in 1793 by which time there was a £10 million reduction in the debt.

Administrative efficiency

Offices, whether sinecures or not, were given as rewards for political services not on merit. Pitt wanted to reduce waste in government. Radical reform would have encountered widespread opposition from the entrenched power of patronage-mongers and consequently Pitt operated in a cautious manner. Sinecures were allowed to lapse on the death of their occupants. Most of the posts the public accounts commissioners recommended should be abolished in 1786 disappeared in the next twenty years. What had gone were 'offices of profit'.

Efficient departmental management was gradually built up with greater Treasury control of public expenditure by the Treasury Commission of Audit created in 1785. The Board of Taxes was reinforced by transfers from the Treasury and the Excise Board. People with talent, like Richard Frewin at Customs, were promoted and encouraged to develop administrative policies on their own initiative. The creation of a central Stationery Office in 1787 secured economies in the supply of stationery to departments. Pitt tightened naval spending where he relied heavily on its Comptroller of the Navy Office Sir Charles Middleton, later Lord Barham, who was largely responsible for the creation of a navy capable of responding to the French challenge between 1793 and 1815.

Before 1787, there were 103 separate exchequer revenue accounts and revenue collectors forwarded funds to 68 different accounts.[21] Under the Consolidated Fund Act of 1787, most revenue collected was paid into a single consolidated Treasury fund account. The exceptions were the Civil List[22] and the land and malt taxes on which specific blocks of funded Exchequer bills were secured. This marked a major step forward in efficient administration and led to economies and reduction of confusion. Initially new taxes were accounted for separately but this was removed in 1797.

---

[21] The Exchequer dealt with national finances.
[22] The Civil List was the money paid by Parliament for the monarch's personal support and for his household. It was introduced in the late-seventeenth century.

Commercial policies

Financial and administration efficiency was paralleled by a commercial policy that encouraged growing trade. The value of imports doubled to £20 million between 1783 and 1790 and exports rose from £12.5 million in 1782 to over £20 by 1790. This was a major achievement. Economic recovery meant protecting British industries and trade and the United States was seen as a threat to British commercial supremacy. Pitt's new Committee of Trade rejected the reduction of trade barriers and the Navigation Acts were maintained with vigour. In 1783, American shipping was excluded from the West Indian islands; trade with America for cheaper meat and fish via the French and Spanish islands was made illegal in 1787-1788. Pitt's protectionist policy towards America trade was shown by the passage of the last Navigation Act in 1786. If America could be prevented from challenging Britain's merchant shipping then, although there had been loss of political control, Britain could retain commercial domination. By 1787, British exports to America had returned to the levels achieved in the early 1770s and by the 1790s the tariffs acted only as a minor irritant. The outbreak of the French war led to the Jay Treaty of 1794 that opened certain markets to American shipping. The effects were dramatic. Britain's exports to America more than doubled between 1793 and 1799 and by 1800, America was taking a quarter of British exports. This more liberal policy recognised the growing economic importance of the American market for exports and the dependence of Britain's textile industry on imported cotton.

The immediate economic advantages of Canada were limited in the 1790s.[23] Its furs, fish and timber were important but its scattered population did not offer a large market for British goods. Yet, relations with Canada were handled with care. An arena of Anglo-French conflict, it was only brought under the British Crown by conquest in 1760. In Quebec, there was still tension between English and French-speakers. Canada's population had been substantially increased by the migration of many American loyalists north: some 25,000 settled in Nova Scotia and a further 20,000 in upper Quebec. The costs of administering the Canadian provinces of Quebec, Nova Scotia and New Brunswick were largely borne by the British government. Canada assumed greater importance after 1783 as a barrier to possible American expansion. The 1791 Canada Act, which radically recast the government of the province of Quebec, reflected an imprecise desire to give some self-determination to colonial

---

[23] Canada was originally a French colony (New France) but was conquered by British troops in 1759-1760. It proved an attractive destination for those American colonists (the loyalists) who had fought with the British during the American war.

development.

The loss of the American colonies focused the attention of government on India and the East, with their potentially large markets. Pitt had come to power because of the abortive Fox-North India Bill and the issue was quickly dealt with in his East India Act of 1784. The East-India Company kept its patronage but political and strategic control passed to a Board of Control made up of ministers of the Crown. Responsibility for Indian affairs passed to Henry Dundas in London and the Governor-General in India. Sinecures were suppressed and able recruits enlisted. Trade in the East improved under Pitt, though this was partly the result of ending tea smuggling.

There was an important commercial thread in ending Britain's isolation in Europe after 1783. Negotiations were opened with all the leading courts of Europe for reciprocally lowered tariff duties. The Eden trade treaty with France, signed in September 1786, was the only real, though temporary, achievement of this policy. French wines entered Britain at the same rates as the Portuguese and, although opposition from manufacturers kept the silk market protected, France was opened to British goods through general tariff reductions of 10-15 per cent. Within three years, French manufacturers were complaining that the treaty was unfairly weighted in favour of British manufacturers. In reality, their complaint was a reflection of Britain's competitiveness in the early stages of industrialisation.

Commercial considerations played a part in challenging French expansion into the Low Countries though Britain also wanted to stop France using Dutch overseas bases like Cape Town. Britain's isolation was emphasised by the French alliance with the Dutch in 1785, which involved a reduction in the powers of the pro-English House of Orange. A successful Prussian invasion in 1787 revived Orange fortunes and was followed by a Triple Alliance between Prussia, the United Provinces and Britain. This ended Britain's diplomatic isolation and enabled Britain successfully to exert her authority in the North Pacific in 1790 when Spain seized ships from a British trading base for furs and fish at Nootka Sound, off western Canada. Pitt was less successful in his support of Anglo-Prussian policy over Russian round Ochakov on the Black Sea. Demands that Russia return the area to the Ottoman Empire were resisted and Pitt abandoned his policy following large-scale opposition to his warlike stance in the House of Commons.

Conclusions

Pitt was an efficient administrator rather than an innovative minister. He improved existing systems of government and taxation, building on the work of previous governments. His approach was cautious and responsive to opposition. Historians frequently argue that Pitt was committed to free trade. This may be true but it did not divert him from the practicalities of politics. Diplomatic and commercial realities meant that his commitment to freer trade was always limited. Britain's commercial success was built on protection and the move to freer trade resulted from British industry no longer needing protection as much as the intellectual attraction of the new system. The outbreak of war in 1793 drove the British government back to protection.

How did Pitt face the French Revolution between 1789 and 1801?

In 1789, the fall of the Bastille[24] foreshadowed revolution in France. Reactions were mixed in Britain but many people were initially well disposed towards the revolution. Pitt saw political advantages for Britain because it weakened France's colonial ambitions. Some thought France should become a 'constitutional' monarchy. Others saw it leading to reform in England. The British believed themselves to be the freest people in Europe, thanks to the 1688 'Glorious' Revolution,[25] and many foreigners flatteringly took the same view. It is not surprising that the opening stages of the revolution looked like a French attempt to copy Britain.

Reacting to revolution: the intellectual debate

The debate began with a 'political sermon' given by the dissenting minister Richard Price on 4 November 1789. He pointed to the 1688-1689 Revolution Settlement as part of the dissenting agitation for repeal of the Test and Corporation Acts. Many opponents of Dissent feared that much more was involved than mere religion. In November 1790, Edmund Burke published his *Reflections on the Revolution in France*. It was an Anglican defence of the state and denied Price's assertion that 'the people' had acquired important rights in 1688-1689, especially the right to choose their own rulers, remove them for misconduct and frame a government for themselves. Religion, not some vague contractual notion, was for Burke at the heart of the civil society. He celebrated aristocratic concepts of paternalism, loyalty and the hereditary principle in which the great social institutions--the Church, the law, even the family--confirmed the

---

[24] The Bastille was the royal palace and prison in the centre of Paris. Its capture on 14 July 1789 by a Parisian mob marked the beginnings of the French Revolution.

[25] The 1688 'Glorious' Revolution occurred when the Catholic James II was replaced by the Protestant William III and Mary so preserving constitutional monarchy and the powers of Parliament.

aristocracy as the ruling class and the protectors of traditional values. The response was immediate.

Thomas Paine wrote the first part of *Rights of Man* as a reply to Burke's *Reflections* and it was published in February 1791. Part Two was published in April 1792. It was only one of the thirty-eight responses to Burke but was the most influential. It merged the debate about the revolution with a programme of practical and radical reform. Paine put forward a simple message. He denounced Burke's idea of society as an association between past and present generations and his view of the role of monarchy and aristocracy. Power lay with the people and their rights. The impact of *Rights of Man* was immediate. It was distributed in cheap editions (50,000 copies of Part One were sold in 1791), read aloud and discussed. To his supporters, Paine was a heroic figure. To his opponents, he became a symbol of the excesses of revolution. He was frequently burned in effigy especially at the end of 1792 and the first few months of 1793. In Nottingham, for instance, Paine was ritualistically killed, stoned by ladies at a dinner and dance. Between 1792 and 1795, the circulation of Paine's work was one of the main reasons given for the passage of repressive legislation.

The debate was not confined to a dialogue between Burke and Paine. Many of the authors knew each other and their work may be seen as a collective project. Paine, William Godwin and Mary Wollstonecraft produced a number of innovative and utopian proposals between 1791 and early 1793--the establishment of a welfare state, the withering away of the centralised state, equality in relationships to remove the automatic obedience of employees to employers and women to men. Thomas Spence's *Meridian Sun of Liberty* cost only one penny and was aimed at a different audience that Burke's *Reflections* at three shillings and Godwin's *Political Justice* priced at a pound. The extent to which the debate reached different sections of the public was largely determined by the cost of the written material.

Government was concerned that 'informed opinion' was in the hands of a closely-knit radical circle. While those individuals were addressing each other, they represented no threat to established order. However, the combination of growing political organisation with a supply of radical writings to politicise the masses was another matter. A loyalist backlash began in late-1792 with John Reeves and the Association for Preserving Liberty and Property against Republicans and Levellers. It commissioned and circulated popularly written anti-radical pamphlets to ensure the loyalty of the labouring population. It maintained pressure on the radical writers while the government controlled radical publishing, processes helped by the patriotic reaction to the outbreak of war with France in 1793. With the publication of Godwin's *Political Justice* in February 1793, innovative radical thinking stopped. Fewer pamphlets were published, repeated old ideas and tried to reassure a moderate audience rather than developing new theories. The objective of many radical thinkers was to attract the widest possible support for an anti-government platform. The radical vision of communicating with a wide audience had been established yet in practical terms, the reforming movement achieved little. By 1800, European societies were destabilised and Burke's fears had apparently been realised.

Reacting to revolution: radical demands for reform

British reformers were roused into action by the events in France. The dissenters' campaign for the repeal of the Test and Corporation Acts was stimulated by events across the Channel. The Society for Constitutional Information (SCI), founded in 1780, began to circulate radical propaganda and in April 1792, some Whig reformers formed the Society of the Friends of the People to campaign for parliamentary reform. However, the Corresponding Societies marked a new departure for radicalism.

The French Revolution stirred people to political action and provided them with an ideology through which to redress their grievances but the economic conditions in the first half of the 1790s also played an important role. The disturbed state of Europe in 1792-1793 led to economic depression in Britain with widespread unemployment and lower wages. War interrupted trade. It also placed increasing tax burdens on the middle- and lower classes. Economic distress reached critical levels in 1795-1796 following harvest failure in 1794, pushing up food prices at a time when the labouring population was already faced with higher taxation and lower wages. It is, however, important not to see the reforming movement simply in terms of a response to economic conditions. What was different about the Corresponding movement was that it crossed the threshold from traditional economic grievances to fundamental political demands.

Corresponding Societies

During the winter of 1791-2, popular radical societies emerged. The London Corresponding Society (LCS) was the most important. Founded in January 1792 by a small group led by the shoemaker Thomas Hardy, membership was open to all who paid a penny at each weekly meeting. Though formed to discuss the poverty faced by many of the labouring population and the high prices of the day, the LCS quickly adopted a political programme for remedying their grievances: universal manhood suffrage, annual parliaments and redistribution of rotten boroughs to the large towns. The LCS spread rapidly across London and developed a sophisticated organisational structure of divisions district committees and general committee.

Two features described the LCS: its size and its social composition. By late-1792, about 650 people regularly attended its meetings. By late-1794, its total active membership was 3,000. By the spring of 1796, this had fallen to about 2,000, by the end of the year to 1,000, to about 600 in 1797 and to 400 active members before it was banned in 1798. LCS membership was confined to a very small proportion of London's working population. To call the LCS a 'working-class' organisation neglects the extent to which its membership was made up of individuals from the 'middling' and professional classes as well as artisans and tradesmen. An analysis of 347 activists shows that only half were artisans and the rest were medical men, lawyers, booksellers, clerks, shopkeepers and printers. There is no evidence that it ever had much appeal to unskilled labourers or the very poor.

Provincial radical societies had begun to spring up before the LCS was founded. The Sheffield Society for Constitutional Information was formed in late 1791. Within a few months, it had grown from a few members to 2,500 members. In the autumn of 1792, the Sheffield SCI could bring 5-6,000 people on to the streets to celebrate the French victory at Valmy and a similar number in February 1794 to press for peace abroad and liberty at home. During 1792, the number of societies mushroomed and regional differences became more obvious. Manchester, with its factory workers, merchants and expanding population, stood at the other end of the scale to Sheffield. It had been Tory since the 1750s and this may account for the slow initial development of the Manchester Constitutional Society founded by Thomas Walker as early as October 1790. In Norwich, the radical cause developed along similar lines. A Revolution Society established in 1788, was dominated by middle-class Dissenters, merchants and tradesmen. It rivalled Sheffield as the pacemaker of radicalism. The textile industry supported artisans of a particularly independent temper and Norwich's Dissent was rooted in a craggy, though surprisingly liberal, tradition. By 1792, forty tavern clubs of shoemakers, weavers and shopkeepers had developed, comprising some 2,000 members.

Organisation

How did the radical societies attempt to achieve their aims? Weekly meetings and the spread of printed propaganda provided focus for their activities. They corresponded regularly with each other and with groups in France. However, their attempt to reach a mass audience was limited. There was, however, no nationwide petitioning campaign. There were only 36 petitions in support of Charles Grey's motion on parliamentary reform in 1793. The reformers seriously overestimated the amount of mass support and dangerously underestimated the fears it would arouse in the authorities. Radical tactics were very restrained. The bulk of the labouring population did not rally behind parliamentary reform and few radical leaders appreciated the power of organised labour. Some radicals did try to whip up food rioters in Sheffield in 1795 to protest against the war and demand parliamentary reform and similar tactics were used in the north-west in 1800. However, these were isolated examples and the radicals made no attempt to co-ordinate popular riots. Most radical leaders, with their middle-class background, were committed to non-violent action. When the governing class refused to concede reform, resorting to repression and persecution, most radicals lost heart or moderated their demands.

Reacting to revolution: the conservative response

The attack on popular radicalism came from three directions. There was an attack on its ideology, a populist and loyalist reaction and a legislative attack by Pitt's government. The reform movement collapsed not simply because of repressive actions but because the opponents of reform developed a defence of the existing political system that was convincing not just to those with property but also to large sections of British society.

Conservative ideology in the 1790s had considerable appeal. A tradition of resistance to constitutional change in Britain existed in the decades leading up to the revolution and events in France, especially after 1791, reinforced this tradition. Radicals at home were seen in the same light as revolutionaries abroad. It was not difficult to persuade people that the radical reform would destroy the established order as the revolution had in France. French anarchy was contrasted unfavourable with British stability and prosperity. Conservative apologists and propagandists appealed to British hatred of France and fear of radical change. There was also an intellectual response contrasting the stability of constitutional monarchy with the anarchy of 'mob' rule and democracy. Anti-radical propaganda, subsidised by the loyalist associations, by government and by private individuals, took many forms. Pamphlets and tracts like the Cheap Repository Tracts, many written by Hannah More, between 1795 and 1798; pro-government newspapers like the *Sun,* the *True Briton* and the *Oracle;* journals like the *Anti-Jacobin* (1797-8) and its successor the *Anti-Jacobin Review and Magazine,* a monthly that lasted until 1821; political caricatures and cartoons by artists like Isaac Cruickshanks. James Gillray and Thomas Rowlandson; and local newspapers like the *Manchester Mercury* and the *Newcastle Courant.* This concerted campaign was outstandingly successful and convinced the majority of English people that the French Revolution was a disaster.

Loyalist associations emerged initially as a response to the Dissenter campaign for repeal of the Test and Corporation Acts but the number of Church and King clubs was given a major boost by the revolution especially the Royal Proclamation against seditious writings on 21 May 1792. By September 1792, some 386 loyal addresses had been received by the king and in November John Reeves formed the first loyalist Association for the Preservation of Liberty and Property against Republicans and Levellers (APLP). By the end of 1793, the total number of APLPs may have reached 2,000 making them the largest political organisation in the country. They spread from London first into the neighbouring counties, then to the west, Midlands and finally the north. Active membership was largely confined to men of property, though they were able to enlist support from across society. They can be seen as far more successful and popular 'working-class' organisations than the radical societies. Loyalist associations adopted the organisation and some of the methods of the reformers. They produced a great deal of printed propaganda but were not content to rely upon persuasion, resorting to intimidation and persecution to defeat their opponents. Calls for loyalty and patriotism proved far more popular with the bulk of the population than demands for radical change.

Government repression.

Pitt acted quickly against the threat pose by the radicals, inaugurating what has been called Pitt's 'Reign of Terror'. The government was convinced it faced a revolutionary conspiracy, a view reinforced by the intelligence received from local magistrates and spies and believed it was justified in taking firm action. In May and December 1792, two Royal Proclamations were issued against seditious writings. The Home Office, especially after 1794 under the strongly anti-radical Duke of Portland, monitored the activities of the radical societies using spies as well as more conventional methods like opening letters, receiving reports from local sources, watching the activities of radicals abroad and infiltrating radical groups. Its resources were very limited with a staff of less than twenty-five. After success in the Scottish treason trials in 1793-1794, Pitt moved against English radicals. Forty-one men, including Hardy, were arrested in late 1794 and charged with high treason but after he was acquitted, further trials were abandoned. The administration had little further success with treason trials during the remainder of the decade but had more success with those for publishing seditious libels. There were less than 200 convictions during the 1790s and whether this constitutes a government-inspired reign of terror is open to debate.

Parliament was prepared to pass legislation in support of the government though, in practice, this often turned out to be far less effective than anticipated. Habeas Corpus was suspended from May 1794 to July 1795 and April 1798 to March 1801 but only a few people were imprisoned without charge. The Two Acts of 1795--the Treasonable Practices Act and the Seditious Meetings Act--proved less than effective weapons despite the wide powers given to central and local government. The Treasonable Practices Act was designed to intimidate and no radical was prosecuted under it. The Seditious Meetings Act failed to prevent the increasing number of meetings organised by the LCS. There was only one prosecution under a 1797 Act rushed through Parliament following the naval mutiny at Spithead and the Nore. It strengthened penalties for attempting to undermine allegiance to the authorities and administering unlawful oaths. The banning of the leading radical societies by law in 1799 was unnecessary, largely because they were already in a state of collapse. The Combination Acts of 1799 and 1800 banned combinations of workers completing the legislative armoury of repression. Radicalism was increasingly driven underground. It did not emerge as a mass movement until the last years of the French wars. Between 1794 and 1800, Pitt had successfully driven radical politics to the margins of political life.

Government legislation was infrequently used but it remained as a threat hanging over radicals, limiting their freedom of action. Its effect was to intimidate and harass. It destroyed the leadership of the radical societies, silenced the ablest propagandists and frightened many into abandoning the reform movement. However, the collapse of the radical movement was not simply a matter of repression by government or magistrates. War revived latent deep-seated patriotism among the most people for whom radicalism was only of peripheral importance.

3 Tory dominance and decline 1815-1830

Lord Liverpool became Prime Minister after Spencer Perceval was assassinated in the lobby of the House of Commons in May 1812. He was the most underrated Prime Minister in the nineteenth century. described later in the century by Benjamin Disraeli as an 'arch mediocrity'. Yet, he was a skilled politician and held together a government of strong personalities with differing opinions more prepared to serve under him than under each other. Between 1812 and 1822, he was faced with economic, political and radical challenges caused by the war against France and the problem of returning to peacetime conditions after the final defeat of Napoleon at Waterloo in 1815. Between 1822 and 1827, the government had considerable energy largely because of the emergence of what has been called 'liberal Toryism'. It was damaged only by divisions within the Cabinet especially over the 'Catholic question' though even here Liverpool was able to head off serious tensions by making it an 'open question'.

Liverpool's stroke in February 1827 released long restrained tensions and rivalries. Within three years, his party was in tatters, divided and without effective leadership. Three Prime Ministers followed in quick succession. Liverpool's successor, George Canning[1] died in August within months of gaining office. His successor, Viscount Goderich[2] was a disaster resigning without ever meeting Parliament. Finally, the Duke of Wellington took the helm in January 1828.[3] His ministry saw the repeal of the Test and Corporation Acts in 1828 and Catholic Emancipation the following year. Wellington's refusal to accept parliamentary reform led to the fall of his government in November 1830. The Whigs were in power.

---

[1] George Canning (1770-1827) entered Parliament in 1784 and held various government offices including Foreign Secretary (1807-1808, 1822-1827). He became Prime Minister and Chancellor of the Exchequer a short time before his death in August 1827.

[2] Frederick Robinson, 1st Viscount Goderich (1782-1859) was Chancellor of the Exchequer between 1823 and 1827. He was asked to serve as Prime Minister after the death of his friend Canning but was unable to control his ministers. He resigned in January 1828. In 1833, he was created Earl of Ripon and served as Whig Lord Privy Seal (April 1833-May 1834) but later joined the Conservative Party serving as a minister between 1841 and 1843 in Peel's government

[3] Arthur Wellesley, 1st Duke of Wellington (1769-1852) rose to fame as a military leader in the French wars culminating in his victory over Napoleon at Waterloo in 1815. He was Prime Minister between 1828 and November 1830. A sound military leader, he lacked the political flexibility to be a good Prime Minister and party leader.

Year	Events
1812	11 May: Assassination of Spencer Perceval 8 June: Lord Liverpool became Prime Minister
1815	Corn Laws passed 18 June: Napoleon defeated at Waterloo
1816	Income tax repealed against government's wishes December: Spa Fields riots
1817	February: Habeas Corpus suspended March: Seditious Meetings Act March of the Blanketeers 9 June: Pentrich rising
1818	General Election
1819	May: Bullion Committee chaired by Peel recommended the phased resumption of cash payments by the Bank of England 16 August: Peterloo Massacre followed by the Six Acts
1820	29 January: George III died, succeeded by George IV; General Election February: Cato Street conspiracy June: beginnings of Queen Caroline affair December: Canning resigned over government's handling of Queen Caroline affair
1821	December: Sidmouth resigned as Home Secretary
1822	Peel appointed Home Secretary 12 August: Castlereagh committed suicide. Canning becomes Foreign Secretary and Leader of House of Commons
1823	January: Robinson appointed Chancellor of the Exchequer October: Huskisson appointed President of the Board of Trade
1826	General Election
1827	March: Liverpool resigned following stroke on 17 February April: Canning became Prime Minister and Chancellor of the Exchequer 8 August: Canning's death. Goderich became Prime Minister
1828	January: Goderich resigned and Wellington became Prime Minister Repeal of Test and Corporation Acts
1829	Catholic Emancipation
1830	June: Death of George IV. William IV succeeds July: Revolution in France August: General Election 2 November: Wellington ruled out parliamentary reform 16 November: Wellington resigned

How did Lord Liverpool's economic policy develop 1812-1822?

Liverpool became Prime Minister towards the end of the protracted wars with France. By 1812, the duke of Wellington was winning the war against the French in Spain. The French defeat at Vitoria in August 1813 allowed him to cross the Pyrenees and invade France. Napoleon had been weakened by his unsuccessful invasion of Russia in 1812 and in early 1813 Liverpool and his Foreign Secretary, Lord Castlereagh[4] were able to set up the Fourth Coalition (Austria, Russia and Prussia). Napoleon was defeated in the three-day 'Battle of the Nations' at Leipzig in October 1813 and faced with a two-pronged invasion of France (Wellington from the south and the coalition partners from the east), he abdicated in 1814. Exiled to Elba, an island in the Mediterranean Napoleon plotted his return while the allies set about redrawing the boundaries of Europe at the Congress of Vienna. In March 1815, Napoleon returned to France but was defeated, in what Wellington called 'a close-run thing' at Waterloo in June. Exile was now permanent and Napoleon was sent to the southern Atlantic island of St. Helena where he died in 1821. Liverpool faced two major problems in the seven years after 1815: he needed to reorganise government finances depleted by the cost of the French Wars; and he had to face and deal with a revival of working-class radicalism.

How did Liverpool reorganise government finances?

The French wars saw two contradictory trends in the British economy. The need for uniforms and weapons to feed the war stimulated demand in increasingly mechanised manufacturing industry, especially textiles and iron and production increased dramatically. Mechanisation led to working-class resistance and Luddism.[5] Because of expansion in the agriculture sector, Britain was less reliant on imported food especially wheat. Large areas of England had been enclosed during the war. This made farming more efficient and allowed farmers to increase the amount of food they were producing. They borrowed money to pay for this but high profits meant that they could easily repay the banks. They could

---

[4] Robert Stewart, Viscount Castlereagh, 2nd Marquess of Londonderry (1769-1822) was Foreign Secretary between 1812 and 1822. He was very influential at the Congress of Vienna at the end of the French wars especially his ideas about a European balance of power. Highly-strung and almost incapable of taking criticism, he committed suicide

[5] The Luddites were machine breakers who operated in Nottinghamshire, south Lancashire and Yorkshire between 1811 and 1813. The term 'Luddism' is often applied more generally to any movement in which machines were smashed to protect existing technologies and employment.

charge high rents for their land and the price of wheat remain high because the war restricted imports. By 1815, both industry and agriculture were outwardly strong but they were geared up for wartime production. The transition to peacetime proved difficult and posed a series of fundamental questions that taxed government until the 1840s. What should the place of agriculture be in an industrialised society? How could the competing claims of farmers and industrialists be resolved? What was the relationship between consumers and producers? What role should government have in determining the overall direction of the economy?

British governments in the late-eighteenth century did not attempt to control change in the economy. After 1815, unemployment rose because of the demobilisation of the armed forces and the need to cut labour costs especially in farming and textiles.[6] In returning the economy to peacetime conditions, ministers were forced to take a more active role. 'Corn' and 'Cash' dominated debates in the 1810s and 'Commerce' became important in the 1820s. Each posed major political problems for the Tories.

'Corn'

Between 1813 and 1815, corn prices fell following good harvests in 1813, 1814 and 1815 and the return to peace in 1814 brought unwelcome foreign grain imports. Farmers and tenants found themselves under pressure. Lower prices and high wartime taxation meant that they often found it difficult to repay bank loans. This had the following consequences for the farming sector. There were many bankruptcies amongst farmers who had borrowed to invest in their land during the war and who now faced with falling prices. Falling prices led to some landowners reducing the rents paid by their tenants. Falling prices and a surplus labour force caused largely by the demobilisation of the armed forces led to farmers reducing the wages they paid resulting in 'distress' in areas where farming was the main occupation.

These events culminated in the passage of the Corn Law of 1815 that prevented the import of grain until the price fell below 80 shillings a quarter (28 lbs.) for wheat. As grain prices rarely rose as high as 80 shillings, this measure effectively ensured that local farmers could get a high price for their grain without foreign competition. Why did Liverpool's government decide to introduce legislation seen as unfair and favouring one sector of society? The protection of farming was not new originating in the Corn Laws passed in 1773 and 1804. Also, Liverpool

---

[6] Up to a quarter of a million soldiers and sailors were demobilised in 1815 and 1816. Unemployment went up dramatically because it did not prove possible to absorb so many people into work

could not ignore the fate of one of the country's largest single economic interests, whose votes mattered in Parliament. A Corn Law was justified on the grounds of national security as Britain might need a reliable domestic supply of food. Finally, legislation was needed to maintain stability, as agriculture was the largest employer of labour and higher prices were justified to protect jobs.

Liverpool saw legislation as temporary to help farming return to normal after the war but the landed interest saw it as permanent or at least long-term. Parliament was dominated by landowners and farmers and they voted for legislation that the government had little option but to accept. Previous Corn Laws had tried to balance the interests of producers and consumers by maintaining prices at levels acceptable to both. The 1815 Act clearly favoured the interests of the producers. Manufacturers attacked the legislation. Parliament was, they argued interfering with the free market in their own narrow interests. Radical politicians regarded it as class legislation keeping corn prices artificially high to help farmers while penalising working people through higher food costs. Reaction was swift. There were petitions and riots in London in March. Politicians' houses were attacked and troops had to be brought to the capital to restore order. Higher food prices fuelled working-class distress especially in rural England and riots in 1816 and again in 1818 were, in part a violent reaction to the Corn Laws.

Even so, there were demands from tenant farmers for further protection of farming after 1815 especially during the agricultural crisis of 1821-1823. However, political attitudes were changing. Liverpool was convinced, largely by the actions of radicals between 1815 and 1821 that governments that pandered to farmers at the expense of working-class consumers or tax-paying industrialists had a dangerously narrow political base. He made his own position clear in February 1822: 'The agricultural is not the only interest in Great Britain. It is not even the most numerous.' Farmers were being told bluntly that they no longer dictated government policies. Abolition of the Corn Laws was not practical but reform was. The government introduced minor changes in 1822 but price levels meant that they never came into operation. Liverpool regarded this as an interim measure while considered a more permanent solution.

Rising wheat prices from 1823, the financial crisis in 1825 and growing depression in manufacturing industry in 1826 brought fresh demands for the abolition of duties on foreign grain. Manufacturers lobbied Parliament and anti-Protectionists tried to make it an issue in the 1826 General Election. Liverpool made it clear in 1826 that he intended to revise the 1815 Act the following year. The 1827 and 1828 Corn Laws introduced by Canning and Huskisson respectively completed the process begun in 1822. These acts provided a sliding scale of duties that operated from 60 shillings and reduced to a nominal rate at 73 shillings a quarter.

They were a compromise because of disagreement in the Cabinet on how best to handle this sensitive issue.

'Finance'

Britain's financial state in 1815 was not healthy: the French wars had been expensive, taxation was high and unpopular and 'cheap' paper money had been circulating since 1797 when Britain had gone off the Gold Standard[7] and the Bank of England had suspended payments in gold and silver and began to issue paper currency (£1 and £2 notes). Income tax (direct taxation)[8] brought in about a fifth of government income. Working-class radicals argued that indirect taxes[9] (duties or tariffs) pushed food prices up and hit working people unfairly. In 1814-1815, government spending exceeded income from taxation by 45 per cent. The national debt had risen from £238 million in 1793 to £902 million in 1816. Roughly, eighty per cent of government expenditure was needed simply to pay the interest on loans.

Reducing public spending and paying off its debts (a process called retrenchment) was a major priority for Liverpool's government after 1815. Liverpool recognised that the transition to lower peacetime taxation would take time. What Liverpool and his Chancellor Nicholas Vansittart needed was a period of financial stability. Income tax was central to this stability. By 1815, it accounted for a fifth of all government income and while it had never been popular, it had been tolerated. With the end of the war, demands for its abolition increased and in 1815 and 1816 the Whigs organised a national campaign against it. This was successful and in 1816, Liverpool failed, by thirty-seven votes, to continue the tax.

Abolishing income tax may have been popular but it left government finances in chaos. To make up the lost income, Liverpool had to reduce government spending, borrow money and increase indirect taxation. £340,000 was trimmed from defence spending in 1816. Government departments pruned and a ten per cent cut was made in official salaries. Liverpool could do little to reduce spending further. By 1818, he controlled only nine per cent of revenue. The rest was swallowed up servicing the interest on the National Debt, war pensions and interest on

---

[7] Gold Standard. System under which a country's currency is exchangeable for a fixed weight of gold on demand at the central bank.

[8] Direct taxation was taxes levied on individuals directly. The most widespread was income tax introduced in 1797 by William Pitt. It was abolished in 1816 but revived by Sir Robert Peel in 1842.

[9] Indirect taxes were taxes imposed on good or services usually collected when the good move from one country to another (customs and excise duties) or at the point of sale. Tariffs are duties paid on goods.

loans necessary to meet the deficit of £13 million. There was an overwhelming need for reform of the financial system.

Liverpool recognised that sustained economic growth meant a return to 'sound money' (low levels of interest and cash payments in gold and silver rather than paper currency). He set up a Select Committee on Currency chaired by Sir Robert Peel. In May 1819, it recommended the gradual resumption of cash payments by 1823. This transition was achieved ahead of time and from 1821, Britain was back on the Gold Standard. Financial experts favoured the end of wartime paper currency arguing that a return to a fixed Gold Standard was essential to a sound monetary policy. The landed interest supported cash payments. For them, it meant a return to 'proper' money and the end of a paper currency that represented financial speculation, industrialisation and uncontrolled urban development. Industrialists in the northern textile towns, by contrast, saw the decision as premature.

By 1818, government income through taxation covered the costs of government spending or a balanced budget. However, Liverpool still faced the problem of having to continue to borrow money from the London money market to pay off existing debts. Interest rates rose after 1815 and the government had to borrow money at high rates of interest to service existing debts. This led to a rising National Debt. The radical press, landowners who had to pay higher interest charges on loans but were faced with lower agricultural prices and industrialists were critical of 'tax eaters' and 'fund holders' who seemed to be holding the nation to ransom. The case of a review of the national system of finance was necessary economically and politically. A second committee looked at government finance (taxation, spending and borrowing). The recommendations of this committee led to Vansittart's budget of 1819 that imposed £3 million of new taxes, including a new malt tax, and took £12 million out of government reserves to balance the budget. This was seen to herald a 'new system of finance'. It established the two principles of fiscal management that dominated the remainder of the century: government should aim for a surplus of income from taxation over government spending; and that a balanced or surplus budget helped to restore public confidence in government.

'Trade'

Liverpool recognised that a revival in trade and manufacture was essential if his fiscal policy was to work effectively. 'Trade' was the third strand of his policies. It was thought that removing tariffs on imports and loosening commercial regulations would stimulate the sluggish economy but Liverpool's approach was cautious. The government derived much of its income from customs and excise. Farmers were suspicious of moves towards freer trade, as they believed this would inevitably lead to the repeal of the Corn Laws.[10] Many merchants and manufacturers supported protection in markets in which they were weak arguing for freer trade only where they had the competitive advantage. Liverpool echoed these attitudes in a speech on trade in the House of Lords on 26 May 1820 that was guarded in its approach. He made clear the advantages of freer trade but he reassured his audience that he was not considering abandoning agricultural protection and believed that absolute free trade was out of the question. Two committees were established to lay down strategies for implementing the move to freer trade. Thomas Wallace, Vice-President of the Board of Trade played a central role arguing that freer trade would help industries out of depression, encourage the search for new markets and generate employment. With Vansittart, he drew up the blueprints for the reforms that Frederick Robinson, Vansittart's successor as Chancellor and William Huskisson undertook after 1823.

In 1819 and 1820, Liverpool had established clear guidelines for the development of new financial and commercial policies. Sound money policy, together with these reforms, led to a dramatic increase in government revenue. By 1822, the government was in surplus and Robinson's budget had excess revenue of £5 million. In 1823, he budgeted for a surplus of £7 million of which £5 million was used to repay debts leaving £2 million for tax cuts. Surplus budgets in 1824 and 1825 allowed reductions in excise duties on a range of consumer goods and raw materials including coal, iron and wood and on spirits, wine, rum, cider and coffee. In fact, there were budget surpluses until 1830 though they were insufficient to allow further tariff reductions. The limits of tax reduction had been reached and Liverpool recognised, as early as 1824 that the only way out of this financial stalemate was the reintroduction of income tax. John Herries, Chancellor of the Exchequer under Goderich was preparing to do so when the ministry collapsed in early 1828 and Henry Goulburn, Wellington's Chancellor was only prevented in doing so in the 1830 budget because of the Prime Minister's opposition.

Changes in commercial policy began in 1821 when Wallace reduced duties on timber imports. The following year he simplified the Navigation Acts allowing the colonies freer trade with foreign countries while Anglo-colonial trade was still restricted to British ships. In 1823, Wallace resigned when William Huskisson[11] became President of the Board of

---

[10] Free Trade--shorthand for the doctrine of laissez-faire—is the doctrine of non-interference by the state in economic matters. It derived from the teachings of classical economists like Adam Smith, Malthus and David Ricardo.

[11] William Huskisson (1770-1830) was President of the Board of Trade 1823-1827 where he continued the work of William Pitt on fiscal reform. He died after

Trade and he has not received the credit for developing the commercial policies that Huskisson then implemented. In 1823, the Reciprocity of Duties Act reduced tariffs if other countries would follow suit and by 1827, most European countries and the United States had negotiated agreements for mutual abolition or adjustment of discriminatory tariffs. Foreign ships were allowed freer access to British ports especially London which became the centre of world trade. The policies of Wallace and Huskisson proved very successful and there was a sixty-four per cent increase in tariff revenue between 1821 and 1827.

Just how committed was Liverpool's government to free trade? Barry Gordon regards Wallace's decision in 1821 to reduce timber duties as 'the first practical step towards implementation of laissez-faire in the post-war period'. Boyd Hilton disagrees seeing the free trade commercial policies of the 1820s as motivated by very practical considerations: the 1821 *Agricultural Report* made it clear that the United Kingdom could no longer feed itself and the Corn Laws were seen as an obstacle to getting the necessary food from the continent. A reliable and cheap food supply was essential to maintain public order. In Boyd Hilton's view, free trade reform was based on fiscal and agricultural policies designed to stabilise rather than expand the economy. Norman Gash argues that Liverpool's economic policies were essentially 'social' in character. His aim was to make the economy more prosperous and as a result reduce working-class discontent.

Liverpool supported the abolition of legal restrictions on the export of machinery, emigration of artisans and trade unions. He was prepared to legislate to deal with particular problems. The Poor Employment Act of 1817 offered government loans for public work schemes to help the unemployed. In 1819, a Factory Act regulated the employment of children in textile mills and the legal position of Friendly Societies[12] was clarified. Restrictions were imposed on trade unions in 1825 a year after the repeal of the Combination Acts. These were limited in scope and largely ineffective in practice. Neither Liverpool nor Huskisson were doctrinaire free traders. Their policies were based on a hard-nosed assessment of the economic advantage Britain could gain, the prosperity and political stability this would bring.

---

being knocked down by a locomotive at the opening of the Liverpool-Manchester railway in September 1830.

[12] Friendly Societies were set up often by working people to provide insurance for workers to cover things like sickness, unemployment and burial costs.

How did the government react to demands for political reform?

Demands for parliamentary reform began in the final years of the war. In 1812, Major John Cartwright, a radical leader who had campaigned for parliamentary reform since the 1760s, began the first of three tours of the Midlands and North. He wanted working- and middle-classes to work together to obtain parliamentary reform. The result was the creation of Hampden Clubs[13] especially in the northern manufacturing districts hit by the slump in trade. These were working-class in composition and moved away from the household or taxpayer suffrages demanded by middle-class reformers towards demands for manhood suffrage. The Political Unions, organised by northern workingmen replaced the Hampden Clubs (they were finally banned in 1817) and helped organise over 2,000 petitions for parliamentary reform between 1817 and 1818.

These two radical organisations raised a series of problems that were to dog radical activity until the 1850s. Was parliamentary reform best achieved by class collaboration (middle and working-classes working together) or by the working-class acting alone? Should parliamentary reform be approached solely through demands for manhood suffrage (one man, one vote) or through achieving limited suffrage (household or taxpayer suffrage) and then moving to manhood suffrage (votes for adult males)? The problem with this approach and class collaboration was that once the middle-classes had achieved limited suffrage, their enthusiasm for further reform waned. This can be seen in the aftermath of the 1832 Reform Act. What tactics should radicals use to achieve parliamentary reform? Should radicals rely on persuasion (the use of petitions and meetings) to achieve their aims or should they adopt a more revolutionary approach using force if the government refused to act on their demands?

It is easy to write off the revolutionaries as a failed minority and in retrospect, their activities can be seen as laughably naïve and doomed to inevitable failure. However, there was a revolutionary underground in Britain that can be traced back to the late 1790s and it was prepared to confront the authorities with armed force. The Luddite attacks between 1812 and 1815 had a revolutionary dimension and the Blanketeers projected march from Manchester to London to present a petition implied the use of force. The fiasco of the Cato Street Conspiracy needs to be seen in the context of the actions of Glasgow weavers who were defeated by troops at the battle of Bonnymuir or the West Riding woollen workers who seized weapons and tried to take Huddersfield in April 1820.

---

[13] Hampden Clubs were first set up in 1812 by Major Cartwright to promote the cause of parliamentary reform. They were named after Sir John Hampden who fought and died for the cause of Parliament in the Civil Wars in the mid-seventeenth century. They were banned by the government in 1817.

The problem that radical faced was that attempts at revolution increased support for firm government action when public order and property were threatened.

The transition to a peacetime economy between 1815 and 1821 severely strained social and economic relationships. Falling demand for manufactured goods, especially textiles and the flooding of the labour market with demobilised soldiers and sailors increased unemployment. In the climate of 'distress', the government found itself under pressure from two quarters. It faced protest that took traditional forms, like the Fenland riots of 1816 that aimed at restoring 'just' wages and prices. There were also growing demands for political reform from the radical platform of Henry 'Orator' Hunt[14] and William Cobbett. Hunt built on the foundations created by the Hampden Clubs and mobilised people around demands for manhood suffrage, annual parliaments and the secret ballot.

Disturbances in 1815 and 1816 convinced Lord Sidmouth[15] that the government faced a revolutionary challenge to its authority. The disorder at the Spa Field meetings calling for parliamentary reform in London in November and December 1816 appeared to confirm his fears. The attack on the Prince Regent's coach in late January 1817 was followed later in the year by the march of the Blanketeers,[16] unemployed workers from Lancashire and Cheshire. These events and Pentrich rising[17] in Derbyshire shifted middle-class public opinion, previously sympathetic to the radical demands behind the government that was committed to preserving public order and defending property. In 1817, Habeas Corpus[18] was suspended and restrictions placed on meetings for twelve months (the Seditious Meetings Act). The opposition Whigs were as worried by events as the government and became more cautious in their approach to parliamentary reform.

---

[14] Henry 'Orator' Hunt (1773-1835) advocated annual parliaments and universal suffrage (one man, one vote). He was the major leader of the radical movement in the 1810s.

[15] Henry Addington 1st Viscount Sidmouth (1757-1844) was an able administrator but a mediocre Prime Minister between 1801 and 1804. He was an effective Home Secretary between 1812 and 1822

[16] March of the Blanketeers. Manchester textile workers decided to march to London to petition the Prince Regent for parliamentary reform. They each carried a blanket but few got beyond Stockport and only one reached London.

[17] The Pentrich Rising was led by Jeremiah Brandreth with little support and was easily put down.

[18] Habeas Corpus. A writ requiring that someone who has been arrested and imprisoned should be examined by the courts to see whether there are sufficient grounds for continued imprisonment. It is an effective means of protecting the individual against arbitrary arrest and detention.

Prompt action by the government only partly explains the decline in radical activities. Economic conditions eased during 1817 and 1818 and this led to a decline in radical activity. William Cobbett maintained that it was difficult to 'agitate a fellow with a full stomach'. Habeas Corpus was revived early in 1818 and the Seditious Meetings Act lapsed in July that year. However, economic distress returned in 1819 and radicalism revived in 1819 reaching its peak in the 'Peterloo Massacre' in August 1819.[19] There was a wave of public support for the radical cause and even *The Times* attacked the actions of the Manchester magistrates. The problem that faced Hunt and the radical leadership was how to translate this support into practical actions. It was clear that the government did not intend to give in to radical demands for parliamentary reform. Liverpool, though Sidmouth had advised the Manchester magistrates against taking any precipitous action, had little choice but to support their actions. Repression was re-imposed in the 'Six Acts' restricting meetings and the press, allowing magistrates to seize weapons, and preventing drilling. They gave the government powers to deal harshly with even slight symptoms of discontent. The radical agitation faltered despite the intense unpopularity of the government.

The Cato Street conspiracy, when a group led by the clearly unstable Arthur Thistlewood planned to assassinate the Cabinet in February 1820, had little impact on public opinion though Liverpool was able to make political capital out of it during the election campaign caused by the sudden death of George III the previous month. More damaging for Liverpool was the unsuccessful attempt by the new king, George IV to divorce his wife Queen Caroline and the successful attempt to prevent her attending his coronation in 1821 (she was locked out of Westminster Abbey). George IV became king on the death of his father in January 1820. He had long lived apart from him wife whose behaviour had been a cause of concern since the mid-1800s. In June 1820, she returned from Italy to claim her rights as queen, to which George IV was totally opposed. The government was instructed to dissolve the marriage. It was forced to abandon its attempts to deprive Caroline of her title and dissolve the marriage in November 1820 after widespread popular and Whig opposition. She died suddenly in August 1821, three weeks after the coronation and the London crowds forced the military to take her coffin through the City on its way to Harwich and to her family home in Brunswick. The Queen Caroline affair made the government very

---

[19] Peterloo Massacre. On 16 August 1819, a peaceful meeting was held at St Peter's Field, Manchester. Local magistrates decided to arrest Hunt who was one of the speakers. The Yeomanry were given this task, in the ensuing chaos, large numbers of people were injured, and at least eleven killed.

unpopular and the Queen's cause provided a rallying point for radical campaigners.

Once again, as the economy revived in the early 1820s, radicalism declined. The public's energies were diverted into other forms of radical action. Some workingmen turned to religion and there were Methodist revivals in Lancashire and Cumberland. Others campaigned against the Combination Acts. Successful parliamentary pressure led to the repeal of the Combination Acts in 1824. A downturn in the economy led to a rapid increase in trade union activity with extensive strikes, including some violence in the winter of 1824-1825. Employers lobbied for the reintroduction of the Combination Acts and in 1825 new legislation was introduced that allowed unions to negotiate over wages and conditions but did not confer the right to strike. This effectively limited trade unions to peaceful collective bargaining with employers over wages and hours. Trade unionists who went beyond this narrow definition of legal activity for trade unions could be prosecuted for criminal conspiracy.

Two linked issues arise from the revival of radicalism after 1815: how revolutionary was it and how justifiable was the response of the government? The radical platform posed a significant threat in that it created a potential for revolution. This was a very real fear for central and local authorities that feared a repeat of events in France thirty years earlier. However, radicals who sought revolutionary solutions were never a leading force in the movement. Far more importantly, the radical platform's grievances challenged the whole direction of social development created by the industrial revolution. There was a growing belief that working-class grievances like discriminatory taxation, the Corn Laws, the game laws, and the legal ban on trade unions could only be resolved by a parliament elected on democratic principles. Unrest and agitation, though they appeared to contemporaries to be part of a nation-wide movement, are best seen in terms of responses to local conditions. In this situation, the local magistrates rather than central government were at the forefront of reaction. The Home Office was prepared to provide advice to local authorities and increasingly its officials became convinced that there was a general desire to begin a national revolution. The problem that Liverpool faced was that he had to rely on information provided by magistrates who reached national conclusions on their basis of their own local experiences, army officers and spies who often exaggerated the nature of the radical threat for financial gain.

Liverpool was therefore responding to a perceived threat to public order based on inaccurate and, on occasions, deceptive information. As a result, the government often overreacted to events as a result and because it did not wish to run any risk of revolution ever happening in Britain. In fact, Liverpool's approach was relatively moderate. When legislation was passed, it was either, like the Seditious Meetings Acts given a time limit or as the Six Acts demonstrated largely ineffective in practice. These radical demands challenged the political and economic power of the landed classes and industrialists and it was this that added a potentially revolutionary dimension of the radical challenge. The reaction of the government though criticised by contemporaries and historians as dictatorial emphasised the need for public order and tried--not always successfully--to distinguish between genuine social grievances and deliberately disruptive radical activity.

How 'liberal' were the Tory governments of 1822-1830?

In the early 1820s, Liverpool made important changes in his Cabinet. Canning became Foreign Secretary after Castlereagh's suicide and Peel replaced Sidmouth at the Home Office in 1822. Robinson took the place of Vansittart at the Exchequer and Huskisson became President of the Board of Trade in 1823. W. R. Brock suggested in 1941 that a 'reactionary' phase (1815-1821) when anti-reforming or 'Ultra' Tory ministers like Sidmouth suppressed liberties in defence of public order was followed by a 'liberal' one (1822-1827) in which 'Liberal Tories' like Huskisson, Peel and Robinson introduced reforms in fiscal policy, trade and the legal system. These were not cosmetic changes but for Brock represented a new style of politics. Castlereagh, Sidmouth and Vansittart supported repression abroad and high taxes at home. Canning, Peel, Huskisson and Robinson championed 'liberal' reforms at home and a 'liberal' policy abroad.

There are, however, several problems with this argument. What was 'Liberal Toryism'? Brock admitted that 'The name is artificial—that is to say it was not found in the mouths of contemporaries.' John Plowright is rightly critical of Brock's use of the 'Liberal Toryism', which 'implies a political philosophy or system of thought that is peculiarly unsuited to the pragmatism of politicians such as Canning.' How far did 'liberals' dominate government? The Cabinet after 1823 was one in which all shades of Tory opinion was represented. Liverpool provided continuity across the period 1815 to 1827 and he was certainly the only man who could hold together the Cabinet between 1822 and 1827. In addition, the 'new' ministers of 1822-1823 had already served in Liverpool's government and the ministers associated with the policy of repression, except for Castlereagh, did not leave the political stage. Finally, the important division within the Cabinet after 1822 was not between 'liberal' and 'ultra' but between those Tories who supported Catholic Emancipation and those who opposed it. Liverpool sensibly made this an 'open question'.[20] On this issue, Peel and Canning who Brock sees as 'liberals' stood at opposite poles.

If Brock's argument about people can be challenged, what about changes in policy? Many of the 'liberal' initiatives of the 1820s were discussed or proposed between 1815 and 1821. Sidmouth had proposed some of the penal reforms later introduced by Peel. Canning's foreign policy was a clear extension of his predecessor Castlereagh. Robinson's fiscal and Huskisson's commercial policies owed much to the general economic strategy and stimulus to trade agreed in 1819 and 1820. What was different in these years was the context. The revival of the economy from 1820-1821 and the decline in the mass radicalism meant that Peel, Huskisson and Robinson were operating in calmer times than Sidmouth and Vansittart. The focus was less on maintaining public order, more on making Britain's economy prosperous. Brock's argument focuses on Liverpool's administration neglecting the three years up to 1830. Fiscal and commercial policies remained largely unchanged and Peel continued his reforms of the legal system with the introduction of the Metropolitan Police in 1829 under Canning, Goodrich and Wellington. The repeal of the Test and Corporation Acts in 1828 and Catholic Emancipation a year later represent a significant shift in policy towards constitutional change.

In practice, Liverpool's administration was neither reactionary nor suddenly reformist in 1822. Any change of ministers, especially in the key positions is going to have an impact on the running of government. There was certainly an increase in the pace of reform and the presentation of policy by the government was improved. However, this did not mean that the substance of government policy and the principles on which it was based underwent radical change. The similarities of the years before and after 1822-1823 outweigh the differences.

Lord Liverpool's incapacitating stroke in February 1827 and his resignation a month later released tensions over religion and constitutional reform he had managed to hold in check. Within three years, his party was in tatters, divided and without effective leadership, leaving the Whigs in power. When Canning became Prime Minister in April, leading Tories including Wellington and Peel refused to serve under him largely because he was a supporter of Catholic Emancipation. The 1826 General Election strengthened the 'Protestant' Tories[21] in the House of Commons and

---

[20] 'Open question'. Catholic Emancipation was such a divisive issue in the Tory Party that Lord Liverpool decided that his ministers could either support or oppose it. This meant that he could keep his Cabinet together.

[21] Protestant Tories' opposed Catholic Emancipation. 'Ultra-Tories' were active in the Tory Party from the 1820s through to the 1850s. They opposed Catholic Emancipation and supported the Corn Laws but were on the losing side in every cause they championed.

Canning had no wish to weaken his position by pursuing a policy unpopular in his own party. Canning was also viewed with suspicion by right-wing Tories in two other areas. He wanted to restructure the Corn Laws and to pursue a foreign policy that improved Britain's global trading position. Both threatened protection and moves towards freer trade at the expense of farmers threatened to split the Tory party.

When Canning died in August 1827, he was succeeded by Frederick Robinson, Viscount Goderich who had been an able Chancellor of the Exchequer. However, he was a disastrous Prime Minister and resigned the following January. The king then turned to Wellington supported by Peel as leader of the Commons. To begin with, Wellington looked as if he could hold the Tories together but cracks soon began to appear. In May 1828, Huskisson and his allies resigned from the government over internal disagreements with colleagues. Wellington found his position weakened by the need to give way over Catholic Emancipation in 1829. 'Protestant' opinion within the Tory party was outraged. The death of George IV necessitated the 1830 General Election that, despite having granted Catholic Emancipation, was not a disaster for the government. However, Wellington's opposition to parliamentary reform was. His statement on 2 November that the existing constitution was in need of no further reform was an attempt to unite his party but it had disastrous consequences. It united all those opposed to Wellington--Whigs, radicals, ultra and 'liberal' Tories. He no longer had the confidence of Parliament and resigned on 16 November 1830. The Whigs returned to government committed to parliamentary reform

How 'liberal' was the government's reaction to the need for legal reform?

There were growing concern about the effectiveness of the legal system. In the civil courts procedures were out of date and cases were frequently subject to long delays. The criminal law was seen as harsh and juries often preferred to find prisoners not guilty rather than sentence them to death for minor capital crimes. There were over 200 capital offences and a further 400 that could lead to transportation. There was no regular police force and the state of prisons had been subject to harsh criticism by John Howard in the 1770s, Sir Frederick Eden in the 1790s and Elizabeth Fry after 1810.[22]

This led to demands for reform of criminal justice from the first decade of the century. Campaigners like Sir Samuel Romilly protested at

---

[22] John Howard (1726-1790) and Elizabeth Fry (1750-1845) were leading champions of prison reform. Howard was especially concerned with improving prison sanitation while Fry was concerned with the treatment of women prisoners.

the 'lottery of justice': there was uncertainty about the punishment for different offences and even when the death sentence was passed it was far from certain that it would be carried out. Judges had too much discretionary power and responded to different offences in different ways. Whig historians[23] of criminal justice have applauded Romilly and the other reformers who were able to get things done because of an increasing level of cross-party parliamentary opinion. The opponents of reform, however, had a strong case. They insisted that justice was not a lottery and that judicial discretion was sensible and conscientiously practised. Reformers could point to injustices but anti-reformers pointed to many examples that showed the system working with mercy and moderation. The problem for the opponents of reform was that moderate and influential Tories like Peel were sympathetic to the reformers' image of justice.

Sir Robert Peel's appointment as Home Secretary in 1822 led to significant reform of the legal system. It is, however, important to recognise that he built on initiatives from the earlier part of Liverpool's government especially the recommendations of Sir James Mackintosh's 1819 committee that the legal system was in need of reform to make it more acceptable, less archaic and fairer in its operation by removing out-dated laws. Peel's reforms fell into two distinct types--reform of the legal system and more efficient policing. The prison system was reformed and central control was tightened. In 1823 the Gaol Act, followed by amending legislation the following year, tried to establish a degree of uniformity throughout the prisons of England and Wales. The legislation laid down health and religious regulations, required the categorisation of prisoners and directed magistrates to inspect prisons three times a year and demanded that annual reports be sent from each gaol to the Home Office. Many local gaols ignored at least some of these regulations and Peel reluctant to antagonise local sensibilities about independence, made no attempt to impose a national system of inspection. It was not until 1835 that the reforming Whig government of Melbourne, with Lord John Russell at the Home Office, established a prison Inspectorate of five with only limited powers. The creation of the Metropolitan Police in 1829 represented a new conception of policing. Full-time, professional and well organised, the police were intended to be the impersonal agents of central policy. However, the 'new' police often turned out to be very similar to the old, in personnel, efficiency and tactics. It was only later in the 1830s that legislation was introduced that would fulfil Peel's intentions.[24]

---

[23] Whig historians interpreted history as a process of improvement and saw the past through contemporary moral ideas.
[24] In the 1830s that legislation. The Municipal Corporation Act 1835 and the Rural Constabulary Act 1839 spread the new police into the provincial boroughs

How significant were the reforms Peel introduced? Compared to Lord John Russell, Home Secretary between 1835 and 1839, some historians argue that Peel merely 'tinkered' with the system by repealing statutes that were no longer used. Peel's reputation as a prison reformer is also suspect as he simply put on the statute book in 1823 and 1824 legislation accepted by the government three years earlier. His introduction of the Metropolitan Police in 1829 built on his experience as Chief Secretary in Ireland where, in 1814, he had established an efficient police system. However, Peel established one important principle. He recognised that an effective legal system needed to operate within a framework of centrally determined policies and that, even if the administration of justice still lay largely at the local level there needed to be central supervision of the process.

How did the government react to demands for religious equality?

Catholics and Nonconformists had long been subjected to discrimination because of their beliefs. In practice, the Corporation Act 1661 and the Test Acts of 1673 and 1678 meant that Nonconformists and Catholics had few political rights.[25] The campaign by Nonconformists for the repeal of this legislation began in the 1780s. The issue of Catholic rights was more complex and in 1801, William Pitt's proposals for Catholic Emancipation were blocked by the king. The Catholic question remained unresolved throughout Liverpool's administration. Between 1812 and 1827, an agreement existed that the cabinet would remain neutral on the issue and would not raise Emancipation as a matter of government business. This did not prevent individual ministers from differing on the issue.

The formation of the Catholic Association in 1823, led by Daniel [26] renewed Catholic agitation in Ireland and revived interest in Emancipation. Bills giving varying concessions to Catholics passed the Commons in 1821, 1822 and 1825 but the Lords rejected them all. While Liverpool was Prime Minister, the repeal of discriminating

---

and enabled counties to establish police forces. The County and Borough Police Act 1856 completed the process subjecting the police to central inspection and allowing grants to police forces certified as 'efficient'.

[25] The Corporation Act prevented Nonconformists being elected to town councils but they could be MPs under the 1678 Test Act because there was no requirement to take the Anglican Communion. The two Test Acts prevented Catholics from membership of either the Commons or Lords unless they took the oath of supremacy and allegiance and an anti-Catholic declaration condemning 'superstitious and idolatrous' Roman practices.

[26] Daniel O' Connell (1775-1847) was known as 'The Liberator'. He founded the Catholic Association in 1823 as a mass movement to campaign for Catholic Emancipation. In the 1840s, he campaigned for the repeal of the Act of Union.

legislation was successfully resisted and he successfully contained differing opinions among his ministers. His resignation in early 1827 and the rapid succession of Canning and then Goderich meant that the Catholic question could no longer be avoided. It is ironic that the most 'Protestant' of Tories, the duke of Wellington first repealed the Test and Corporation Acts in 1828 and the following year conceded Catholic Emancipation.

In 1828 and 1829, Wellington was faced by a stark dilemma. He was aware that if he took any action that threatened the supremacy of the Church of England, he would face widespread opposition from his own MPs. A strong alliance of extra-parliamentary Nonconformists championed the well-organised campaign for the repeal of the Test and Corporation Acts. Peel piloted the legislation through the Commons and in the Lords where the bishops overwhelmingly supported the proposal. Catholic Emancipation was, however, a different matter.

By 1828, resistance to Catholic Emancipation was crumbling. Repeal of the Test and Corporation Acts established the principle that the constitution could be changed. When Huskisson resigned from the Board of Trade in May 1828, he was replaced by Vesey Fitzgerald, an Irish Protestant MP who favoured Catholic Emancipation. In the subsequent County Clare by-election, O'Connell stood against him and won. As a Catholic O'Connell could not take his seat in the Commons and Wellington and Peel were faced with two alternatives. They could use force to ban the Catholic Association, but there were insufficient troops in Ireland to do that or they could concede Emancipation. Calling a General Election on the issue would have solved nothing--the 1826 Election showed the strength of anti-Catholicism on the mainland--but it was likely that British rule in Ireland would be challenged if large numbers of ineligible Irish Catholic MPs were elected. Wellington concluded that Emancipation was necessary to prevent civil war in Ireland. Despite opposition in both Commons and Lords, Emancipation was easily achieved largely because Wellington could count on the support of the Whigs.

This undermined the Protestant basis of his government and split the Tories. By early 1829, the Ultras were a party within a party. The cost for Wellington and Peel was high. They had betrayed their party and although his ministry limped on for over a year it was barely supported by many Tories and vigorously opposed by the Whigs. Wellington hoped that things would improve before the next General Election scheduled for 1832-1833 but the death of George IV at the end of June 1830 ended this hope.

4 The Whig reforms 1830-1841

The Whigs supported the idea of both parliamentary and social reform. When they came to power in late 1830, they put parliamentary reform at the centre of their political agenda and it dominated debate until the Reform Act was passed in 1832. In addition to parliamentary reform, there was reform of the local vestries in 1831 and municipal government in 1835.

Constitutional reform

Reform of parliament in 1832 and of towns and cities, three years later and important developments in dealing with the poor, factory conditions and education marked the Whig governments as 'reforming' administrations and the 1830s as 'the decade of reform'. The measures they introduced began a process of reform that was not completed until the 1870s.

1830 November	Wellington speaks against the need for parliamentary reform (2 November); government defeated on a vote (15 November); Wellington resigned the following day. Whig administration formed under Earl Grey.
1831 March	First Reform Bill introduced into House of Commons; passes Second Reading but only by one vote (302 to 302).
April	Government defeated on an amendment objecting to the reduction in the number of MPs for England and Wales at the Committee Stage. Parliament dissolved.
June	Whigs returned after General Election: the MPs split into 370 pro-reformers, 235 anti-reformers and 53 undecided. Second Reform Bill introduced into Parliament 24 June.
July	Second Reading carried 367 to 231.
September	Third Reading carried by 345 to 236 (22 September).
October	House of Lords reject the Bill by 41 votes (199 to 158) (8 October); widespread rioting in Nottingham and Derby (8-10 October) and Bristol (29-31 October) as a result of the rejection of the Bill.
December	Third Reform Bill introduced into Commons (12 December) and passes its Second Reading in the Commons before Christmas.
1832 January	William IV agrees to the creation of peers in order to ensure Reform Acts can be passed.
March	Reform Bill passes Third Reading in the Commons by 355 to 239 votes (22 March).
April	Reform Bill passes Second Reading in the Lords by nine votes (13 April).

May	Government defeat on Lord Lyndhurst's motion led to the resignation of ministers. 'Days of May' (9-15 May) when Wellington asked to form an administration but is unable to do so. The King is compelled to recall Grey and confirm that peers will be created to ensure the passage of the Bill.
June	Reform Bill passes Third Reading in the Lords (106 to 22) and receives Royal Assent (4 and 7 June)
July	Scottish Reform Act passed.
August	Irish Reform Act passed.
December	General Election under the new franchise: Whigs 483 MPs, Tories 175.

The death of George IV and the accession of William IV in early 1830 had two important consequences. There had to be a General Election within six months of the death of the monarch. This meant that Wellington had to fight an election at least two years earlier than he expected with his party still deeply divided over the passage of Catholic Emancipation. George IV's long-standing veto on the Whig leader was removed as William IV was prepared for Earl Grey to become Prime Minister.

When Wellington conceded Catholic Emancipation in 1829, he made himself very unpopular with his party and with the British people. His problems were made worse by the outbreak of revolution in France in July 1830[1] and the 'Swing' riots in August, both of which raised the threat of widespread public disorder in Britain. Despite his unpopularity, Wellington did well in the election and the Tories gained 21 seats. Parliamentary reform had been an important issue in some constituencies but concerns about economic conditions, the continuation of the Corn Laws and the effects of Catholic Emancipation and of the ending of slavery in the British Empire were also evident.

It was clear when Parliament reassembled in October 1830 that the question of parliamentary reform could not be ignored but Wellington ruled this out in a speech he gave on 2 November. This led to the fall of his administration when he was defeated on a crucial vote of the Civil List (monies paid to the monarchy) on 15 November. Both the Huskisson Tories and some ultra-Tories were prepared to vote against their party because of his attitude to further reform. Wellington no longer had the confidence of the House of Commons and resigned the following day. The Whigs formed a government making the introduction of parliamentary reform inevitable. The Whigs long-standing commitment to reform led to 18 months of frenetic activity inside and outside

---

[1] The July Revolution in France resulted in the removal of the last Bourbon king, Charles X and his replacement by the more liberal Louis Philippe.

Parliament that culminated in the passage of the Reform Acts in mid-1832.

The Reform Act 1832

1. **Disfranchising clauses**
   - 56 rotten or nomination boroughs returning 111 MPs lost their representation.
   - 30 boroughs with less than 4,000 inhabitants lost one MP each.
   - Weymouth and Melcombe Regis gave up 2 of their 4 members.
   - 143 seats were made available for redistribution.

2. **Enfranchising clauses**
   - 65 seats were awarded to the counties.
   - 44 seats distributed to 22 large towns including Manchester, Leeds, Birmingham and Sheffield and to new London metropolitan districts.
   - 21 smaller towns were given one MP each.
   - Scotland given 8 extra seats.
   - Ireland gains 5 extra seats.

3. **The franchise**
   - In the boroughs, the franchise was given to all householders paying a yearly rent of £10 and, subject to a one year residence qualification, £10 lodgers (if sharing a house and the landlord not in residence).
   - In the counties, the franchise was given to 40s freeholders[2]; £10 copyholders[3] and long-lease holders and £50 short-lease holders or tenants-at-will.[4] Borough freeholders could also vote in the counties where they held land if their freehold was between 40s and £10 or if it was over £10 and occupied by a tenant.
   - Registration of electors for each constituency on an electoral roll revised annually.
   - Those with 'ancient rights'[5] retained their vote until their death.
   - No secret ballot.

   The Reform Act redefined who had the right to vote in both counties

---

[2] Freeholders owned their own land.
[3] Copyholders were tenants who had a lease for 20 to 25 years giving them considerable security of tenure.
[4] Tenants-at-will had short-term leases and were consequently more easily 'influenced' by their landlords to vote the way they wanted with the threat of eviction of tenants did not.
[5] 'Ancient rights' applied to those who had the right to vote under the pre-1832 system.

and boroughs. The electorate of England and Wales increased by 78 per cent between 1831 and 1833 rising from 366,250 to 652,777 but this still represented only five per cent of the population of England and Wales in the 1831 census. Parliamentary seats were redistributed, especially in England, provided MPs for areas of growing population and economic influence. 56 rotten boroughs lost both their MPs and 40 smaller boroughs lost one MP. These seats were then given (or redistributed) to places previously without their own MPs. While the Acts removed the most obvious defects of the unreformed system, they did not remove all the inequalities of representation: they did introduce democracy nor did not give the middle-classes control of the political system. As Earl Grey,[6] the Whig Prime Minister, observed that the Reform Acts were essentially 'aristocratic measures', which aimed at preserving the power of the landowner by aligning them with the propertied middle-classes.

Their achievement lay in establishing a political climate in which questions about reforming the constitution and discussion of new political ideas were acceptable and no longer considered revolutionary. Radical working-class opinion was disappointed by the attitude of the Whigs to their demands but they had not united in their attitude to reform between 1830 and 1832. Some radicals were prepared to accept limited household suffrage and to work with middle-class reformers; others led by Henry Hunt demanded manhood suffrage and were unwilling to collaborate. Either way, working-class aspirations were not met by the Reform Act and it was subsequently seen as the 'great betrayal'.

Was 1832 an expression of change or continuity? Although contemporaries thought that the Reform Acts were middle-class measures, the reality was somewhat different. The urban middle-class were happy to elect MPs from the landed interest. The composition of the 1833 Parliament was not very different from the unreformed one. Between 70 and 80 per cent of MPs were still from the landed interest and no more than a hundred were from the professional and industrial middle-classes, a number comparable with elections before 1832.

Municipal reform

In July 1833, a Royal Commission was set up to consider the question of municipal reform. Its report, published in 1835, formed the basis of the Municipal Corporations Act that extended the principles of the 1832 Reform Act. Many towns were unincorporated. They had no charter giving them independent rights and under the control of the local

---

[6] Charles Grey, 2nd Earl Grey (1764-1845) held office in 1806-1807 but had to wait until 1830 until he became Prime Minister, a position he held until 1834.

magistrates and paid the county rate.[7] Corporate towns, so called because they were run by an elected corporation had charters, many of them dating to the Middle Ages. The distribution of incorporated and unincorporated towns was an accident of history rather than a consequence of size or importance. Many of the rapidly growing cities, like Birmingham, Manchester and Sheffield, were without corporations. Reform was necessary to take account of changes in population and the move from a rural-agrarian economy to and urban-industrial one.

There were pressing arguments for reform. Law and order was a growing problem for both national and local government. Many feared that large towns were increasingly ungovernable because of their undisciplined populations. The unreformed corporations tended to be largely Tory and Anglican which, was unacceptable to the emerging industrial urban elites with their Whig and Nonconformist sympathies. They believed that reform would allow for a degree of equity between the economic interests in towns. The corporations were generally self-electing. For radicals, this meant that urban elites could maintain themselves in power and exclude others (especially the middle-classes). Municipal reform was seen as a necessary part of parliamentary reform.

The Royal Commission criticised the inefficiency and corruption of the existing corporations. The government accepted the its proposals and the bill quickly passed the Commons. However, it met substantial Tory opposition in the Lords. Its passage was eased when the Whigs compromised on some of the contentious issues: aldermen were retained and made up a quarter of a council, councillors were to have substantial property qualifications and in boroughs with over 6,000 inhabitants the town was to be divided into wards. The bill became law in September 1835. Twenty-two new boroughs were incorporated within twenty years, including Manchester and Birmingham in 1838.

- 178 corporations were abolished and replaced by elected councils.
- A uniform household franchise was established by which all occupiers with a three-year residence qualification could vote for the first council and after that annually for one third of the council.
- Each council elected its own mayor and aldermen.
- All debates would be open and accounts publicly audited.
- Corporations could take over the duties of local improvement commissions. Few councils took advantage of this permissive clause.
- Corporations could levy rates.
- Councils must form watch committees and could establish borough

---

[7] Local government taxes were raised for either specific purposes (like building a local bridge) or to cover general spending. The county rate was a general tax.

police forces.
- The Act laid down procedures by which a town could petition for incorporation.

Whig reforms 1832-1841

During the 1833 and 1834 sessions Lord Althorp,[8] leader of the House of Commons, showed that the energy for further reform remained strong. Although ministers sympathised with and even promoted specific bills in general, legislation to improve the condition of the 'lower orders' such as factory, education and Poor Law reform resulted partly because of extra-parliamentary pressure and fact-finding Royal Commissions. Althorp's record suggests, however, that the Whig government did have certain political principles as well as humanitarian concerns and that their actions cannot be seen simply as a response to external pressures.

Melbourne, Prime Minister briefly in 1834 and between 1835 and 1841 led a government that was far less radical that Grey's.[9] There were various reasons for this. Melbourne fought General Elections in 1835 (called by the Conservatives after the minority government of Sir Robert Peel was defeated) and in 1837 (after the death of William IV). This reduced the Whig majority to 32 after 1837 and Melbourne had to rely on the support of the Irish MPs or the agreement of the Conservatives to get legislation through Parliament. By temperament Melbourne was not a radical reformer preferring gradual to fundamental change. By 1835, Britain had experienced almost a decade of frenetic change and need a period of stability. Lord John Russell[10] offended radicals in the autumn of 1837, acquiring the nickname of 'Finality Jack', when he strongly defended the reform settlement and declared himself against further reform.

---

[8] John Charles Spencer, Viscount Althorp, 3rd Earl Spencer (1782-1845) preferred private life to politics but played a central role in Grey's and Melbourne's ministries as Chancellor of the Exchequer. She succeeded his father as Earl Spencer in November 1834 and left political life. He was not an eloquent speaker but had the confidence of the House of Commons because of his honesty.

[9] William Lamb, 2nd Viscount Melbourne (1779-1848) was Home Secretary 1830-1834 and Prime Minister in 1834 and against from 1835 to 1841. Though he led a Whig government, he was by nature conservative in his attitudes. He holds the distinction of being the last Prime Minister to be dismissed by the monarch (William IV in 1834).

[10] Lord John Russell, 1st Earl Russell (1792-1878) was a radical Whig politician, at least in his youth. He was Postmaster General 1830-1834, Home Secretary 1835-1839 and Colonial Secretary 1839-1841. He served as Prime Minister between 1846 and 1852 and again in 1865-1866.

By the late 1830s, however, the Whigs were showing signs of stress. Unemployment and manufacturing depression deepened after 1838 and the government appeared to have no answers to the economic and social problems facing Britain. However, Melbourne's government did introduce important reforms on church matters. The Ecclesiastical Revenues Commission that had been established in June 1832 to investigate the financial structure of the Church of England was not very effective and, during Peel's minority administration in early 1835, a new Commission was set up to 'consider the State of the Established Church'. Made permanent in 1836 as the Ecclesiastical Commission, it introduced a series of major reforms of the Church's structure. These measures reinforced State control over the Church.

The following is a summary of reforming legislation passed between 1832 and 1841:

1833	Slavery abolished throughout the British Empire and £20 million allocated as compensation for slave owners. The abolition of slavery was clearly influenced by the extra-parliamentary campaign. It also redeemed pledges given to the electorate by many Whig candidates in the 1830 and 1832 General Elections. The measure disappointed humanitarians by delaying full emancipation of slaves until a period of 'apprenticeship' in limited freedom had been served (seven years for slaves who worked on the land, five years for the rest).
	Factory Act passed but it applied only to the textile industry. It restricted the employment of young children and established an inspectorate to enforce the act. This laid the foundation for later social and industrial legislation.
	£20,000 was granted to the voluntary societies providing elementary education. This established the principle of state-assisted education.
	Reform of the law by Henry Brougham,[11] Lord Chancellor establishing the central criminal court and the Judicial Committee of the Privy Council.
	Irish Church Temporalities Act abolished 10 Church of Ireland bishoprics and reduced the revenues of the remainder. Surplus revenues to be used for purely church purposes.
1834	Poor Law Amendment Act reformed the existing system of poor relief. It introduced workhouses and said that all relief should be in the workhouse. Parishes were grouped together into Poor Law Unions to improve efficiency and reduce costs.
1835	Municipal Corporations Act

---

[11] Henry Brougham, 1st Baron Brougham and Vaux (1778-1868) was a barrister and writer by profession. He helped found the *Edinburgh Review* in 1802 and London University in 1828. He was Lord Chancellor between 1830 and 1834 introducing radical reform of the legal system and supervising the passage of the Reform Act but never held office again.

1836	Commutation of Tithes Act legislated for tithes to be paid in money (a rent charge) based on the average price of corn in previous seven years. Tithes were paid to the Church of England and consisted of a tenth part of the main produce of the land (corn, oats, wood etc.) and a tenth part of the profits of labour. They were very unpopular, especially with Nonconformists and often difficult for clergymen to collect. The rent charge was abolished in 1925 and any remaining tithes in 1936.
	Dissenters' Marriage Act allowing Nonconformists to be married outside an Anglican church, in special circumstances by a civil ceremony.
	The registration of births, marriages and deaths made compulsory with the introduction of civil registration. This ended the Anglican Church's monopoly of the registration of baptisms, marriages and burials.
	Act enabling London University to grant degrees. This broke the monopoly of Oxford and Cambridge universities where students had to be Anglicans to take a degree. London University was open to all Protestants.
1838	The Pluralities Act placed restrictions on clerical pluralism (clergymen having more than one parish). Acts for building and enlarging churches were also passed.
1839	Education grant increased to £30,000 and government inspectors appointed to supervise the schools receiving the grant.
1840	Excess revenues of cathedrals were distributed to parishes with the greatest needs.

Problems for the Whigs

The Whigs faced threats to public order and property. They inherited the Swing disturbances across southern England when they came to power in November 1830. Melbourne, as Home Secretary urged local magistrates to act vigorously against rioters. Of the 1,976 prisoners tried in thirty-four counties 252 were sentenced to death though only 19 were hanged, 505 were transported and 644 were imprisoned. No other protest movement in this period was treated as severely.

The Whig governments faced other challenges to its authority in the first half of the 1830s. There were campaigns against stamp duties[12] on newspaper taxes, for factory movement, trade union activity on an unprecedented scale and the anti-Poor Law agitation, as well as the campaign for parliamentary reform. Radical working-class opinion was disappointed by the attitude of the Whigs to their demands. The Reform

---

[12] There was a stamp duty on newspapers. This was very unpopular as it pushed up prices. Many believed it was a government device for keeping information out of the hands of the working-class

Act was seen as the 'great betrayal'. The 1833 Factory Act did not meet the aspirations of the extra-parliamentary factory reformers. The 1834 Poor Law Amendment Act led to widespread opposition and attacks on trade unions culminating in the case of the Tolpuddle Martyrs.[13] Chartism posed a more serious challenge to the government. Russell, as Home Secretary until late August 1839, initially behaved with restraint, assuming that its appeal was limited. By mid-1839, however, a harder policy had emerged as the Home Office recognised that local authorities could not manage without support. Drilling was banned. Six thousand regular troops were stationed in the north and leading Chartists were arrested, tried and imprisoned or, in some cases, transported.

The Whig party found itself under attack from a revitalised Tory party led by Sir Robert Peel and by internal divisions. The Tory party, trounced in the 1832 General Election revived and the Whigs saw their majority in the Commons gradually eroded. The number of Conservative MPs rose from 150 after the 1832 election to about 290 in 1835 and then 313 in 1837 and finally 370 when they won in 1841. Some MPs who had voted for reform in 1832 returned to Conservative ranks. There was a long-running battle between Edward Stanley, the Irish Secretary, and Lord John Russell over the direction of Irish policy especially lay appropriation[14] contained in the Irish Temporalities Bill of 1833 but later dropped when it encountered opposition in the House of Lords. Russell, however, continued to urge the principle. This led to the resignation of four cabinet ministers, Edward Stanley,[15] Sir James Graham, the Duke of Richmond and the Earl of Ripon, the so-called 'Derby Dilly'.[16] Policies, largely initiated by Russell, towards Ireland and in favour of nonconformists led to a gradual alienation of some of the government's more moderate supporters in the House of Commons. Over thirty MPs

---

[13] The Tolpuddle Martyrs were six farm labourers from Dorset transported to Australia for trade union activity. Their plight, seen by many of grossly unfair, proved an important focal point for radical activity in 1834 and 1835. Lord Melbourne refused to pardon them as Home Secretary but when Prime Minister he allowed Lord John Russell, his Home Secretary to do so.

[14] Lay appropriation meant using the revenues of the Church of Ireland for non-church or temporal activities such as funding non-denominational schools.

[15] Lord Edward Smith-Stanley, (1799-1869) 14th Earl of Derby (1851-1869) was Chief Secretary for Ireland 1830-1833 and Colonial Secretary 1833-1834 but resigned over the question of lay appropriation. He served in Peel's government as Colonial Secretary 1841-1845 before resigning over the proposal to repeal the Corn Laws. He was later Prime Minister of Conservative governments in 1852, 1858-1859 and 1866-1868.

[16] Sir James Graham (1792-1861) backed Canning in the 1820s but supported the Whig government until 1834. He was Peel's Home Secretary between 1841 and 1846.

who had voted for reform in 1832 crossed to the Conservative benches between 1833 and 1837.

In July 1834, the government was embarrassed by revelations that it had negotiated with O'Connell when deciding whether to renew the Irish Coercion Bill. This led to Grey's retirement and his replacement by Lord Melbourne. Melbourne proposed that Russell should become leader of the House of Commons in November. William IV objected to this and Melbourne resigned. Peel formed a minority Conservative administration and gained about 100 seats in the early 1835 General Election. This did not give him a parliamentary majority and was forced to resign in April 1835. His defeat was made possible by the 'Litchfield House compact' of March 1835 when the Whigs and O'Connell's Irish MPs agreed to cooperate to remove Peel. Melbourne returned with Russell as Home Secretary.

The Whigs' relations with the Crown improved with the accession of Victoria in June 1837. A close personal relationship developed between Melbourne and Victoria. This was exploited in the 'Bedchamber crisis' of 1839. In May 1839, the Whig majority was reduced to five and Melbourne decided to resign. The Queen, however, refused to change any of the Ladies of her Bedchamber who were all Whigs. Peel would not form a government under such circumstance—a very useful excuse for him as he would again lead a minority government--and Melbourne returned to office. This gave the Whigs two more years in power but Peel no longer supported them on moderate issues.

5 Redefining Toryism

Peel is generally recognised as the founder of modern Conservatism. He saw the need for the Tory party to adapt itself after its disastrous showing in the 1832 General Election when 175 Tory MPs were elected out of the 658 MPs in the House of Commons. In successive elections in the 1830s, the Conservatives increased their support in the House of Commons eventually defeating Melbourne's Whig government in 1841.

Peel was prepared to put the interests of the nation above those of the Tory party and on two occasions introduced policies that went against the basic tenets of Toryism. In 1829, he pushed through Catholic Emancipation against the wishes of the Protestant Tory majority and 17 years later, he ignored its belief in protection for agriculture by repealing the Corn Laws exposing divisions within the developing Conservative party.

1832	Electoral disaster for the Tories in the December General Election (175 Tory, 483 Whig).
1833	Peel stated that he would support the Whig government when it acted in defence of law, order and property.
1834	William IV dismissed Melbourne's government [November] and Peel became Prime Minister of a minority Tory government; the Tamworth Manifesto.
1835	Ecclesiastical Commission set up. The Tories gained seats in the General Election (273 Tory, 385 Whig) but Peel is defeated by an alliance of Whigs and Radicals; return to opposition.
1836	Peel, with the support of Wellington in the Lords worked for greater co-operation between Tories in the two Houses of Parliament to coordinate their attack on the Whigs.
1837	Further gains in the General Election (313 Tory, 345 Whig).
1839	Bedchamber Crisis.
1840	Disagreements between Peel and Wellington over various issues; Wellington persuade to compromise to maintain Conservative unity.
1841	Whigs defeated on vote of no confidence in June leading to a General Election in July. Conservatives win (367 Conservative, 291 Whig) and Peel became Prime Minister of a majority government.
1842	Reintroduction of income tax, reduction of duties on wheat and a general reduction in tariffs in Peel's first budget. Mines Act banned women and children from working underground
1843	Graham's Factory Bill provoked widespread opposition from Nonconformists over its educational clauses.
1844	Factory Act reduced working hours in textile mills. Significant Tory support for the ten-hour working day. Government defeat reversed when Peel threatens to resign. Backbench revolt on sugar duties. Bank Charter Act and Joint Stock Companies Act

1845	Budget renewed income tax and further reduced tariffs including abolishing many import duties. Gladstone resigned on proposal to increase grant to Roman Catholic seminary at Maynooth; 149 Tories voted against the grant. Irish Famine began and Peel committed Cabinet to repeal Corn Laws in December.
1846	Widespread opposition among Tories, to repeal of the Corn Laws [January-February]. Only 112 Tories supported Peel on Corn Law vote and repeal was only carried by Whig votes. Peel resigned after defeat on Irish Coercion Bill in June.

How effective was Peel as a party leader in the 1830s?

In the 1830s, Peel was not a 'leader of the opposition' in its modern sense. He was not the official leader of the Tories until the end of 1834. Wellington led the Tories in the House of Lords and, as a previous Prime Minister was regarded by some as the Tory leader. Peel led the Tories in the Commons and was prepared to support government legislation when it was aimed at maintaining law and order. Considerable distrust existed between Peel and the ultra-Tories. They feared that Peel would betray the party, as they believed he had in 1829 over Catholic Emancipation. Peel, on the other hand, did not believe that the Ultras would act as part of a responsible opposition in Parliament and rejected their view that politics should be determined largely by the interests of English landowners.

When George IV dismissed Melbourne's government in November 1834, he first turned to Wellington to form a new government. Wellington refused because he believed that Prime Ministers must carry authority in the House of Commons. The King then appointed Peel. Peel did not become Prime Minister because he was leader of a party in the Commons; instead, his authority as leader of the Tories was the result of his appointment as Prime Minister by the king. This reinforced his view of the executive nature of government. Strong government, he thought, not only achieved more but also was preferred by the governed. This meant efficient administration to maintain public order in the interests of the country. His financial and commercial reforms in the 1840s were designed to promote public order as much as relieve the economic complaints of manufacturers and consumers. This same concern can also be seen in his Irish policies. His first loyalty was to the king, rather than to the Tory party. This was an important distinction and proved central to his decisions during the 'Bedchamber crisis'[1] in 1839 and the crisis over

---

[1] A close relationship grew up between the young Victoria and Lord Melbourne after she became Queen in 1837. This was exploited in the 'Bedchamber crisis' of 1839. In May 1839, the Whig majority was reduced to five and Melbourne

the repeal of the Corn Laws in 1845-1846. Peel's minority administration lasted just a hundred days ending in April 1835 after which the Conservatives returned to opposition.

Peel's attitude to parliamentary reform

In late 1832, the Tory party was in a demoralised state. Although the party had opposed parliamentary reform, there were nevertheless those who did not condemn the principle of reform entirely but believed the Whigs had gone too far. Unquestionably, there were die-hard opponents of reform among the Tories: the ultras-Tories in Lords and Commons, opposed parliamentary reform, municipal reform, church reform, factory reform and Poor Law reform. The clearest statement we have of Peel's attitude to reform came in his response to the King's speech at the opening of Parliament in early 1833: 'He [Peel] was for reforming every institution that really required reform; but he was for doing it gradually, dispassionately and deliberately, in order that reform might be lasting'. Change, if necessary, must reinforce not undermine the Constitution and Britain's governing elite. This was not designed to pacify the Ultras within the party

Peel was dedicated to good government by men of integrity. He believed that power should be held by an elite with the education and expertise necessary to act in the national interest. Public opinion had its place but Peel sought to find the proper balance between executive government and public opinion that he believed had been altered by the crisis over reform. Like most of his contemporaries, Peel was not a democrat. The 'people', he believed, did not have the necessary education or judgement to make central decisions and if Parliament surrendered to outside pressure, the quality of its judgements would be weakened and the interests of the nation jeopardised.

Reconstructing the Tory party

Peel's achievement in the 1830s was to make the Tory party more relevant to a changing society. He recognised that staying in opposition would not restore the fortunes of the Tories and that it was necessary to alter the widely-held view that the Tory party was reactionary and supported by only a small part of the population. To do this, Peel needed to broaden support for the party amongst the newly enfranchised urban middle-classes and

---

decided to resign. The Queen, however, refused to accept Conservative ladies in waiting rather than her existing Whig ladies. Peel regarded this as a matter of principle and refused to form a government under such circumstances. Melbourne returned to office for a further two years.

rekindled support among the landed interest who had voted Whig in the 1832 General Election. He did this by linking the interests of all property owners--whether landed, industrial or commercial--firmly to the necessity of public order through the maintenance of the existing Constitution.

His appointment as Prime Minister in 1834-1835 gave him the opportunity of making his position clear to the new electorate in the Tamworth Manifesto of December 1834.[2] Peel used the manifesto to make his position on three issues clear to the nation. He maintained that it was essential to broaden the appeal of the Tory party and the manifesto contained a direct bid for uncommitted middle-class voters.

'I gladly avail myself also of this, a legitimate opportunity, of making a more public appeal -- of addressing, through you [his own electorate in Tamworth], to that great and intelligent class of society of which you are a portion, and a fair and unexceptionable representative -- to that class which is much less interested in the contentions of party, than in the maintenance of order and the cause of good government'.

Peel was also anxious to emphasise that he accepted the Reform Act and that there would be no attempt to reverse the changes already made by the Whigs. He committed himself and his party to moderate reform where there was a strong case for it. This was designed to gain the support of the middle-classes who wanted further reforms.

'I consider the Reform Bill a final and irrevocable settlement of a great Constitutional question -- a settlement which no friend of the peace and welfare of this country would attempt to disturb, either by direct or insidious means..... But if the spirit of the Reform Bill implies merely a careful review of institutions, civil and ecclesiastical, undertaken in a friendly temper, combining, with the firm maintenance of established rights, the correction of proved abuses and the redress of real grievances -- in that case, I can for myself and colleagues undertake to act in such a spirit and with such intentions...'

Finally, he made his support for the Church of England clear, essential if he wanted the cooperation of the Ultras but was prepared to support reform of its abuses.

'Then, as to the great question of Church reform...I cannot give my consent to the alienating of Church property, in any part of the United Kingdom, from strictly Ecclesiastical purposes [he opposed lay appropriation] ...With regard to alterations in the law which govern our Ecclesiastical Establishment.... It is a subject

---

[2] The Tamworth Manifesto was an address by Peel to his constituents at Tamworth. On taking office, he was legally required to seek re-election but it had been approved in advance by the cabinet and sent to leading London newspapers for publication on 18 December 1834.

which must undergo the fullest deliberation and into that deliberation the Government will enter, and with the sincerest desire to remove every abuse that can impair the efficiency of the Establishment, to extend the sphere of its usefulness and to strengthen and confirm its just claims upon the respect and affections of the people.'

The Manifesto was too liberal by some but the majority of the Ultras went along with Peel.

Throughout the 1830s, Peel sought to broaden Tory support in the country and convince dissidents within the party that he had taken account of both their interests. This was accompanied by the gradual introduction of the term 'Conservative' in place of 'Tory'. Tories believed in the uncompromising defence of the privileges enjoyed by institutions connected to the Anglican landed interest while Conservatives accepted the need for gradual and cautious change designed to reconcile those institutions with the needs of the modern world. The strategy of reforming to conserve, Peel believed, was an effective way of preventing radical reformers who threatened to erode or even destroy the traditional ruling institutions of the country. Conservatism may be seen as an extension of the 'liberal' Tory administrative reforming impulse of the 1820s.

The 1841 election

Peel is credited with the Conservative victory in 1841: without his leadership, many contemporaries believed that the Tories could have been assigned to permanent opposition. Peel's parliamentary performance during the 1830s was an important element in this revival. His grasp of economics let him capitalise on the growing economic problems the Whigs faced after 1838. Nevertheless, there were other pressures at work over which Peel had little or no control. After the 1832 election, the Whigs rapidly found their dominant position eroded. Forty MPs who has supported the Reform Act moved to the Conservative benches between 1832 and 1837. Four Whig cabinet ministers resigned over Irish appropriation in June 1834, two of whom became Conservative supporters by the late 1830s and ministers in the 1840s. In addition, the Whigs were seen as unable to control the radicals that Tory propaganda played on.

The unexpected frequency of General Elections after 1832 also aided the Conservative cause. Peel used William IV's invitation to form a government in late 1834 to call an election in 1835. A further election was held on William's death in 1837. These gave those voters, concerned that the Whigs wished to push reform further and threaten their position as property-owners, the opportunity of voting Tory. The Conservatives increased their MPs by about 100 in the 1835 election and added 40 more in the election two years later. By-election successes between 1837 and 1841 further improved their position. Between 1837 and 1841, they were only 30 votes short of the Whigs and their normal voting allies. The electoral tide was running in their favour.

The emergence of an organisational structure also played an important part in reviving Tory fortunes. Peel played little part in organisational change in the 1830s and the initiative came from individuals like Francis Bonham. The Reform Act required voters to register and this provided opportunities for local supporters to organise and consolidate their party's voting strength. Peel recognised the need for party organisation but was, at least initially, ambivalent in his attitude. He was suspicious of extra-parliamentary pressure and this meant that his relations with many local Tory organisations were not particularly close but by 1837, Peel was urging his supporters to register. The fact that Conservatives were a much better organised party in 1841 was an important factor in their victory. During the 1830s, Peel turned the Conservatives into a viable party of government and established a sense of direction and leadership. However, there were important divisions of principle between Peel and the right of the Conservative party that were to re-emerge, with disastrous consequences, after 1841.

Why is Peel's ministry of 1841-1846 considered so successful?

When Peel took office in 1841, he recognised that the major problem facing Britain was economic, and his priority was to make the country debt-free and affluent. He set about establishing a government based on administrative effectiveness. The focus of his administration before the Corn Law crisis was on fiscal and economic reform. A prosperous country, he believed, was one where social distress and disorder would be reduced.

Although Peel had attempted to broaden the base of the Conservative Party in the 1830s, this was not evident in the election results: the election was a triumph for Protectionist Toryism.[3] The party did best in the English and Welsh counties and in those boroughs, little changed by the 1832 Reform Act. The MPs elected were largely from the 'Tory' wing of the party who had no interest in change and little sympathy for reform. Above all many were ardent Protectionists. Tory votes had been cast in favour of a party that was most likely to protect landowners and defend the Established Church. Theirs was a far narrower perspective than Peel's. Nevertheless, Peel appointed those in the party who supported his policies and beliefs to important positions. His only

---

[3] Protectionist Tories argued for retaining the Corn Laws to protect British farming

concession to party feeling was the appointment of a leading Protectionist, the Duke of Buckingham, to the post of Lord Privy Seal.

Peel increasingly adopted policies out of sympathy with the majority of his MPs. Public duty on behalf of the monarch and in the interests of the nation was his first priority; party came a poor second. This proved a problem particularly as the election had been fought largely on the question of Protection. The route from the electoral triumph of 1841 to the political disaster of 1846 was, in retrospect, predictable.

Economic and financial reform

The economy had slumped in the late 1830s and Peel inherited a budget deficit in 1841. Peel recognised that the only way he could remedy this was to introduce tariff reform, building on the work of Huskisson in the 1820s and to reintroduce income tax to generate the income needed to make tariff reductions possible. Parallel to his budgetary programme, Peel reformed the business practices of banks and companies. The 1842 Budget sought to restore prosperity to the manufacturing sector and so promote social stability.

Income tax[4] was reintroduced at 7d (3 per cent) in the pound on annual incomes of over £150 excluding most of the working-classes and would raise £3.7 million. Peel assured MPs that it would not be made permanent and would only be retained for three years. This significantly reduced opposition from the Whigs and from within the Conservative ranks. Customs duties were reduced on about 750 items and maximum duties on imported raw materials, partially manufactured goods and manufactured items were set at 5 per cent, 12 per cent and 20 per cent respectively. Duties on imported timber and all export duties on manufactured goods were abolished. Peel argued that reduced import duties would both encourage trade and provide cheaper goods for British consumers stimulating demand. Changes were made to the scale of duties on corn reducing the level of tax paid and as a result, Buckingham resigned from the Cabinet. These proposals were controversial especially to Protectionists who saw the proposals as an abandonment of protection for farming and to Free Traders who did not think Peel had gone far enough. They were, however, popular and certainly politically astute.

The 1842 Budget did not produce immediate improvements in trade or employment. The economy remained sluggish throughout 1842 and trade did not revive until late 1843. By 1844, however, there was clear evidence that the economy was recovering helped by good harvests in

---

[4] Income tax had previously been introduced by William Pitt during the French wars as a wartime tax. In 1816, against the wishes of the Tory government of Lord Liverpool, Parliament had voted against its continuance.

1843 and 1844 and by a boom in railway investment. Government finance moved into profit and 1844 and further changes took place in the 1845 Budget. The estimated budget surplus of around £3.4 million for 1845-1846 was sufficient for Peel to dispense with income tax but he argued that it should be renewed for a further three years to allow further reductions in tariffs. This, Peel argued would result in greater economic prosperity. There were further reductions in tariffs. All surviving import and export duties on raw materials, like cotton and coal, were abolished. Duties on colonial sugar from the West Indies and foreign sugar were both reduced. Further reductions followed and when Peel fell in 1846, Britain was almost a free-trading country.

Peel's economic liberalism had its origins in the 1820s. At its heart were the notions of 'sound money' through low levels of taxation and freeing of trade to produce a balanced budget. Without monetary control and stability there would be inflation and this, Peel maintained, would limit economy growth. He thought it was necessary to restrict the Bank of England's power to issue money 'to inspire just confidence in the medium of exchange'. The Gold Standard linked sound money to cheap government and low rates of direct and indirect taxation. If businessmen and industrialists were given freedom to exploit the market, Peel suggested this would increase profitability, improve employment and lead to economic growth for everyone's benefit.

Peel considered the Bank Charter Act 1844 as one of his most important achievements. Its aim was to establish a more stable banking system by preventing the excessive issuing of paper money that had led to some crises in the past. Between 1826 and 1844, over-issue by provincial banks had caused the failure of a quarter of all banks entitled to issue their own notes. The 1844 Act defined the position of the Bank of England in the British economy very carefully. The Bank could issue notes to the value of its gold reserves to a limit of £14. No new English provincial bank was allowed to issue its own notes. The Act recognised 279 banks with note-issuing powers and Peel aimed to reduce their rights of issue and concentrate them within the Bank of England. The effect of the 1844 Act could have limited the scope of banks to finance economic growth but the new gold discoveries (in California and Australia) from the late 1840s increased the Bank of England's reserves enabling an increase in the issue of notes. Without this, the economic expansion of the 1850s and 1860s that Peel is often credited with would not have occurred.

The repeal of the Bubble Act in 1825 freed joint-stock companies from the regulations that had prohibited their growth for over a century.[5]

---

[5] Joint-stock companies raised capital by issuing shares. Investors purchased these shares and received a dividend from the profits made by the company based

The result was increased often speculative investment in projects of every sort: docks, gas and water companies and especially after 1830, railways. Many of these companies collapsed because they were poorly organised or fraudulent and many people lost their savings. William Gladstone,[6] President of the Board of Trade introduced the Joint Stock Companies Act in 1844. The Act established the Registrar of Companies and all companies with more than twenty-five members and freely transferable shares were required to register. Company directors had to submit fully audited accounts to the Registrar. This Act helped protect the public from unscrupulous companies and created a more responsible climate for company development.

Poor Law and factory reform, 1842 and 1844

Peel believed that social reform was linked to successful economic conditions. These would enable economic growth, create new jobs and so stimulate consumption. Government support for social reform was lukewarm and Peel was sceptical of the value of direct government intervention in solving social problems. Free market answers were more effective. He recognised that government could not abdicate all responsibility in the 'social question' but, like many contemporaries, believed that its role should be severely limited and definitely cost-effective. Peel supported the Whig government when the Poor Law Amendment Act was passed in 1834. In 1842, the operation of Poor Law was tightened to reduce excessive costs while Peel argued, without reducing the generosity and fairness of the system of relief, compared to other countries.

Although Peel's government was not known for its support for social reform, publication of reports from committees originally set up by the Whigs in the late 1830s and extra-parliamentary pressure from radicals as well as Tory politicians, led to two important acts being passed. The Mines Act 1842, which banned women and children from working below ground, was not a piece of government legislation. Factory reforms introduced by the government caused much controversy. In 1843, Sir James Graham, the Home Secretary--who had defected from the Whigs in 1834--sought to reduce the hours worked by women and children. This

---

on the number of shares they owned. It was the failure of the South Sea Company in the early 1720s that led to the Bubble Act.

[6] William Ewart Gladstone (1809-1898) was in office every decade from the 1830s to the 1890s and was Liberal Prime Minister on four occasions (1868-1874, 1880-1885, 1886 and 1892-1894). He was Vice-President and then President of the Board of Trade between 1841 and 1845 and supported Peel over the repeal of the Corn Law.

was linked to proposals for compulsory schooling provided largely by the Church of England. Nonconformists did not intend to allow the Church of England to take control of all factory schools and organised widespread opposition and the Bill was withdrawn. The following year it was reintroduced without its education clauses. The legislation was in effect the first health and safety act in Britain. All dangerous machinery was to be securely fenced off and no child or young person was to clean mill machinery while it was in motion and failure to do so was a criminal offence

There was a well-organised campaign inside and outside Parliament to restrict the maximum working day for all to ten hours and include this in the Factory Act. Peel disagreed: he was prepared to pass laws preventing exploitation of children and women but he argued adult males were free agents and the law should not interfere with market forces. The Commons did not agree with Peel's position and Ashley's Ten Hours' amendment was carried with the support of the Whigs and Protectionist Tories. It was only Peel's threat of resignation that persuaded Tories to overturn the amendment. The passage of the Factory Act established a maximum working day of twelve hours.

Why did Corn Law repeal lead to the end of Peel's government?

Relations between Peel and his backbenchers were strained from the early days of his ministry. Peel was insensitive to their interests of many Conservative MPs and made little attempt to court backbench opinion. He took the loyalty of Conservatives in Parliament for granted and was irritated when this was withheld. Peel managed his government but he made little effort to manage his party. Conservative whips warned Peel of the unpopularity of his 1842 Budget among Protectionists and 85 Conservatives failed to support him. Poor Law and factory reform also led to backbench discontent. These rebellions did not threaten Peel's position in 1842 and 1843 but divisions between Peel's government and his Protectionist MPs widened further.

In March 1844, 95 Tories voted for Ashley's amendment to the Factory Bill and in June 61 Tories supported an amendment to the government proposal to reduce the duty on foreign sugar by almost half. Both amendments were carried and though Peel had little difficulty in reversing them his approach caused considerable annoyance. He threatened to resign if they refused to support him. Reluctantly they fell into line. Party morale was low in early 1845 and party unity was showing signs of terminal strain. On the Corn Laws, Peel pushed his party too far.

Arguments for repeal

By 1845, it was increasingly recognised that repeal was in the national interest. The Corn Laws were designed to protect farmers against the corn surpluses, and hence cheap imports, of European producers. By the mid-1840s, there was a widespread shortage of corn in Europe and Peel reasoned that British farmers had nothing to fear from repeal because there were no surpluses to flood the British market. The nation would benefit, the widespread criticism of the aristocracy would be removed and the land-owning classes were unlikely to suffer.

By 1841, Peel had, in fact, recognised that the Corn Laws would eventually have to be repealed. The moves to free trade in the 1842 and 1845 Budgets were part of this process. Since corn was one of the most highly valued import Peel needed to include it. He argued that tariff reform did not mean abandoning protection for farming, but he called for fair, rather than excessive protection. In 1842, Peel reduced the levels of duty paid under the existing sliding scale on foreign wheat from 28s 8d to 13s per quarter when the domestic price of what was between 59s and 60s. The Whigs favoured a fixed duty on corn but were defeated and the expected protectionist Tory rebellion did not occur. The following year, the Canadian Corn Act admitted Canadian imports at a nominal duty of 1s a quarter. Peel argued that this was a question of giving the colonies preferential treatment rather than freer trade. Protectionist backbenchers were not convinced and though their amendments were easily defeated, they demonstrated a growing concern about the direction of Peel's tariff policies.

Yet, Peel did not announce his conversion to repealing the Corn Laws until late in 1845. Why? There are different possible explanations for his decision. Peel had accepted the intellectual arguments for free trade in the 1820s supporting the commercial policies put forward by Huskisson. His later thinking was influenced by Huskisson's view that British farmers would eventually be unable to supply the needs of Britain's growing population and that imports of foreign grain would be essential. In which case, the repeal of the Corn Laws would then be inevitable. Peel may have accepted this but he was the leader of a Protectionist party. According to this view, Peel intended to abandon its commitment of agricultural protection before the General Election due in 1847 or 1848 with repeal following during the next Parliament, probably in the early 1850s. This might have given Peel the time to convince his own MPs.

Time ran out when famine broke out in Ireland. By October 1845, at least half of the Irish potato crop had been ruined by blight and this led to a major subsistence crisis since large numbers of people depended entirely on the potato for food. If the government was to act quickly to reduce the worst effects of famine, every barrier to the efficient transport of food needed to be removed. The most obvious barrier was the Corn Laws and this meant either their suspension or abolition to open Irish ports to unrestricted grain imports. Suspending the Acts was not a viable option as Peel maintained it would be impossible to reconcile public opinion to their re-imposition later. However, there is a problem with this view. The failure of the potato crop meant that those Irish did not have any way of earning the money to pay for imported corn, even if it was sold more cheaply. The £750,000 spent by Peel's government on public work projects, cheap maize from the United States and other relief measures were of far more practical value to Ireland than the repeal of the Corn Laws. Peel used the opportunity provided by the Famine to introduce a policy on which he had already made up his mind and the crisis merely accelerated this process.

Peel disapproved of extra-parliamentary pressure and viewed the lobbying of the Anti-Corn Law League with considerable suspicion. The success of the League, especially between 1841 and 1844, may have persuaded Peel not to move quickly to repeal. He saw it as his duty to act in the national interest and did not want to be accused of acting under pressure. The activities of the League threatened to divide propertied interests and Peel saw that social stability was essential for economic growth. Giving in to the League was an unacceptable political option. Peel was also critical of the League's propaganda especially its language of class warfare. The strident, anti-aristocratic attacks by the League and the creation of a Protectionist Anti-League raised the spectre of commercial and industrial property pitted against agricultural property. This, Peel believed, would significantly weaken the forces of property against those agitating for democratic rights. However, Peel recognised that the Anti-Corn Law League might exploit the crisis in Ireland. Repeal was therefore a pre-emptive strike designed to take the initiative away from middle-class radicals and as a result help to maintain the landed interest's control of the political system.

The politics of repeal

Peel told his cabinet in late 1845 that he proposed repealing the Corn Laws outlining that it was in the national interest to do so. This was too sophisticated for the Protectionists. For small landowners and tenant farmers, the most vocal supporters of protection, repeal meant ruin. Peel's argument that free trade would offer new opportunities for efficient farmers made little impact. Although only Viscount Stanley and the Duke of Buccleuch resigned on the issue, Peel nonetheless felt that this was sufficient for him to resign.

He hoped that Lord John Russell and the Whigs would form a government, pass repeal through Parliament and perhaps allow him to keep the Conservative Party together. Lord John Russell had recently announced his conversion to repeal in his 'Edinburgh Letter' in December 1845 but was unwilling to form a minority administration. This meant that Peel had to return to office. Predictably, repeal passed its Third Reading in the Commons in May 1846. The Whigs voted solidly for the bill but only 106 Tories voted in favour of repeal compared to 222 against. The great landowners voted solidly for repeal as they recognised that it did not threaten their economic position. The bulk of the opposition came from MPs representing the small landowners. Retribution was swift. In June 1846, sufficient Protectionists voted with the Whigs on an Irish Coercion Bill to engineer Peel's resignation. He did not hold office again dying in 1850 after a horse riding accident

6 Pitt, Peel and Ireland 1789-1846

Ireland posed three problems in the period between the 1780s and the famines in the mid-1840s. First, there was the question of how Ireland should be governed. There was also the highly emotive question of the rights of the Catholic majority in Ireland. Finally, the nature of Ireland's economic and social structure was brought into high relief by the disastrous events of the 1840s. In addition, events in Ireland had a profound effect on mainland politics.

Why was Ireland a problem for William Pitt?

Ireland was important to Pitt throughout his first ministry and led to his resignation in 1801. Three things were important. Pitt wanted to establish good relations with the Irish Parliament that had been given considerable legislative freedom in 1782. The loss of America in 1783 meant that Ireland took on a more important role in Britain's trading empire. Finally, there were important security issues and after 1793, Pitt had to be wary of plans for a French invasion using Ireland as a base.

In the early 1780s, Ireland had a rapidly growing population of around four million. Most were Roman Catholic but it was the Anglo-Irish Protestant landowners[1] who controlled about eighty percent of the land. They were often absentee landlords and were bitterly resented by their Catholic tenants, who generally lived in poverty. This Protestant elite governed Ireland largely for its own benefit and strongly resisted interference from Britain. Relations between the Irish and Westminster Parliaments were strained throughout the eighteenth century. In the 1770s and 1780s, the Irish Parliament enthusiastically supported the Americans in their fight for independence turning Ireland into a pro-American colony on England's doorstep.

Demands for parliamentary reform especially the campaign to open up Parliament to other forms of property besides land in the mid-1780s failed. The major reason for this was sectarian. Catholics had been deprived of their political rights in the late-seventeenth century and Protestants, who had more to lose, were unwilling to change this. Middle-class political identity had been created in the late 1770s and early 1780s but this had not led to an opening up of the political system. The Anglican 'ascendancy' was unwilling to share power with the middle-classes. The reforms of 1782-1783 led to a narrowing of the political elite in Ireland. Catholics were totally excluded from political power by the Penal Laws

---

[1] Anglo-Irish Protestant landowners. Protestant control over the institutions of Ireland is known as the Protestant Ascendancy.

and Dissenters had only limited access.[2] No Presbyterians sat in the Dublin Parliament. Anglican landowners controlled parliamentary seats and this control increased dramatically after 1782. The result of the failure to take the reforms of 1782-1783 forward was an increasing polarisation of Irish politics between Catholics and Protestants and between those with access to power and those denied it.[3]

Politicians agreed on two things, both designed to prevent Ireland following the American colonies into independence. Ireland should have a significant amount of self-government and that it should have greater access to British markets. Pitt saw the second issue as a way of strengthening the British Empire as well as creating political stability. In 1785, he proposed free trade between England and Ireland. This, he maintained, would benefit Irish trade and, from its profits, a contribution could be made for the defence of the Empire. However, the Irish disliked the idea of contributing to imperial defence intensely drawing parallels with proposals to tax the American colonies in the 1760s. British manufacturers organised a vigorous campaign against the threat from Ireland especially to the woollen trade. Pitt had little choice but to withdraw his proposals. Despite this, Ireland's trade with Britain increased significantly in the 1780s. Irish linen exports trebled between 1781 and 1792. During the 1780s, Pitt's control over Irish politics was severely limited by the independent actions of the Dublin Parliament.

The effects of the French Revolution.

The French Revolution renewed demands for political and parliamentary reform. Pitt did not accept the view of the Dublin Parliament that the security of Ireland could be guaranteed only by continued Catholic oppression and he attempted to win over the Catholic gentry. In 1792, an Irish Catholic Relief Act freed Catholics from remaining disabilities relating to mixed marriages, education and the law. The following year they were given the same municipal and parliamentary franchise as Protestants. However, these concessions did little to improve their status and they were still debarred from membership of the Irish Parliament. These concessions were wrung out of an unwilling Irish Parliament and many in the Protestant Ascendancy felt betrayed. Their insecurity was

---

[2] Catholics had been deprived of their political rights. Most of the population of Ireland was Roman Catholics but their rulers were Protestant. Catholics were denied access to public offices, to ownership of land and to full involvement in the running of their country. The existence of disabilities against Catholics was used by the minority Protestants to maintain their political dominance

[3] Sectarian. Divisions in Ireland were based on religious belief and conflict generally followed the lines of religion. Catholics versus Protestants.

reinforced by the actions of Earl Fitzwilliam, briefly Irish Chief Secretary in 1795. Fitzwilliam supported religious toleration and, having assured Pitt that he would not meddle with the Irish administration quickly began to do precisely that. Pitt had little choice but to recall him. Pitt's reforms whetted the appetite of the more radical Irishmen but satisfied few. Protestant fears of eventual Catholic domination were heightened. Sectarian divisions were increased by measures designed to protect Ireland from invasion after the outbreak of war with Catholic France. Between 1793 and 1796 a Militia Act was passed, a new Protestant Yeomanry formed, an Insurrection Act that made oath-taking a capital offence became law and Habeas Corpus was suspended.

Irish reformers believed in Irish nationalism and more democratic institutions. Demands for reform straddled the religious divide and, during the 1790s support for Irish nationalism was non-sectarian. The two societies of 'United Irishmen' formed in late 1791 in Belfast (mostly Presbyterian and middle-class supporters) led by the lawyer Theobald Wolfe Tone and Dublin (mostly Catholic supporters) led by Napper Tandy, an ironmonger. Their non-sectarian approach had little appeal to most Irishmen. Secret societies of Catholic 'Defenders' and Protestant 'Peep o' Day Boys' were responsible for rural atrocities. In September 1795, the Protestant Orange Order was formed dedicated to maintaining Protestant dominance at all costs. The failure of the Irish government to address the twin issues of 'Emancipation' and 'parliamentary reform' helped push Catholic and Protestant radicals closer together and encouraged the growth of more extreme demands.

The United Irishmen became increasingly nationalist in ideas appealing to all Irishmen, irrespective of religion to establish an independent Irish republic. Freedom from English rule appealed to both the middle-class radicals who had been denied access to political power and the Catholic peasantry who had largely economic grievances against Protestant landowners and the Anglican Church. Officially suppressed in 1794, the United Irishmen went underground and its leadership accepted French assistance to achieve revolution in Ireland. Bad weather prevented the French troops landing in December 1796 and British repression in Ulster in 1797 and around Dublin the following year significantly weakened the United Irishmen. The 1798 Rising was, in many respects, a prolonged and flabby failure. The United Irishmen was largely leaderless and its organisation was in disarray. It was unable to impose any real control over the rebellion when it finally began in late May. The result was a series of separate risings based largely on local grievances. The risings in Ulster and in the west of Ireland were very limited affairs. The Catholic rising in the south-east was, after some initial success, defeated at Vinegar Hill in June and the French landed too late to be of any real value.

The rebellion lasted barely a month but some 30,000 people were killed or executed.

Union

The 1798 Rising convinced Pitt that the Dublin government could not keep Ireland loyal. Constitutional union of the two kingdoms became increasingly attractive and by June 1798, it was the only real option. Pitt believed that removing the remaining disabilities against Catholics was essential to ensure their support for union. In this, they faced opposition not only from the Protestant minority in Ireland and politicians in Westminster, but also from George III. Pitt decided that he would concentrate on getting the support of the Irish Parliament for union and would work for Catholic Emancipation once union had been achieved.

A narrow rejection of a Union Bill in Dublin in January 1799 was followed by a year of negotiation and bribery. Castlereagh as Chief Secretary was largely responsible for winning over public opinion. Critics denounced his activities as pure corruption but recent investigation has shown that the swing of Irish parliamentary opinion between 1799 and 1800 cannot be explained simply in these terms. The bulk of support for the 1800 Act came from MPs elected to the 60 seats that changed hands between the two votes on Union. More important was the inability of those opposed to Union to come up with any real alternative. This ensured the passage of the bill a year later. At Westminster, the Act of Union was approved with little difficulty and constitutional union occurred on 1 January 1801.[4]

Committed as Pitt and some of his colleagues were to Catholic Emancipation in 1800 they were unable to win over the king. In March 1801, Pitt resigned over the policy that he saw as necessary. Far from eliminating the Catholic question, Union merely pushed it more directly on to the British political scene. The Catholic community felt betrayed by the British government and soon became increasingly anti-unionist in attitude developing a sense of its own separate religious and national identity.

---

[4] In the Act of Union, the separate Irish Parliament disappeared. Each of the 32 Irish counties kept their two MPs. Two were given to Dublin and Cork and one to Dublin University and the 31 single-member Irish borough constituencies. This gave a total representation of 100 Irish MPs in the House of Commons. Twenty-eight Irish peers were elected for life to the House of Lords. One archbishop and three bishops spoke for the Irish Anglican Church. Irish peers, who were not representative peers, could sit in the Commons for mainland constituencies. The Anglican Churches of England and Ireland were united. The Act gave full equality of commercial rights and privileges though Castlereagh did secure twenty years' protection for Irish textile manufacturers.

Why was Catholic Emancipation such a contentious issue?

The Catholic question was left unresolved by Union and until 1823 the issue stagnated. There were two main reasons why the campaign for Catholic Emancipation before the formation of the Catholic Association by Daniel O'Connell in 1823-1824 made little headway. The leaders of the campaign were very cautious. The British Catholic upper-class supported a compromise bill giving Catholics Emancipation but allowing the British government the right to veto appointments to the Roman Catholic Church in the United Kingdom. Daniel O'Connell denounced this approach.[5] By the early 1820s the Catholic cause in Ireland was divided and bankrupt. In addition, Parliament would decide Catholic Emancipation in London. Between 1815 and 1827 the Catholic question was a major problem for Lord Liverpool's government. The electorate voted overwhelmingly against Emancipation in the General Elections of 1818, 1820 and especially 1826. The Cabinet was divided on the issue.[6] Between 1815 and 1822, an open agreement existed that Emancipation would not be raised as a matter of government business but that when it was raised independently ministers could vote as their consciences dictated. Emancipation Bills passed the Commons in 1821, 1822 and 1825 but were all rejected in the Lords. The 1825 Bill precipitated a major political crisis for Liverpool with 'Protestant' Peel and then 'Catholic' Canning threatening resignation. Canning argued that the government could no longer remain neutral on the issue. His 'Catholic' colleagues persuaded him otherwise and the 'agreeing to disagree' formula was re-established.

O'Connell and The Catholic Association.

O'Connell recognised that even with a majority in favour of Emancipation, with or without the veto in the Commons, the House of Lords and the

---

[5] Daniel O'Connell (1775-1847) came from the Irish Catholic gentry, his father was a small landowner and shopkeeper. Educated in France, he studied law at Lincoln's Inn in London between 1794 and 1796 qualifying as a barrister at the Irish Bar in 1798. He was involved in drafting the 1805 Petition and was increasingly involved in the Emancipation debate. In 1823, he established the Catholic Association. He was known as 'The Liberator' because of his success in getting Emancipation. He was much less successful in his campaign for Repeal of the Act of Union in the 1840s

[6] In broad terms 'Protestants' like Peel and Wellington did not agree with Catholic Emancipation on principle. 'Catholics' like Canning took a more pragmatic view arguing that Emancipation was necessary for the stability of Ireland.

king could obstruct change. The result was the formation of the Catholic Association in the spring of 1823. Its main aim was Emancipation. O'Connell, however, took a broader view of the Catholic problem and included electoral reform, reform of the Church of Ireland and tenants' right. This allowed him to advance the interests of the whole Catholic community. It was the introduction of the 'Catholic Rent' of one penny a month for supporters that proved crucial. Some £20,000 was raised in the first nine months of collection in 1824-1825 and a further £35,000 was collected between 1826 and 1829. It enabled the Catholic Association to become a truly national organisation run from Dublin with support across the Catholic community. O'Connell realised that making the Irish Catholic Church an integral part of the movement was essential. Parish priests were made members of the Association. They could mobilise the mass of the Catholic population, something the Establishment viewed with some alarm. The great open-air meetings often addressed by O'Connell played a central part in the work of the Catholic Association. This allowed him to demand justice for Ireland but also let him to make veiled threats to the British government. Mass support could lead to mass disobedience, the possibility of violence and growing demands for separation from Britain.

The 1826 General Election.

Growing support for the Association across Ireland allowed O'Connell to intervene in the Irish elections in 1826. He called on voters in certain areas to support only pro-Emancipation candidates. The votes of tenants had been taken for granted by their landlords but in many places, Catholics voted for candidates favoured by local Catholic agitators. Four pro-Emancipation candidates were returned. It was clear that the backing of the Association enabled Catholic voters to defy their landlords with relative immunity.

The support for Emancipation demonstrated in Ireland was not evident on the mainland. The 1826 General Election showed the depth of anti-Catholic sentiment among the British electorate, attitudes not helped by the steady influx of Irish immigrants after 1800 and especially after the 1821 famine. Irish Catholics concentrated in London and other cities, were seen as a political threat and, for much of the nineteenth century, government was haunted by the spectre of union between Irish nationalism and radical agitation. After Lord Liverpool's resignation in early 1827, tensions over Emancipation could no longer be contained. Peel and Wellington opposed Emancipation on principle while Canning was more pragmatic recognising that Emancipation would strengthen the Union and allow the government to deal with Ireland's economic problems. Peel and Wellington refused to serve in either Canning's or

Goderich's administration. Wellington himself became Prime Minister in January 1828 with Peel as his Home Secretary. Canning's former supporters soon resigned from the new government. The Tory party was in turmoil.

Emancipation achieved 1828-1829.

In early 1828, Parliament repealed the Test and Corporation Acts. This ended all legal restrictions on the civil rights of Dissenters and made it extremely difficult for Wellington and Peel to ignore Catholic Emancipation. Resistance to Catholic Emancipation inside Westminster had been crumbling since 1812. In 1813, a motion had passed the Commons only to fail by one vote in the Lords. In 1823 Nugent's Bill, supported by Peel, passed by 59 votes only to be wrecked in the Lords and in May 1828 there was a majority of six for Emancipation in the Commons. It is, however, ironic that it was finally carried by perhaps the most 'Protestant' Commons elected since 1800.

Wellington and Peel were now faced by two contradictory pressures. O'Connell's victory brought the prospect of civil war in Ireland closer. Yet, English public opinion was overwhelmingly opposed to further concessions. In the event, County Clare was a fortunate accident.[7] It allowed Wellington and Peel to introduce Emancipation to prevent widespread disturbances in Ireland. This led to a widespread petitioning campaign and by March 1829, when the first reading of the bill took place, there had been 957 petitions in opposition compared to 357, mostly from Ireland, in favour. Emancipation was easily achieved despite opposition in the Commons (142 Tory MPs voted against) and the campaign led by Winchelsea and Eldon in the Lords. The cost for Wellington and Peel was high. Both were criticised as betrayers of the ancient constitution and Church. Peel felt obliged to offer himself for re-election at Oxford University and was defeated. Wellington fought a duel with the Ultra Lord Winchelsea. More important was the legacy of bitterness within the Tory party. A group of Ultra-Tories announced their conversion to parliamentary reform as the only way of defending what was left of the existing constitution.

---

[7] The County Clare election in July 1828, caused by the promotion of Vesey Fitzgerald to the Board of Trade, brought the issue to a head. O'Connell decided to stand against Fitzgerald. This placed the government in an awkward position. Fitzgerald was a popular landlord and a supporter of Emancipation. If O'Connell won, as a Roman Catholic he could not take his seat in the House of Commons. However, the government would run of risk of widespread disorder in Ireland with the inevitable prospect of further Catholic election candidates in the future. With the support of the Catholic Association and the local priests, O'Connell won easily beating Fitzgerald by 2,057 to 982 votes.

The Roman Catholic Emancipation Act 1829 gave full civil and political rights to Roman Catholics. They could now become MPs and occupy public offices with a few minor exceptions such as the office of Lord Chancellor. O'Connell believed that Catholic advancement in politics, government service and the professions would eventually lead to the end of Protestant dominance. There was, however, a change in voting qualification that was raised from a forty-shilling freeholder to a ten-pound householder. This cut the Irish electorate to a sixth of its former size. Despite this, Emancipation was seen as a victory for Catholicism and this further increased sectarian tension.

Why was Ireland so important in Peel's career?

The Conservative victory in 1841 brought the conflict between Peel and O'Connell that had festered for twenty-years centre stage. Peel was not prepared to compromise on Repeal of the Act of Union. However, he recognised the need to build confidence in the benefits of the Union. Peel's Irish policy was therefore a combination of strong opposition to O'Connell and the Repeal movement combined with legislation that addressed some of Ireland's problems.

Calls for Repeal.

The creation of the Repeal Association in 1840 and the reduction of his MPs to 18 in the 1841 Election led O'Connell to concentrate on extra-parliamentary agitation. There is a problem with what Repeal meant to O'Connell. He never came down firmly on the side of repeal or reform. O'Connell wanted the restoration of an Irish Parliament but with a more representative structure. This Parliament would then be able to legislate to improve conditions for the Irish people. O'Connell was vague and inconsistent in his statements on Repeal. Some historians have suggested that he was not seriously committed to Repeal and that the whole campaign was a ploy to get the British government to introduce further reforms within the framework of the Union.

The Repeal campaign was closely based on the Emancipation movement of the 1820s though on a much larger scale. It was financed by the 'Repeal Rent' and used 'monster meetings' to get its message across and put pressure on the British government. Support came from the Catholic peasantry, for whom Repeal appeared to offer the loosening of landlord control, and the Catholic Church. He also had the support of 'Young Ireland', a small group of more radical nationalists. The Catholic middle-classes were less committed than in the 1820s. They were far more concerned with retaining the gains they had achieved because of

Union and were suspicious of the suggested advantages of Repeal. There was, however, an important difference between the Repeal campaign in the 1840s and the successful Emancipation campaign. In 1828-1829 Wellington led a divided and, to some degree demoralised party. Peel, by contrast, had the support, especially between 1841 and 1844 of a strong and united Conservative Party with a large majority in the House of Commons. Peel was prepared to tolerate the Repeal campaign as long as it remained within the law. The 'monster meetings' and O'Connell's claim that 1843 would be the 'Year of Repeal' worried Peel's administration. A mass meeting at Clontarf on 7 October was banned. O'Connell accepted the decision, though many of his supporters were disappointed and was arrested, tried, imprisoned and then released.

Clontarf marked the end of an effective Repeal campaign. O'Connell did not have the united support he had in 1828-1829. The Catholic middle-classes were ambivalent in their attitudes. 'Young Ireland' differed sharply with O'Connell over long-term aims and tactics. In 1846, its leaders came out in favour of the possible use of force and seceded from the Repeal Association. Peel's reforms and then the Famine took the sting out of the campaign. O'Connell could do little to alleviate conditions during the Famine and his parliamentary party was eclipsed after his death in 1847. O'Connell's enduring achievement was to make clear that the grievances and claims of Ireland were now an intrinsic part of British domestic politics.

Peel's reforms.

Peel had considerable first-hand experience of Ireland and recognised that there were two main obstacles to good government there: poor relations between tenant and landlord, and bad relations between the British government and the Catholic middle-class and moderate clergy. Responsibility for the first problem was delegated to a Royal Commission headed by the Earl of Devon set up in 1843. Peel's solutions for the other half of his programme were put forward in a series of cabinet memoranda in the spring of 1844. Only if, Peel argued, the moderate Catholic clergy could be detached from the Repeal movement would the Church of Ireland be able to retain its privileges. But a policy of religious concessions had difficulties. Irish Conservatives were unwilling to give offices to Roman Catholics. Some members of his cabinet, especially Stanley and Gladstone, were implacably hostile to concessions. The changed state of British public opinion towards Catholicism was equally important. Anti-Catholic feeling had hardened since 1829 because of the violence of O'Connell's movement and increasing numbers of Irish Catholics on mainland Britain.

Peel identified charitable endowments as an area of reform that would benefit Irish Catholics and the 1844 Charitable Bequests Act aimed to remove obstacles to endowments to the Catholic Church. Without directly recognising the Roman Catholic hierarchy, a supervisory Charitable Trusts Board was created with Catholic members to facilitate endowment of chapels and benefices. Many Catholic bishops and clergy did not immediately welcome the Act but it was soon recognised as a useful working solution and as the first gesture of conciliation.

In 1845 Peel turned to Irish education, both to the better training of Catholic priests at Maynooth College, near Dublin, and to the creation of improved higher educational facilities. Each proposal ran into strong opposition. The principle of state support for Maynooth went back to 1795 but the annual grant of less than £9,000 was inadequate. Peel wanted it increased to £26,000 plus a special building grant of £30,000 and aimed to raise the social and intellectual level of the priesthood, hoping this would make priests more moderate. In late 1844, he had pulled back from this proposal in the face of opposition from Stanley and from William Gladstone, who left the cabinet in January 1845. Peel introduced his Maynooth Bill in April 1845 without fully appreciating the nationwide hostility to the proposal. Anglicans saw it as implicit official recognition of the Catholic Church and as a challenge to the position of the Church of Ireland. Nonconformists opposed the payments because they disliked any link between Church and state. A joint central Anti-Maynooth Committee was set up and over 10,000 petitions poured into Parliament between February and May.

Peel pressed ahead with his plan. For opponents Maynooth was yet another example of Peel's 'flexibility'. They pointed to 1829 when he had argued that Maynooth's charter should be revoked and Irish priests brought under government control. Despite widespread extra-parliamentary opposition from the Anti-Maynooth Committee the bill went through, as Emancipation had in 1829, with large cross-bench majorities. The debate on Maynooth is important less for the discussion of the principles of the bill than for the vehemence of attacks on Peel's 'betrayal'. The Conservative Party split 159 to 147 in favour of the bill on the second reading but 149 to 148 against it on the third.

Peel's third proposal, the Academic Institutions (Ireland) Act intended to improve the education of the Irish middle-classes by establishing non-denominational university colleges at Belfast, Cork and Galway. The hope was that this would make it more resistant to political extremism or clerical influence. Anglicans were damning in their criticism of the idea of the non-denominational 'Godless colleges'. Irish Catholic attitudes were split and in July 1846 the Vatican decided that such institutions would be harmful to the Catholic faith.

Peel's policies for Ireland in 1844 and 1845 attempted to kill repeal and detach moderate Catholic clergy and middle-class from the repeal movement. Of his three reforms, only two proved successful. The price of concessions to Ireland was the break-up of Peel's own party. It never recovered from the shock administered by the Maynooth grant. The Famine administered the *coup de grace*. Famine with its deep social, economic and psychological effects changed Ireland's political agenda. Under O'Connell Ireland had been generally loyal and pacifist. That loyalty and pacifism perished in the Famine. Whether English rule was in fact to blame for the Famine mattered less than the widespread belief that it was. John Mitchel was not alone in believing that 'the Almighty indeed sent the potato blight, but the English created the famine'

Peel, the Corn Laws and the Famine.

The impact of Ireland on British politics was at its starkest in Peel's response to the Great Famine. By the summer of 1845 the press and many politicians were predicting the ending of the Corn Laws and that Peel would attempt further revision in the 1846 session. The news of the potato blight in September 1845 and imminent and widespread famine merely brought matters to a head. Peel had no illusions about the effects of blight. As Irish Secretary, he had lived through the famine of 1817. A scheme of national relief at the taxpayers' expense would have to be organised before the full effects of famine were felt the following spring. Could the taxpayer be asked to contribute to the feeding of Ireland and still tolerate the existence of the Corn Laws? Peel had three alternatives open to him. He could leave the law intact, suspend it until the Irish problem was resolved or abolish it. Leaving the law intact while the Irish starved was a non-starter. Suspension posed political problems. The length of suspension was unpredictable but was likely to be for more than a year. This meant that an unpopular resumption of the law would occur in 1847 when a General Election was due. Peel already intended to prepare the country gradually for a change of policy and fight the elections due in 1847-1848 on a platform of free trade. This would deprive the Whigs of the electoral advantage from cries of 'cheap bread'. The problem with abolition was that the Conservatives were wedded to Protection. Peel also recognised that repeal in itself would not alleviate the problems facing Ireland, as the Irish affected by the famine would not be able to afford to buy the cheap grain from Europe. In that respect, the repeal of the Corn Laws in 1846 had little to do with the situation in Ireland. The Famine was the event that precipitated repeal; it was not its cause.

What were the social and economic effects of the Famine?

The 'Great Famine' began unexpectedly in the late summer of 1845. By September, potatoes were rotting in the ground and within a month blight was spreading rapidly. Three-quarters of the country's crop, the chief food for some three million people was wiped out. The following year blight caused a total crop failure. In 1847, the blight was less virulent but in 1848 a poor grain harvest aggravated the situation further. 1848 proved to be the worst year in terms of distress and death during the whole history of the Great Famine. Both 1849 and 1850 saw blight, substantial in some counties, sporadic in others.

Why was there famine?

Famine caused by potato blight was nothing new to Ireland. There had been failures in 1739, 1741, 1801, 1817 and 1821. In 1741, perhaps 400,000 people died because of famine. The Great Famine in the 1840s was only one demographic crisis among many but most historians regard it as a real turning point in Irish history. It was simply a disaster beyond all expectations and imagination.

Contemporaries and historians have considerable difficulty in explaining why the Famine took place. It is, however, generally agreed that the structure of the Irish economy and especially its system of land tenure played a significant part. Most of the cultivated land in Ireland in the 1840s was in the hands of Protestant landowners. Estates were regarded as sources of income for these landowners, many of them absentees in England rather than long-term investments. This led to a failure to invest in Irish farming. Tenants were unable to invest in their land because of high rents. Where improvement in farming did occur in Ireland, it proved very profitable. Irish agriculture promised returns of between 15 and 20 per cent compared to 5 to 10 per cent yields in England. There was insufficient land available to satisfy demand, despite the conclusion of the Devon Commission that over 1.5 million acres of land suitable for tillage was uncultivated. This led to the division and sub-division of land. By 1845, a quarter of all holdings were between one and five acres, 40 per cent were between five and fifteen acres and only seven per cent over thirty acres. This created under-employment and forced many of the labourers to become migrant workers in England for part of the year. They became navvies for road building, canal digging and railway construction. Many turned seasonal migration into permanent settlement and were largely involved in work English people found dirty, disreputable or otherwise disagreeable--jobs like petty trading, keeping lodging-houses and beer-houses. Inadequate investment meant that Irish industrialisation could not provide the employment necessary to absorb its growing population.

The potato made the division and sub-division of land possible. It was easy to grow even in poor soil and produced high yields. Two acres of land could provide enough potatoes for a family of five or six to live on for a year. Potatoes could also be used to feed pigs and poultry. Subsistence on the potato allowed tenants to grow wheat and oats to pay their rent. The precise relationship between the potato and population growth in Ireland is difficult to establish. It is clear that there was a dramatic rise in Irish population in the eighteenth and early nineteenth centuries. The high birth rate and the early age of marriage were largely responsible for dramatic growth. Between 1780 and 1841, Ireland's population increased from about five million to over eight million people, despite the emigration of one and a half million people in the decades after Union. This placed even greater pressure on land and greater reliance on the potato.

How did the British government react?

Peel's response was rapid and, within limits, imaginative. The crisis convinced him finally of the necessity for dismantling the Corn Laws but he realised that this would, because of its contentious nature, take time. Immediate solutions were needed. In November 1845, a Special Commission was established to co-ordinate relief efforts. It did two things. First, work was needed so that labourers could afford to buy food. The government established public work schemes but on a much larger scale than before. These were the boom years of Irish railway construction. Food had also to be kept at a level that prevented profiteering. £185,000 was spent on supplies, chiefly Indian meal. These measures, however, only met the immediate crisis. Lord John Russell succeeded Peel in mid-1846 but he lacked Peel's Irish experience. Economy and efficiency replaced Peel's more humane policy. The full extent of the Famine was seriously underestimated in official circles. The problem, however, was not the shortage of food in Ireland--between September 1846 and July 1847 five times as much grain was imported as was exported--but of ensuring that those in need had access to that food. The failure was one of awareness, not compassion.

What were the consequences of the Famine?

Between 1841 and 1851, the population of Ireland fell from over 8 million to some 6.5 million. Emigration accounted for perhaps 1.5 million and became an accepted part of Irish life. This leaves about a million deaths as a result of the Famine. Actual starvation rarely caused death but weakened people sufficiently for diseases like typhus and fever to take their toll. In early 1849, a serious outbreak of cholera added to the problem. The impact of famine was felt differently in both regional and social terms. Western and south-western counties were hardest hit. Counties on the east coast, where food could be more easily imported, were least affected. The north-east did not suffer a crisis, despite its high density of population, because of the more industrial nature of its economy. But it was not unaffected. Many disease-ridden migrants crowded into Belfast, where poor living conditions helped spread disease, but this was a public health not an economic problem.

Labourers and small farmers were the chief victims of the Famine. In 1841, 71.5 per cent of holdings were less than 15 acres but by 1851 the figure was 49.1 per cent. There was a consequent increase in the number of holdings over 15 acres from 18.5 to 50.9 per cent. Livestock farming expanded encouraged by attractive prices in Britain and by reductions in transport costs. In 1851, the agricultural economy was apparently still in a state of crisis: the potato had lost its potency, low agricultural prices gave little promise of recovery to those who had survived, and slightly larger holdings hardly made up for increased Poor Law rates. But from the 1850s change was rapid. Livestock increased in value and numbers, arable farming declined slowly and tenant farmers, whose numbers remained relatively stable for the next fifty years, enjoyed some prosperity.

The Famine marked a watershed in the political history of modern Ireland. The Repeal Association of O'Connell was dead. Young Ireland made their separatist gesture in the abortive rising of 1848. A sense of desolation, growing sectarian divisions, the rhetoric of genocide and the re-emergence of some form of national consciousness eventually led to the emergence of a movement dedicated to the independence of Ireland from English rule.

7 Britain at War 1793-1815

In the fifty-four years before 1793, Britain had fought three major wars with France lasting some twenty-three years. Britain could not ignore France and the threat to European security posed by the expansion of the French Revolution. Lord Auckland declared in Parliament in 1799: 'The security of Europe is essential to the security of the British Empire'.

What were British interests between 1793 and 1841?

What strategies underpinned British foreign policies between 1793 and 1841? Contemporaries identified blue-water or maritime and continental policies. Colonial expansion was in Britain's economic interest and colonial wars were fought largely for wealth, raw materials and markets. Britain lost the American colonies in 1783 but had already gained Canada and Newfoundland with their furs and fisheries. She was dominant in the Caribbean with its sugar and cotton and in India and was opening trade links with China. However, the key to Britain's security lay in its continental policies.

Since the loss of Calais in 1558, Britain had no realistic territorial ambitions on the continent. However, her security from invasion and her continental markets meant that Britain needed allies in Europe and be prepared to aid them with subsidies and with force. By doing this, she prevented French expansion especially into the Low Countries where Britain had important interests. The Low Countries provided routes and markets for her exports and the harbours of the Scheldt estuary provided an enemy with invasion bases north of the Straits of Dover. For Pitt, continental markets seemed especially threatened and it was to save Holland that the British government entered the war in January 1793. A balance of power in Europe was central to British foreign policy. It was a necessary for expansion overseas and trade in Europe, and for security at home including security from subversive ideas.

There were important respects in which Britain's history in the eighteenth and early-nineteenth centuries differed from continental experiences. By the 1790s, Britain was already well advanced industrially and commercially. Economic and population growth meant that Britain was increasingly dependent on international trade for both food and industrial raw materials. Britain had no large army but to protect trade routes Britain felt that she must be supreme at sea. What Britain regarded as the pursuit of a vigorous trading position was seen differently by foreigners. To them it was downright aggressive.

Economic change in Britain had resulted in social transformation, in particular the emergence of an articulate middle-class public opinion.

Castlereagh recognised as early as 1820 that public opinion could not be ignored. Canning and Palmerston made conscious efforts to woo and direct public opinion by the publication of the documents explaining their policies and by a judicious use of the press. Public opinion was, however, frequently uninformed, prejudiced and xenophobic. It was firmly convinced of the superiority of Britain and its institutions to other countries in the world. This enabled both Canning and Palmerston to appeal to public sympathy when acting in defence of 'constitutional states'.

Contemporaries liked to see Britain as the greatest power in the world in the first half of the nineteenth century. This is clearly an overestimation. Commercial interests often compelled Britain to assume a role in the world which politicians did not always seek but in terms of the continent she was always only one among five great powers: Britain, France Austria, Prussia and Russia.[1] It was the 'balance' between these five powers that dominated much of Britain's foreign policies. This 'Concert of Europe' became an important concept in the course of the nineteenth century. Initially it meant the coalition against Napoleonic France but gradually it came to define the permanent relationship between the great powers.

Its development and acceptance was, however a slow process. It frequently reverted to being a coalition for specific purposes. In the 1820s, when the government of most European countries was in the hands of conservatives, the Concert tended to be the means through which the status quo was maintained. This attitude brought it into conflict with the growth of nationalism. Austria, Russia and Prussia certainly had a more interventionist view of the Concert that Britain. They wished to use it as the basis for the defence of the whole existing structure of society and of 'legitimate', by which they meant 'Conservative' authority. Britain could agree with this position when it came to the containment of France and was quite prepared to support the Bourbon restoration in 1814. However, the principle of legitimacy did not have the same ideological appeal to the British government as it did to the other European powers. In fact, all the great powers were prepared to depart from the principle when it conflicted with other national interests or ambitions. British statesmen believed that the Congress of Vienna had created a desirable territorial 'balance of power'[2] in Europe and that peace could be preserved as long as no power

---

[1] The 'Great Powers'. These were regarded as Britain and France (the 'Western powers' with their systems of government based on constitutional monarchies) and Russia, Austria and Prussia (the 'Eastern powers' with systems of government based on the absolute power of the ruler).

[2] Balance of power. Contemporaries believed that if the power of the leading states in Europe was 'balanced' then expensive and unnecessary wars could be avoided and peace maintained.

threatened it. Consequently, there were no permanent blocs of power in this period. France sided with the Eastern Powers over Spain in 1822 but with Britain twelve years later. Britain sided with Russia over the Eastern Question in 1840 but with France against Russia in 1854. All British governments found it inconvenient to seek allies. It was more flexible and more valuable to support a 'balance of power' policy in Europe and participate only when that balance seemed threatened by an actual or potential aggressor from among the Great Powers. Pragmatism and the specific interests of the great powers rather than adherence to a particular ideology marked foreign relations after Waterloo.

As far as Britain was concerned, the Congress of Vienna defined the limits of her continental ambitions and, while a general peace was maintained, British trade could expand unhindered. Britain was quite prepared to see the Vienna Settlement altered if its basic aims were still fulfilled. In the 1830s, Britain was prepared to see an independent Belgium as long as its neutrality was guaranteed. Palmerston would have liked to see Austrian influence removed from Italy so long as French ambitions did not fill the political vacuum. By 1841, he clearly regarded some parts of the 1814-1815 Settlement as obsolete but he, like his predecessors at the Foreign Office, did not adopt a 'revisionist' approach to European affairs.

British foreign policy throughout the late-eighteenth and nineteenth centuries has been criticised for being pragmatic, as it was not based on any long-term ideological or systematic considerations. It is, however, possible to identify two general principles that did underlie the actions of successive Foreign Secretaries: security and trade. These tended to be implicit in policies, underlining and on occasions determining action. Pitt, Castlereagh, Canning and Palmerston all accepted that they had a responsibility for ensuring that British trade could be carried on throughout as much of the world as possible without interference. Free trade was not simply an economic dogma. It was also seen as a means of achieving international peace. Destructive economic competition--a prime cause of war--would be replaced by trade for mutual advantage.

There was an essential continuity between Britain's foreign policy before and after 1815. The French Revolution and Napoleonic Wars did not induce Britain to abandon the balance of power, though it sought to eliminate melding and ineffectiveness. William Pitt provided the foundations for this development in the plans he made for peace, guidelines put into practice by Castlereagh and Canning. Pitt planned for a concert among the Powers to provide a more effective system of European security, with a new distribution of power in order to contain future French aggression and a guarantee between the Powers to maintain it.

Why did Britain not win the war with France 1793 and 1802?

The outbreak of the French Revolution in 1789 was initially welcomed by most politicians. The Whigs saw it as the dawn of liberty. For Pitt, the revolution would be a useful distraction for Britain's major rival. Edmund Burke found in 1791 that 'there was no moving ministers from their neutrality'. Attitudes were slow to change. In his budget in early 1792, Pitt planned to reduce defence spending. It is important to see Pitt's actions not with hindsight but in the context of traditions of non-interference in the affairs of European powers unless there was a direct threat to British interests. Pitt did not participate in the war for ideological considerations. No action was taken when first Prussia and then Austria declared war on revolutionary France in 1792. It was the French victory over Austrian forces at Jemappes in November 1792 followed by the fall of Antwerp and the opening of the Scheldt estuary in defiance of treaty to all shipping that upset the balance of Britain's diplomacy. In addition, the French showed themselves willing to export their revolutionary ideas by assisting all people seeking to break the yoke of monarchy and tyranny.

In two important respects France now posed a potent threat to what Pitt perceived as Britain's 'security' and once France declared war in February 1793 he could justify his actions as self-defence. From November 1792 Pitt and his Foreign Secretary, Lord Grenville showed themselves willing to let France resolve her own internal problems if she withdrew her forces from Belgium and renounced interference with the internal government of other countries. Pitt's objective was to restore the balance of power in the Low Countries and remove the French threat from the United Provinces. French domination of the entire coastline of north-west Europe was a threat both to Britain's domestic security and trade and it was to contest the ambitions of France in an area sensitive to British interests that Pitt went to war. France also posed a threat to the stability of Britain's constitution through its revolutionary ideology. In 1792, Pitt had failed to predict that war with France was inevitable. He was now astonishingly wrong about its nature believing that the war would be quickly over.

Fighting France 1793-1802

Pitt and Henry Dundas, his Secretary of War, thought of war in a traditional eighteenth-century way. This entailed a three-pronged approach. The first two had been used against France earlier in the century. The third strategy was something new. The 'blue-water' maritime strategy was employed with the Royal Navy blockading the French coast and picking up enemy colonies especially in the Caribbean. Attacks on her colonies weakened France's commercial base and could later be used as bargaining counters in subsequent peace negotiations. A continental war was also fought using small units of British forces, paid mercenaries and subsidised allies. Finally, Pitt supported opponents of the revolution inside France especially in the west where there was considerable opposition to revolutionary change. Broadly the first part of this strategy was successful, the others less so.

The major problem facing Pitt in the summer of 1793 was which of the various conflicting war aims to pursue. Should he concentrate his energies in securing the Low Countries against French aggression? Should he aid counter-revolutionary forces within France to destabilise the revolutionary regime, as urged by Burke and Windham? Should the main thrust of the campaign be against French colonies? The first and third options reflected the approach used throughout the century. It was the second option that was different and brought to the war an ideological element. Both sides could see their actions in crusading terms, for and against revolutionary and republican dogmas. The conflict between the two options--peace either through military and naval victory or through the restoration of the Bourbon monarchy--was reflected within the coalition ministry. Pitt and Dundas supported the former while Burke and Windham saw the war as the means of eliminating the revolutionary threat.

The First Coalition 1793-1797

Britain could not defeat revolutionary France, with its new armies, a 'nation in arms' led by generals using unorthodox and mobile tactics, alone. The British army was too small and poorly trained to provide an effective continental force. Of the 50,000-strong army, half were needed for police and garrison duties in Britain and the rest were scattered abroad. The government therefore turned to German allies for mercenaries: 14,000 Hanoverians and 8,000 Hessians were taken into pay. Britain could only raise 7,000 men under the Duke of York for the Flanders campaign that began in April. The result was the creation of the First Coalition.[3]

Pitt believed that he could successful defeat the revolution from within France. Support for French royalists in the Vendée and in Toulon were both inadequate and too late. A plan to land French émigré troops in southern Brittany in mid-1795 was also unsuccessful. The revolutionary forces were better prepared than expected and their earlier successes gave them higher morale. In addition, Pitt failed to grasp the power of French

---

[3] The First Coalition against France was signed in February 1793. It consisted of Britain, Austria, Prussia and Holland. Spain and Sardinia also entered the coalition strengthening Pitt's belief that the war would not last long.

patriotism in the 1790s. Many people in France preferred the revolutionary to the Bourbon government. They certainly favoured any French government to the restoration of monarchy engineered by Britain, the national enemy.

The anti-French coalition proved very fragile. The campaign in Flanders continued in 1794 but it was increasingly clear that Prussia and Austria were more concerned with the affairs of Poland than with the west. Austrian defeat at Fleurus compelled York to retreat across Holland, though he evacuated most of his force from Bremen in April 1795. Between 1795 and 1797, the First Coalition collapsed. Prussia made peace at Basle in April 1795. Holland, which had a strong pro-French party, was taken over in January 1795 and declared war on Britain in May 1795. Prussia made peace with France in April 1795. Spain followed suit in July and made a defensive-offensive alliance with France. The utter defeat of Austria in 1796 and 1797 led to peace at Campo Formio. The collapse of the Coalition changed the basis of British strategy. It imposed constraints from which successive governments were unable to escape. Britain had lost her bridgeheads into western Europe. Holland and Belgium were now in French hands. This left Britain to fight on alone. A Second Coalition[4] was created at the end of 1798 but also collapsed within a few years.

Colonial and naval success 1793-1801

What gains Britain made between 1793 and 1801 were either colonial conquests or naval victories. Sea power cut the French off from their overseas empire. French and later Spanish and Dutch colonies were occupied. French settlements at Pondicherry and Chandernagore in India were secured in 1793 though French influence remained, especially in Mysore.[5] In the West Indies Britain took Tobago in 1793 and supported a rebellion in Santo Domingo. Control was extended over the French islands of Martinique, St Lucia and Guadeloupe in 1794, though it had abandoned the last two by the end of the year. Haiti, rich in coffee, sugar and cotton, seemed to have been wrested from France and Spain when the coastal towns were captured in 1794 but it was never secured.[6] With

---

[4] The Second Coalition consisted of Britain, Russia, Austria, Turkey, Portugal and Naples and proved to have even fewer unifying features than the first.

[5] Britain had fought a long war with France for dominance in India culminating in the battle of Plassey in 1757 when Robert Clive defeated a combined Indian-French army. Some French settlements remained though they were quickly taken in 1793-1794.

[6] The Caribbean was always a graveyard of troops and seamen largely from malaria and yellow fever. Between 1793 and 1801, the British army sent 89,000

40,000 men killed and a similar number incapacitated by disease, Britain lost more men in the West Indies than Wellington was to lose in the Peninsular campaigns after 1808. The Franco-Dutch alliance of 1795 led to Britain's seizure of Dutch colonies at the Cape of Good Hope, in Ceylon and in the West Indies. From the British point of view, even before the Austrians made peace, the war was reaching a stalemate. British trade and empire had been maintained and extended through military operations backed by naval supremacy.

Nevertheless, French mastery of western Europe seemed complete. Two attempts were made to make peace in 1796-1797: in October 1796 Lord Malmesbury was sent to Paris and this was followed by a second series of negotiations the following July at Lille. French resolve was hardened by the *coup d'etat* of 18 Fructidor that marked the reassertion of Jacobin influence in the Directory government of France and negotiations foundered on demands that Britain should surrender all her conquests while France should keep all hers. Events became increasingly unfavourable to Britain. From late-1796, Pitt faced what was perhaps the greatest threat to national security between 1588 and 1940. The external threat of invasion was made worse by problems in Ireland, which France was willing to exploit, naval mutinies, high prices and inflation. Naval victories over the Spanish at Cape St. Vincent and the Dutch at Camperdown in February and October 1797 ended French hopes of invasion.

Napoleon Bonaparte persuaded the Directory of the merits of an attack on British power in India and in early 1798, French agents began to intrigue with the East India Company's greatest enemy in southern India, Tipu of Mysore.[7] Napoleon invaded Rome and extinguished the freedom of Switzerland and, using his naval control of the Mediterranean, took Malta and defeated the rulers of Egypt. The military advantage that he had gained was eliminated by the destruction of the French fleet by Nelson[8] at Aboukir Bay (Battle of the Nile) in August 1798. The implications of Nelson's victory were far-reaching. The French lost their naval supremacy in the Mediterranean and their army was stranded, though not actually defeated until 1801. Tipu was defeated and killed at Seringapatam in 1799 and the territorial power of the East India Company extended. In Europe,

---

men to the Caribbean and lost 70 per cent of them. The total loss for army, navy and transport crew was probably over 100,000.

[7] Tipu 'the Lion' of Mysore was the cruel, yet enlightened ruler of Mysore. He was strongly pro-French.

[8] Horatio, Lord Nelson (1759-1805) was the most successful and popular naval figure during the war. His victories at Aboukir Bay in 1798, Copenhagen in 1801 and Trafalgar in 1805 played a central role in preserving British freedom. His death at Trafalgar achieved mythic proportions.

the failure of the Egyptian expedition encouraged those states with grievances to show their hand. The Ottoman Empire declared war on the invaders of their Egyptian province.

The Second Coalition 1798-1801

Coalition warfare was the only way to achieve outright victory and end French expansion. The experience of the First Coalition showed how difficult this was going to be. Lord Grenville reassembled a Second Coalition against France. As with the First Coalition, early limited success was followed by disunity and defeat. Austria was defeated at Marengo and Hohenlinden in 1800 and made peace at Lunéville in 1801. Russia withdrew her support and during 1800. France cultivated good relations with Russia, Prussia and Denmark with a view to closing northern Europe to British trade. These moves threatened Britain's domestic stability since poor harvests increased the importance of imports of Baltic grain. Retribution for the formation of the 'Armed Neutrality of the North' and the invasion of Hanover by Danish and Prussian troops was swift. In March 1801, the Danish fleet was destroyed by Nelson at anchor at Copenhagen, invading troops were withdrawn from Hanover and relations between Britain and Russia thawed. The consequences of the formation of the First and Second Coalitions were similar. In both 1797 and 1801, Britain was left isolated after France had successfully defeated the coalition armies and countries that lacked trust in each other. France's grip on Europe had been gradually tightened. The British Navy had saved Britain from invasion in 1797 and had successfully defeated the navies of France, Spain, Holland and Denmark. It had secured Britain's colonial possessions and enabled the conquest of enemy colonies in the West Indies, Africa, India and Ceylon. However, it could not defeat Napoleon in Europe and its success encouraged France to concentrate more on its armies, thus increasing pressure on Britain's allies. Sea power and land power had fought each other to a standstill, each dominant in its own sphere. A compromise peace was a logical option in 1801-1802 to give both sides breathing space.

Was Pitt a good war leader?

Pitt had left office before the Treaty of Amiens of 1802. He fought the French between 1793 and 1801 much as his father would have done, using Britain's naval supremacy to blockade Europe and pick off enemy colonies while subsidising allies to fight the land war. Yet, he has been dismissed as a 'disastrous' war leader. How true is this? In two respects, Pitt proved successful. He put national finances on a wartime footing through direct taxation rather than loans. He also showed considerable tenacity in pursuing the war. This was evident in 1797 when the First Coalition collapsed and Britain was alone. His actions established a sense of national purpose and raised levels of patriotism to new heights.

In other respects, he was much less successful. In 1793, Britain was unprepared for war and Pitt did not understand the need for more military and naval training. It took Pitt until 1795 to appreciate that this was going to be a long war. Pitt has been unjustly criticised for an indiscriminate and poor use of subsidies. Of the £66 million paid in subsidies between 1793 and 1815, only £9.2 million was provided before 1802. The lack of military success, which these bought, was a consequence of several things. Pitt's concern to keep the Low Countries out of French control was not shared by members of the two coalitions, both of which were loose federations of distrusting states. Prussia was more interested in the Baltic than the North Sea and looked to the partition of Poland to pick up more territory. Austria wished to sever her connections with Belgium and consolidate her position in central Europe.

In addition, the French had superior armies, generals and tactics. The British commanders of the 1790s were, with notable exceptions like Nelson not particularly able and the British army was in no position to sustain a long continental campaign. In Europe, reliance on others was unavoidable. This led to the coalitions and they were very fragile. Pitt also faced conflicting advice from his chief ministers. Dundas favoured the colonial strategy. Grenville wanted a continental policy believing that France could only be defeated in France. Pitt could see the advantage of both strategies and failed to decide decisively between them. Pitt's success as Prime Minister between 1783 and 1793 came largely from his control of events. This allowed him to take decisive, quick decisions. After 1793, his ability to control events was more limited and he often failed to give decisive leadership. He misjudged the military capacity of revolutionary France in 1793. Perhaps the best thing that can be said about Pitt's leadership is that at least Britain had not been defeated by 1802.

The cost of war

The war was expensive for Britain and ended Pitt's economic reforms. He was hesitant about pushing up taxes and relied heavily on borrowing to finance the war that increased from £4.5 million in 1793 to £44 million by 1797. The effect was inflationary and in 1797, following a run on the banks occasioned by the French landing at Fishguard, the government authorised the Bank of England to suspend cash payments and to issue notes for small denominations (£1 and £2). Inadvertently Pitt had stumbled upon one aspect of successful wartime fiscal policy. It was not until he announced his proposals for an income tax in 1798 and its collection in 1799 that Pitt pursued other aspects of wartime fiscal policy.

This graduated tax was a logical, if unpopular, solution and was only accepted on the understanding that it was a temporary wartime expedient. It raised about half the £10 million Pitt had hoped to raise annually and one explanation of the support for the negotiations leading to the Peace of Amiens between 1801 and 1802 was the belief that income tax would be abolished. Wartime ministers, especially if they do not provide outright victory, have rarely been seen as successful. Pitt may well fall into this category. However, to condemn him outright as inadequate fails to acknowledge his appreciation of the commercial implications of the war, the advantages that colonial conquests were to bring and the naval supremacy for which his reforms in the 1780s and early 1790s had laid the foundations. War was a necessity forced upon Pitt, who needed to make commerce and constitution secure.

Amiens to Waterloo 1802-1815

The Peace of Amiens, negotiated by Hawkesbury (later Lord Liverpool) and Cornwallis and ratified by Parliament in May 1802, received a poor press from contemporaries and subsequently from historians. The surrender of Austria deprived Britain of any leverage in Europe and Addington accepted terms which recognised French predominance on the continent and agreed to the abandonment of all overseas conquests. Grenville and Windham regarded these concessions as a disgrace and refused to give the ministry further support. This opened a split between them and Pitt, who was still prepared to give Addington assistance. Viewed simply in territorial terms Amiens was disastrous but Addington and his ministers saw it as a truce, not a final solution. Britain had been at war for nine years and Addington, previously Speaker of the House of Commons, was fully aware of growing pressures from MPs and from the nation at large for peace. Canning, one of the most vehement critics of the Peace, willingly admitted that MPs were in no mood to subject its terms to detailed scrutiny and that they would have ratified almost anything.

Amiens to Trafalgar 1802-1805

In the twelve months between Amiens and the inevitable renewal of the war, Addington made military and fiscal preparations that placed Britain in a far stronger position than it had been in 1793. British naval and military strength was not run down. The remobilisation of the fleet proceeded well in 1803. Addington retained a regular army of over 130,000 men of which 50,000 were left in the West Indies to facilitate the prompt occupation of the islands given back in 1802 when the need arose. 81,000 men were left in Britain that, with a militia of about 50,000, provided a garrison far larger than anything Napoleon could mount for invasion in 1803. The 1803 Army of Reserve Act produced an additional 30,000 men. He revived the Volunteers, backed by legislation giving him powers to raise a levy *en masse*. This raised 380,000 men in Britain and 70,000 in Ireland and by 1804, they were an effective auxiliary force. Reforms by the Duke of York improved the quality of officers and in 1802, the Royal Military College was set up. Addington improved Pitt's fiscal management of the war in his budgets of 1803 and 1804 by deducting income tax at source. This was initially set at a shilling and raised by Pitt in 1805 at 1/3d, in the pound on all income over £150. Fox, who bitterly denounced Pitt's 25 per cent increase in 1805, had now to defend a further 60 per cent increase the following year. Once war was renewed in 1803, Addington adopted a simple strategy of blockading French ports. The navy swept French commerce from the seas. Colonies recently returned to France and her allies were reoccupied. He sought allies on the continent who were willing to resist French expansion.

Continuity of strategy

From 1803 until about 1810, there was little difference in Britain's strategy to that employed in the 1790s or its level of success. Addington gave way to Pitt in April 1804. Napoleon recognised that final victory depended on the conquest of Britain and during early 1805, preparations were made for an invasion. To succeed he needed to control the Channel and to prevent the formation of a European coalition against France. He failed on both counts. The destruction of a combined Franco-Spanish fleet at Trafalgar in October 1805 denied Napoleon naval supremacy and the hesitant moves of Russia and Austria against him meant that troops intended for invasion had to be diverted. Between late 1805 and 1807, France confirmed its military control of mainland Europe. The Third Coalition was quickly overwhelmed in 1806 and 1807. Austria was defeated at Ulm and Austerlitz in October and December 1805 respectively and in January 1806 Austria made peace at Pressburg. Prussia, which had remained neutral in 1805, attempted to take on France single-handed and was defeated at Jena in October 1806; Russia, after its defeat at Friedland, made peace at Tilsit in 1807. Britain once again stood alone.

'Economic warfare'

With the prospect of successful invasion receding as a means of defeating Britain, Napoleon turned to economic warfare. The Berlin Decree (November 1807) threatened to close all Europe to British trade. This was not new. Both Pitt and the Directory had issued decrees aimed at dislocating enemy trade and food imports. The difference between

Napoleon's continental system and the attempts in the 1790s was one of scale. Between 1807 and 1812, France's unprecedented control of mainland Europe meant that British shipping could be excluded from the continent. In practice, however, there were major flaws in Napoleon's policy. It was impossible to seal off Europe completely from British shipping. Parts of the Baltic and Portugal remained open and in 1810 Russian ports were reopened to British commerce. In the face of French agricultural interests, Napoleon did not ban the export of wines and brandies to Britain and during the harvest shortages of 1808-1810, he allowed the export of French and German wheat under license. Most importantly, he had no control over Britain's trade with the rest of the world and it was to this that Britain increasingly looked. Though the Continental System and particularly Britain's Orders in Council were blamed for economic crisis in 1811-1812 by both manufacturers and the Whigs, it has been suggested that a better explanation can be found in industrial overproduction and speculation in untried world markets. Napoleon failed to achieve an economic stranglehold because he did not have naval supremacy and because Britain's economic expansion was directed at non-European markets. The British blockade inflicted far more harm on France, whose customs receipts fell by 80 per cent between 1807 and 1809 than exclusion from Europe ever did to Britain.

The British response to the creation of the Continental System came in the form of Orders in Council. In January 1807, the 'Ministry of all the Talents' banned any sea borne trade between ports under French control from which British shipping was excluded. To avoid unduly antagonising the United States trade by neutral shipping from the New World to French-controlled ports was unaffected. The Portland ministry took a harder line. Under pressure from Spencer Perceval, the Chancellor of the Exchequer far more strict Orders were issued in November and December 1807. This extended exclusion to all shipping from French-controlled ports, paying transit duties in the process. The major purpose of the Orders was to dislocate European commerce and as a result create discontent with the Napoleonic regime. Success was achieved at the cost of further deterioration in relations with the United States. Demand for British goods meant that trade was largely uninterrupted until America passed a Non-Importation Act in 1811. British exports to her largest single market plummeted from £7.8 million in 1810 to £1.4 million in 1811. There was a corresponding reduction in imports of raw cotton, which was 45 per cent lower in 1812-1814 than in 1809-1811. The Anglo-American war of 1812-1814 was fought largely about the Great Lakes, since the primary objective of the American 'hawks' was the conquest of Upper Canada. The New England states opposed the war vigorously and had the Orders in Council been withdrawn a few weeks earlier it would probably not have been approved by Congress. Little was achieved militarily and the most famous incident of the war, the repulse of a British attack on New Orleans, was fought a month after the war ended but before news of the Peace of Ghent reached America. The peace settled nothing. None of the original causes of the war, for example, the boundaries between the United States and Canada or maritime rights, received any mention.

Total victory 1808-1815

The final phase of the war began in 1808 when Napoleon attempted to exchange influences for domination in the Iberian Peninsula. Nationalist risings in Spain against the installation of Napoleon's brother Joseph as king and anti-French hostility in Portugal, which had been annexed the previous autumn, prompted Castlereagh, Secretary of War for the Colonies, to send 15,000 troops in support. This approach conformed to the strategy used since 1793 of offering limited armed support to the opponents of France. In the next five years, British troops, at no time more than 60,000 strong, led by Arthur Wellesley (created Viscount Wellington in 1809) and his Portuguese and Spanish allies fought a tenacious war with limited resources. Wellington's victory at Vimeiro in August 1808 was followed by the Convention of Cintra, negotiated by his superior, which repatriated the French troops and set Portugal free. By the time, Wellington returned to the Peninsula in April 1809, it seemed that this campaign was to be no more successful than the Walcheren expedition to the Low Countries was to prove later that year.

The Peninsula campaign drained Napoleon's supply of troops that he had to divert from central Europe. Calling the war the 'Spanish Ulcer' was no understatement. Wellington gradually wore down French military power and it was from the Peninsula that France was first invaded when Wellington crossed the Pyrenees after his decisive victory at Vitoria in August 1813. Napoleon's position in Europe was weakened by the unsuccessful and costly Russian campaign of 1812 and by the spring of 1813, the British government was absorbed in creating a further anti-French coalition. The Treaty of Reichenbach provided subsidies for Prussia and Russia. Separately negotiated treaties, usually under French military duress, had been a major problem of the three previous attempts at concerted allied action. Castlereagh, now foreign secretary, saw keeping the allies together long enough to achieve the total defeat of France as one of his primary objectives. Austria was at first unwilling to enter the coalition, fearing the aggressive aspirations of Russia as much as those of France. Castlereagh knew that a general European settlement was impossible without total victory. When he arrived in Basle in February 1814 French troops were everywhere in retreat--Napoleon had been defeated in the three-day 'Battle of the Nations' at Leipzig the previous October and Wellington had invaded south-west France--but the allies were no more trusting of each other's motives. Castlereagh demonstrated his skills as a negotiator and achieved the Treaty of Chaumont in March by which the allies pledged to keep 150,000 men each under arms and not to make a separate peace with France. Napoleon's abdication and exile to Elba in 1814 allowed Castlereagh to implement his second objective: the redrawing of the map of Europe to satisfy the territorial integrity of all nations, including France. The Congress of Vienna of 1814-1815, within limits, achieved this. Napoleon's final flourish in 1815 that ended at Waterloo made no real difference.

8 Foreign Policy 1815-1841

After the defeat of France in 1814 and 1815, Britain played a central role in redrawing the map of Europe at the Congress of Vienna.

1814-1815	Congress of Vienna
1818	Congress at Aix-la-Chapelle
1820	Congress at Troppau
1821	Congress at Laibach
1822	Castlereagh committed suicide; Canning became Foreign Secretary
1823	Congress at Verona Monroe Doctrine
1827	Battle of Navarino; Canning's death
1830	Palmerston became Foreign Secretary
1833	Treaty of Unkiar Skelessi
1839	Treaty of London
1842	Treaty of Nanking

Castlereagh, Britain's Foreign Secretary from 1812 until his suicide in 1822 wanted stability and peace in Europe leaving Britain free to pursue its global commercial and imperial interests. The idea of a 'balance of power' between the great powers in Europe--Austria, Russia, France, Britain and Prussia--was at the heart of his thinking. Co-operation between the great powers was enshrined in the idea of regular congresses to resolve areas of dispute. The problem Castlereagh, and subsequently Canning and Palmerston, Foreign Secretaries between 1822 and 1827 and 1830 and 1841, respectively faced was that the great powers in Europe meant that they were prepared to intervene, diplomatically and militarily in support of their own interests. This meant that Britain also had to intervene in support of its own European interests. This was especially the case in the Low Countries (Belgium and Holland), the Iberian Peninsula (Portugal and Spain) and in the Near East (the Ottoman Empire) where Britain had either commercial or strategic interests. The continuities in foreign policies between 1815 and 1841 were important but the ways in which those policies operated depended on the contrasting personalities and styles of Castlereagh, Canning and Palmerston.

Did Castlereagh secure an effective peace 1814-1822?

Castlereagh was Foreign Secretary from February 1812 until August 1822. Napoleon's failure in Russia in 1812, Wellington's victories in Spain and Portugal and the creation of the Fourth Coalition (Britain, Austria, Prussia and Russia) in 1813 brought defeat for France. Napoleon abdicated in

1814 and the Bourbon monarchy was restored. The 'Hundred Days'[1] in 1815 culminating in the final French defeat at Waterloo ended the threat from Napoleon. The post-war settlement was the result of the Congress of Vienna.[2]

Britain, Austria, Prussia and Russia had fought against France to ensure their own survival and independence. As winners, they expected to strengthen their own positions by acquiring land either in Europe or as colonies. What they feared was a repeat of French domination of Europe. This provided the impetus for creating a balance of power between the five great European powers. For Castlereagh, this meant a settlement in which each of the mainland powers were satisfied and so were unlikely to dispute it in the future. He believed that, 'It is not the business of England to collect trophies, but to restore Europe to peaceful habits.' It was in Britain's interests to have a peaceful Europe as this secured her defences and to remain free from European commitments leaving the country free to develop its colonial empire and increase its wealth through overseas trade. Britain's security may have been the major priority of Castlereagh's policies but he was also concerned to encourage liberal ideas, something the other great powers viewed nervously. Economic liberalism through freer trade was seen by the other great powers as a ploy to help Britain win commercial advantage. Political liberalism and the creation of constitutional monarchies were even more suspect and Castlereagh approached them with great care. He was aware that the other great powers saw great danger in sudden political change. The French Revolution had clearly shown this. He was ready to see other countries adopt more liberal constitutions but only where appropriate and in Britain's interest. Britain also pressed for the abolition of the slave trade but Castlereagh was only able to obtain vague promises of action by the other powers.[3]

---

[1] The 'Hundred Days' was a three-month period in 1815 during which Napoleon escaped from his exile on the Mediterranean island of Elba, returned to France, took back power for himself and relaunched the war. He was defeated at Waterloo in June. He was exiled again, this time to the island of St. Helena in the southern Atlantic where he died in 1821.
[2] The territorial settlement of the Congress of Vienna consisted of three agreements signed in 1814 and 1815. The first Treaty of Paris (30 May 1814) was the peace treaty with France after Napoleon's abdication. The Final Act of the Congress of Vienna (9 June 1815) contained most of the post-war settlement, the result of negotiations in Vienna between October 1814 and June 1815. The second Treaty of Paris (20 November 1815) revised the peace terms with France making them slightly harsher after Napoleon's 'Hundred Days'. The Vienna settlement evolved over more than a year.
[3] The abolition of the British slave trade took place in 1807. Britain paid off other countries that practiced the trade. Spain was given £400,000 in 1820 and

Britain did not want any territory on the mainland of Europe. However, it wanted the independence of Belgium, especially the port of Antwerp to protect the British coastline and to guarantee access to European markets. Britain also wanted to see Spain and Portugal free from French influence. Castlereagh accepted that Italy should be an area of Austrian influence and that Prussia should be expanded. They could then guard against Russia aggression. Canning's involvement in Spain and Portugal and Palmerston's concerns about the Low Countries and the Ottoman Empire show the essential continuity of Britain's European policies.

The Vienna Settlement brought Britain few territorial gains though their location emphasised Britain's major interests. The Cape of Good Hope (South Africa), Ceylon (now Sri Lanka) and Mauritius were of strategic and commercial importance in relation to India. Britain's special interest in the Low Countries (modern day Belgium and the Netherlands) was central to her trade with Europe. Most British exports entered Europe through the Scheldt estuary. This was safeguarded by the possession of Heligoland and by Austria's decision not to take back the old Austrian Netherlands (later Belgium), which was united with the United Provinces (the Netherlands). As a result, no great power controlled the Low Countries. Malta and the Ionian Islands provided bases in the Mediterranean guarding against the advance of Russia. The West Indian islands of St Lucia, Trinidad and Tobago reinforced Britain's commercial control over the Caribbean. The centre of Europe was bolstered against aggression from east and west by strengthening the position of Austria in Germany and Italy and by guarding against Russian advance into the Balkans. In broad terms, Castlereagh had secured the settlement he wanted.

The Congress system.

The territorial settlement, though inevitably a compromise satisfied the great powers. Russia gained Poland and Finland. Austria's influence in Italy and Germany was strengthened. Prussia, the most successful of the great powers in 1815 doubled in population. France lost territory in Europe and some colonies, had to pay an indemnity (compensation) or 700 million francs and ensure an army of occupation for between three and five years but was not treated too harshly and the Bourbons were

---

Portugal followed Spain's lead by accepting £300,000. The Dutch were not paid cash but ended the trade in their colonies in 1815 in return for keeping most of their colonies in the East Indies, such as Java that Britain had captured during the war.

restored.[4] The main aim of the great powers was European political stability, a balance of power. The Congress system was premised on this.

Holy and Quadruple Alliances.

By the end of 1815, two further alliances had been signed: the Holy Alliance of Austria, Russia and Prussia established in September and the Quadruple Alliance signed in November The Holy Alliance was the idea of Tsar Alexander I. He wanted to establish an alliance of Christian kings who could work together to keep order, peace and friendly relations between the states of Europe. Britain did not sign and Castlereagh described it as a 'piece of sublime mysticism and nonsense'. The Holy Alliance was a reactionary move reflecting anxieties about all revolutionary movements. It had two important results. It was used to justify intervention by the Great Powers in the affairs of smaller states in the 1820s if a revolutionary change seemed likely. The Congress System became a means for maintaining established order and authority. It also led to liberalism and nationalism being repressed.

The Quadruple Alliance was signed by the four victorious great powers. It was more specific and practical than the rather vague notions of 'Justice, Christian Charity and Peace' of the Holy Alliance. Article VI was drawn up by Castlereagh and was a crucial element in organising the congresses: the four victorious powers 'have agreed to renew their meetings at fixed periods...for the purpose of consulting on their common interests.' The vagueness was deliberate. Castlereagh recognised the advantage of keeping the allies together but anything more specific would have been overruled in Cabinet by colleagues opposed to further involvement on mainland Europe.

In practice, there was no 'system'. The congresses met in different places: Aix-la-Chapelle, Troppau, Laibach and Verona. There was no permanent staff to support them. Meetings were held at irregular intervals, in 1818, 1820, 1821 and 1822 with the Congresses in 1820 and 1821 almost merging. The meeting at Aix-la-Chapelle was called to deal with outstanding problems that arose from the treatment of France. There was no clear reason for calling any of the other three, other than considering revolution. There were no congresses after 1822, though attempts were made to call them. Congresses proved unworkable largely because the great powers wanted to pursue their own interests and were no prepared to surrender this except when it was to their advantage to do so. Normal

---

[4] The Bourbons were restored: the Bourbons were the royal family of France. Louis XVI had been executed in 1793 and in 1814, his brother Louis XVIII was restored. He died in 1824 and was succeeded by Charles X. Louis Philippe finally replaced the Bourbons in the Revolution of 1830

diplomatic channels proved to be a far more effective way of maintaining the balance of power in Europe.

Britain and the four Congresses.

In 1818, at Aix-La-Chapelle, France was brought back as one of the great powers in the Quintuple Alliance in part to balance what Castlereagh and Metternich[5] saw as the growing power of Russia. Both Austria and Britain were concerned about Russia expanding further westwards and this ensured that Castlereagh and Metternich worked closely together until 1820. Tsar Alexander[6] wanted to guarantee existing rulers their thrones and frontiers arguing for regular congresses that could direct the use of troops to restore deposed leaders. Castlereagh opposed this proposal vigorously and it was, for the moment dropped. The Congress at Aix-la-Chapelle was the most successful of the four.

The second Congress at Troppau in 1820 was concerned with how the balance of power in Europe should be maintained. It was unclear whether the balance of power created at Vienna in 1815 was to be maintained indefinitely or whether it should be open to limited change. The Congress was called because the rebellions in Spain, Naples and then Portugal threatened the rulers there. Castlereagh made his position clear in the State Paper of 5 May 1820:

'it (the Quadruple Alliance) never was intended as a Union for the government of the world, or the superintendence of the internal affairs of other states.'

Castlereagh was prepared to support change in the balance of power as long as they did not threaten the overall peace of the continent. Russia, Prussia and Austria took the opposite view and signed the Troppau Protocol committing them to intervene if revolutionary changes in any state threatened other states or international peace. Britain saw its obligations as limited to guaranteeing the territorial integrity of the Vienna Settlement and that, since the Spanish revolution was an internal matter intervention was unjustified. In practice, British foreign policy in the 1820s and 1830s took a more pragmatic attitude to intervention.

The Troppau meeting was adjourned to Laibach reassembling in January 1821. Castlereagh's brother Lord Stewart the British Ambassador

---

[5] Metternich was the Austrian Chancellor and a key player in European diplomacy from 1815 to 1848.
[6] Alexander I, tsar of Russia from 1801 to 1825 took a leading part in the defeat of Napoleon in 1815. His approach to foreign policy after 1815 was motivated by a belief in Christian brotherhood.

in Vienna represented Britain. Ferdinand of Naples appealed to the Congress for help and, though Britain could not object to the dispatch of an Austrian army in view of Austria's treaty arrangements with Naples, the British opposed the use of international force. Suppression of the rebellion was, according to Castlereagh, an Italian question and that intervention by the Austrians in their sphere of influence was not an issue as far as British foreign policy was concerned. This did little to help Castlereagh's reputation in Britain where he was seen as an arch-reactionary. The outbreak of a revolt in Wallachia and Moldavia was followed by the Greek revolt. This had the effect of uniting British and Austrian policy, as both were anxious that the Russians should not profit from the situation the expense of Turkey. Laibach settled little and a new congress was arranged to meet at Verona in 1822. The threat to British interests in the Near East obliged Castlereagh to consider attending in person. However, on 12 August 1822, he killed himself throwing British policy into some confusion. Canning, his successor did not go to Verona and quickly recalled Wellington, who had gone in his place. He maintained that this ended the Congress System but this overestimated his achievement. Doubts on the part of the Tsar, reinforced by Metternich's arguments, prevented Russia from intervening in Greece. Wellington's argument against French intervention in Spain was also unsuccessful and the Bourbon army found little difficulty in subduing the country in mid-1823. The Verona Congress maintained the façade of unity but it was increasingly clear that the interests of the great powers had diverged.

How did Canning secure British interests 1822 -1830?

George Canning had already held the post between 1807 and 1809. Only his unwillingness to serve with Castlereagh prevented his reappointment in July 1812. By 1816, Canning and Castlereagh appeared to have made up their differences, at least outwardly, and Canning joined the cabinet. He had a hand in drafting the 1820 State Paper and accepted it as the basis for his own policies once in office. The real contrast between Castlereagh and Canning was not in policy but in personality and public image. Castlereagh was hesitant and shy, Canning was a speaker with a strong sense of humour. Castlereagh was popular at Court but largely because as Leader of the House of Commons he had had to defend the government's repressive policies against radicalism, unpopular in the country. Canning was very popular with the public. Castlereagh was cautious and was only pushed into disagreement with Britain's allies by the pressure of public opinion. Canning was more flamboyant, setting himself vigorously in the van of public opinion and ruthlessly pursuing British interests and gained a reputation as a crusader for liberalism and nationalism. Metternich saw him as the evil genius of revolution, 'a malevolent meteor, this scourge of the world, a revolution in himself'.

This contrast exaggerates differences between Castlereagh and Canning. Both were well aware of the limitations of both British interests and power and were pragmatic in their approach. Both sought to pursue Britain's aims of security, trade and support for liberal causes. The difference between them was over how policy should be put into practice. Castlereagh and Canning represented the alternative approaches that ran through nineteenth century British foreign policy. Castlereagh, Aberdeen and Gladstone sought cooperation with foreign states. Canning, Palmerston and Disraeli were more competitive and belligerent in approach.

Canning and the Americas

Britain feared the extension of the forces of reaction to Portugal and Spanish America where she had important economic interests. Castlereagh had been anxious about this but for Canning, spokesman for Britain's commercial interests and MP for Liverpool, it was of central importance. The United States had already recognised the rebel governments in Latin America. Canning moved more cautiously. He was opposed by the king and Wellington but exerted sufficient diplomatic pressure on France to get agreement that its intervention should not be extended to the rebel Spanish colonies. The uneasiness of Anglo-American relations and American suspicions of Canning's motives led President Monroe to issue his famous message (the Monroe Doctrine) in December 1823 banning European assistance to Spain in her struggle against the rebels and any transfer or extension of European possessions to the New World. Canning's defence of the rebel colonies and his pose as a true friend of the United States were not very convincing. By mid-1823, he was isolated from the European powers. His attacks on French intervention caused criticism at home and he needed to drum up popular support against opponents in his own party. Support for the rebels had commercial and political advantages for Canning and it was popular outside Parliament. His claim that he had 'called the New World into existence, to redress the balance of the Old' must be seen in this domestic context.

Canning and Portugal

The Royal Navy allowed Britain to intervene in Portugal where revolutionaries and reactionaries were struggling for power. Canning wanted to maintain the 'special relationship' between the two countries. He sent the fleet to Lisbon to support King John VI in 1824 and helped to arrange the peaceful separation of Brazil from direct Portuguese rule. King John's death in 1826 saw the accession of the eight-year-old Donna Maria. Her father Pedro renounced the throne preferring to remain as Emperor of Brazil. This led to a revival of the claims of her uncle Miguel. Spanish interfered in support of Miguel and this led to direct British action. Canning rushed 5,000 troops to Lisbon and threatened Spain with war. This ensured Maria's succession and the acceptance of the 1826 liberal constitution. British naval power played a major role in the success of Canning's actions and a naval presence at Lisbon maintained British influence. Events in Portugal and the New World made the weaknesses and strengths of Britain's position very clear. Naval power let her operate effectively only where water dominated communication.

Canning and Greece

Canning's influence on European countries was, by contrast limited. Britain remained isolated as long as the conservative alliance of Russia, Austria and Prussia was united. Disagreement between Austria and Russia over the Greek revolt against the Turks permitted Canning to take a leading role.

Greece was a major problem for Canning. It was in Britain's interest to prevent Russia becoming a Mediterranean naval power and to secure the stability of the Ottoman Empire, opening it to British trade.[7] The Greek revolt roused mixed feelings in London. Canning agreed with Castlereagh that preserving the Ottoman Empire offered the best hope of stability in the area. There was, however, a great deal of sympathy for the Greeks among the educated classes. Turkey's refusal to compromise combined with a growth of popular philhellenism[8] in Britain, personified by the poet Lord Byron who died in Greece in 1824, threatened to undermine British policy.

Russia was sympathetic to the Greek struggle and had an interest in eroding the boundaries of the Ottoman Empire. This broke the conservative alliance with Austria against revolution. Canning recognised the Greeks in March 1823. Tsar Alexander tried first to get the British to agree to joint intervention, but by the end of 1824, he abandoned this strategy. The Greeks suffered from Ottoman military victories and in July 1825 appealed for protection and mediation directly to Great Britain.

---

[7] Ottoman Empire. The Ottoman Turks controlled large parts of the Balkans throughout the nineteenth century. The Eastern Question reflected concerns about the future of these Balkan territories. Britain was concerned about Russian expansion into the Balkans and often supported Turkey against Russia aggression.

[8] Philhellenism or love of things Greek.

Canning wanted to avoid a Russo-Turkish war and the possibility of Russian territorial expansion. The St. Petersburg Protocol of April 1826 gave him roughly what he wanted. Nicholas I, who had succeeded Tsar Alexander in late 1825, agreed that Greece should become an autonomous state, nominally under the sovereignty of the Sultan, and that Russia should support Britain's mediation to achieve this. Austria and Prussia refused to accept this. This was formalised in the Treaty of London in 1827. The Turks, strengthened by further victories over the Greeks, refused the demands of the great powers and British, French and Russian ships were sent to the east Mediterranean. On 20 October 1827, a combined Turkish and Egyptian fleet was annihilated within two hours at Navarino. This was followed by the outbreak of war between Russia and Turkey in April 1828.

Canning did not live to see the breakdown of his policy. Navarino changed the balance of power in the eastern Mediterranean and outbreak of war between Russia and Turkey marked an end to the policy pursued since 1826. Canning might have been able to limit the effects of this situation but under Wellington, Britain's Greek policy simply drifted. Domestic issues rather than foreign policy dominated Parliament and Lord Aberdeen, who became Foreign Secretary in June 1828, though sympathetic to Greek demands, believed that a narrowly defined state would limit Russian influence. Russia made small territorial gains from the war with Turkey that ended with the Treaty of Adrianople in September 1829. Greek independence was achieved the following year. Little of the limited success Wellington and Aberdeen had between 1828 and 1830 was the result their efforts. They badly bungled the situation in Portugal by withdrawing the British naval presence and giving the initiative to the reactionaries. They almost destroyed Canning's achievement in dismantling the conservative alliance and, over the Greek issue, came close to restoring Britain's isolation.

How did Palmerston secure British interests 1830-1841?

Henry John Temple, Lord Palmerston, became the Whig Foreign Secretary in late 1830. Born in 1784, Palmerston entered Parliament in 1807. In 1809, he became Secretary at War, without a seat in the cabinet. He remained at the War Office until 1828. He was generally regarded as hard-working and competent but in the late 1820s seemed destined to be only a minor political figure.

Canning brought Palmerston into the Cabinet in April 1827 but his unexpected death in August 1827 led to political disarray. Canningites led by Huskisson and Palmerston remained in office under Goderich and continued under Wellington until May 1828. The five months the

Canningites were in Wellington's Cabinet frustrated Palmerston and, freed from the constraints of office, he vigorously attacked government policy over Greece and Portugal, arguing for an extension of Greek territory and against Wellington's support for the absolutist Miguel. His speech of 1 June 1829 was a comprehensive denunciation of foreign policy on both these issues, in which he presented his interpretation of Canningite foreign policy.

The speech had little impact at the time. Wellington did not take it too seriously. This was not Palmerston's view and he circulated copies to the press and later provided a version for inclusion in *Hansard*.[9] Palmerston saw himself as Canning's true successor but his emphasis was different. Canning was aggressive in his approach but his policies were cautious. Palmerston was more uncompromising arguing for intervention in support of Britain's vital interests. He gave the foreign policy debate a distinctly ideological slant, insisting that Britain stood for the defence of constitutional rights in other countries and for the extension of 'liberty and civilisation'. There is little evidence that Palmerston was making a play for the Foreign Office in preference to any other offices. Grey had considered him as Leader of the House of Commons, Chancellor of the Exchequer and Home Secretary before making him Foreign Secretary.

Palmerston did not take a prominent part in the reform debates in the early 1830s. He had reservations about parliamentary reform though he did believe that 'piecemeal' reform could prevent revolution. Grey had a major influence on foreign policy between 1830 and 1834 and his support and often-detailed guidance were central to Palmerston's success. He did not control Palmerston's actions but a kind of inner cabinet consisting of Grey, Lansdowne, Holland and Palmerston was largely responsible for foreign policy decisions. Certainly, Palmerston did not have the prestige he enjoyed later but even under Melbourne from 1834 to 1841, he was still engaged in trying to balance often-contradictory opinions.

In the 1830s, Palmerston was faced with the results of a series of challenges to the Vienna Settlement. The July Revolution of 1830 in France was seen by Palmerston, and ironically by Wellington and Aberdeen as a limited political revolution, which the Bourbon king had brought upon himself. He also recognised that the new government of Louis Philippe was not aggressive and that the best way of maintaining stability in Europe was to recognise the *fait accompli*. Revolution had, however spread from France into Belgium, where riots broke out in August.

---

[9] *Hansard*. A written record of what was said in the two Houses of Parliament

The Belgian problem

The decision to unite Belgium and Holland in 1815 under the Dutch House of Orange provided a barrier to French expansion into the Low Countries. The two countries had economies that were complementary and religious and linguistic divisions did not correspond to existing boundaries. However, it proved a difficult union and the Belgians increasingly felt repressed by the Dutch. In early 1830, Wellington had established an ambassadorial conference in London to discuss the problem that Palmerston inherited. The outbreak of revolution in Poland in mid-1830 distracted the eastern powers that would have supported Holland had France intervened and Louis Philippe's government was too insecure to risk a serious quarrel with Britain.

The Belgians drew up a new constitution and in February 1831 elected the Duke of Nemours, the son of Louis Philippe, as their king. Knowing this would prove unacceptable to the other Powers, Louis Philippe vetoed it and Leopold of Saxe-Coburg became Leopold I of the Belgians. William I of Holland accepted Belgian independence in January 1831 but his claims over the Duchy of Luxembourg led to a Dutch invasion in August 1831. Leopold appealed for aid and while the British fleet blockaded the coast, the French army forced the Dutch to withdraw.

The great powers agreed as early as January 1831 that Belgium should become an independent state and that they should guarantee its neutrality. The details of the agreement were modified in June and again in October 1831. The terms were acceptable to the Belgians but not to the Dutch. William I, who still controlled Antwerp, stubbornly refused to withdraw and the French intervened again in 1832. Palmerston was prepared to accept limited French military intervention but, he had considerable difficulty in persuading both king and Parliament of the policy, which seemed a complete reversal of the 'containment' of France, agreed in 1815. A new armistice was agreed in 1833 but a final settlement was delayed until the Treaty of London of 1839.

Revolutions in 1830

Revolution also erupted in Poland, Germany and Italy in 1830. Public opinion in Britain was generally on the side of the Poles and radical groups urged Palmerston to act. In practice, there was little that he could do other than stress that as a signatory of the Treaty of Vienna Britain had the right to be consulted before Poland's status was changed. By 1832 the Poles had lost their independence and became yet another Russian province. Palmerston did little to support liberal groups in Germany and by 1832, the conservative stability had been restored.

He had little success in his policies over Italy. In 1831-1832, there were a number of unsuccessful risings in the Papal States and in Modena and Parma. Anti-papal feeling in Britain ran high and again the radical groups in Parliament urged Palmerston to take action. From the Foreign Office viewpoint, the important thing was to prevent conflict between France, which showed some gestures of support for the rebels, and Austria, which gave military aid to the recently elected conservative Pope, Gregory XVI. Palmerston argued that moderate reform would stave off revolution. The Pope took no notice and absolutism was re-established throughout Italy. War between France and Austria had been averted but the cause of liberalism here, as in Poland and Germany, had been put back.

The Iberian Peninsula

Palmerston's reputation was improved by his handling of problems in Portugal and Spain where, as in the Low Countries, Britain had long-established strategic and commercial interests. In Portugal, British support for Maria had collapsed with Canning's death and by November 1830 Miguel, the conservative claimant was in control of the whole of the country. Maria's supporters held only Terceira in the Azores. In 1831, the French, with British approval, sent a fleet to Lisbon. This coincided with the French invasion of Belgium and again Palmerston came under attack from the Tory opposition because of his support from France. British opinion was better pleased when he extended his support to Pedro, who abdicated his Brazilian throne to come to the assistance of his daughter. He landed at Oporto in July 1832 and Palmerston made little attempt to stop British volunteers, notably Charles Napier, from enlisting under Pedro. Napier defeated Miguel's fleet off Cape St Vincent in July 1833 and took possession of Lisbon three weeks later.

Spain was also divided between liberals and absolutists in the 1830s. King Ferdinand VII died in September 1833. The succession was disputed between the supporters of his young daughter, Isabella and her mother Christina who had been proclaimed Regent and the supporters of Ferdinand's younger brother, Carlos, who argued that the Salic Law forbade the accession of women to the throne. Carlos had the support of conservatives and the Catholic Church while Isabella was supported by the liberals. For Palmerston the attitude of Russia, Prussia and Austria was more disturbing. They had signed an agreement at Munchengratz in September 1833 pledging them to uphold conservative causes and one effect of this was that they provided financial assistance to Carlos. In April 1834, Palmerston countered this by establishing the Quadruple Alliance of Britain, France and the queens of Portugal and Spain. This prevented the intervention of the Eastern Powers and established, in an embryonic form, the idea of two balancing power blocs, the absolutist powers of Eastern Europe and the constitutional powers of the West. Despite this, the conflict between Christina and Carlos continued until late 1839. Palmerston's influence on Spain was less than in Portugal, but in both countries, he had prevented unilateral intervention by France.

Palmerston's actions in his early years as Foreign Secretary were dominated by either revolutions that had swept Louis Philippe to power in France and then spread to the Low Countries, to Poland, Germany and Italy or by the conflict between 'liberals' and conservatives in the Iberian Peninsula. His degree of success was, however, limited to the western edge of Europe where French military and British naval power and influence could be exerted. In Eastern Europe Palmerston could do little more than protest at the suppression of the Polish Revolt while in Italy, Austria and the Pope were able to restore the status quo. In Belgium alone was a solution found that was completely in line with his plans.

The Eastern Question

Palmerston, however, took a more decisive stand on the Eastern Question and here his influence on events was undeniable. The basic questions remained as they had done under Castlereagh and Canning: could the Ottoman Empire survive and, if not what would take its place? Palmerston hoped that the Turks would leave Europe. However, he recognised that this would leave a political vacuum that would benefit Russia and, as a result adopted a policy of support for the empire. In the 1830s, the Turks were under serious attack from rebellious Pasha of Egypt, Mehemet Ali, who had ruled Egypt since 1805.

Mehemet Ali had used his large army on behalf of the Sultan in Greece in the 1820s, aid that would probably have been successful but for the intervention of the great powers. In return for his assistance, the Sultan had promised him Syria and Crete. After the Greek settlement, Mehemet Ali demanded his reward but in view of his limited success, the Sultan refused to give him Syria as well as Crete. In 1831, he invaded Syria and the following year defeated the Turkish army at Koneih. Constantinople was threatened and the Sultan appealed to Britain for assistance. Palmerston would have been willing to provide aid but the Cabinet overruled him. It was the middle in election campaign after the Reform Act and the Whigs were unwilling to accept commitments where British interests were not directly affected. The Cabinet also rejected French offers of joint intervention.

In desperation, the Sultan turned to Russia. A Russian naval squadron entered the Bosphorus, the strait separating the Black Sea from the Mediterranean. Mehemet Ali's forces retreated and with the worried British and French pressing him to compromise, peace was made at

Kutahiya in May 1833. This gave the Egyptians what they wanted in Syria. The Treaty of Unkiar Skelessi in July 1833 formalised Russian influence in Constantinople, an agreement that aroused considerable suspicion in Britain and France. Though it was essentially defensive, there were secret clauses of which the most important was an Ottoman undertaking to close the Dardanelles, the western end of the Bosphorus to foreign warships if Russia requested it. The three Eastern Powers publicly agreed to maintain the integrity of the Sultan's dominions and in secret clauses to oppose any further advance by Mehemet Ali.

Central Asia

Russia had established a dominant influence at Constantinople and the revival of the conservative alliance provided sufficient justification for Palmerston's alarm. Britain was concerned by threats to communications with India. Between 1833 and 1839, Palmerston pursued a policy in Central Asia which aimed at the containment of Russia. In Persia, Britain was concerned to prevent Russia's advance both on her lines of communication with India and on the frontiers of India itself. In 1809, Britain had secured treaties with Persia, Sind and Afghanistan to hold off the Russian advance but its victories against Persia between 1826 and 1828 upset this arrangement. Russian influence in Teheran was as powerful as in Constantinople further undermining Britain's previously dominant position in Persia. Both Tories and Whigs were worried by this development. Under Wellington, Grey and Melbourne there was a conscious policy of extending British power into Central Asia to counteract the threat from Russia. As a result, Palmerston gained control of the Khyber Pass linking Afghanistan to India. Palmerston pursued this policy with some vigour, opening up the River Indus to British trade and influence as a counter to Russian advances. Though Britain and Russia cooperated in the Persian succession in 1834, Palmerston remained suspicious of Russian intentions and believed that their representatives were pressing the Shah of Persia to renew his attack on the strategic Afghan fortress of Herat, which he did in July 1837.

By 1836, Palmerston wanted to retaliate against Russian policy but the internal chaos in Afghanistan proved a major difficulty. Despite their encouragement of the Persian attack on Herat, the Russians had also gained ascendancy in Kabul, the Afghan capital. British intervention in support of a favourable candidate occurred in 1839 but it proved impossible to maintain this position and in 1841, the British suffered a series of military defeats in the First Afghan war. It was not until late 1842 that Kabul was reoccupied. Britain eventually accepted a compromise that restored the former pro-Russian candidate to power. The events of 1837-1842 demonstrated the extent of the Russian threat in Central Asia and the difficulty of dealing with it diplomatically and militarily. St. Petersburg had little control over the actions of over-zealous agents in Teheran or Kabul. The real aims of Russian expansionism--whether determined from the centre or locally--was contrary to Britain's quest for security for India.

The Eastern Question revived

An uneasy peace prevailed in the Near East until 1839. Neither the Sultan nor Mehemet Ali was content to leave things as they were. The former wanted revenge against an ambitious subject while Mehemet Ali continued to press, if not for complete independence, at least for hereditary possession of Egypt under nominal Ottoman sovereignty. By 1839, the Sultan's army had been reorganised and, recognising that he was a dying man, he invaded to drive the Egyptians out of Syria. Mehemet Ali's son Ibrahim had little difficulty defeating him and once again, the road to Constantinople lay open. On 1 July 1839, the Sultan died and was succeeded by Abdulmejid I, a sixteen-year-old boy. The Ottoman Empire seemed on the point of total collapse and the great powers were seriously alarmed.

Palmerston was in a difficult position. He recognised that the crisis gave Russia further opportunities to strengthen its position in Constantinople but by 1839, he was more suspicious of France than Russia in the Mediterranean. The agreement reached between Britain and France in the 1834 had gradually been eroded. The French had consolidated their bold over Algeria after 1830 and favoured giving considerable concessions to Mehemet Ali who posed a real threat to British economic and strategic interests. He directly threatened British routes to the River Euphrates and the Persian Gulf, which his forces reached in 1838. At the same time, he was also threatened the Red Sea route to India. To offset this, British forces had occupied the important strategic position of Aden in 1839. The means of defending Britain's interests in the Near Fast and of resolving the contest for supremacy in Constantinople were not to be found in the Western Alliance.

Palmerston attempted to co-ordinate his policy with France, as he had done over Belgium, but during 1839 and early 1840 he moved closer to Russia. Increasing divisions between Britain and France were reinforced by the appointment of Thiers as French Prime Minister in March 1840 and French support for Mehemet Ali now became more open. Palmerston did not hesitate to join with the Eastern Powers and Turkey in an agreement to which France was not a party, the Convention of London, on 15 July 1840. Mebemet Ali was offered the hereditary possession of Egypt and the possession of Syria during his lifetime. He failed to respond in the twenty days given and on 3 November, a British fleet bombarded Acre.

Palmerston again found himself in a difficult position. The French, angered by the attack on Acre, increasingly spoke in warlike terms. However, the French cabinet was equally divided between peace and war parties. Though contemporaries criticised Palmerston for his threatening approach to France, Thiers' policy in Egypt was a direct threat to British interests. Just before the bombardment, Thiers was replaced by Guizot, who was a more pacific individual and had been recalled as French ambassador to London to head the ministry. Instead of ending the crisis without directly involving the French, Palmerston allowed them to re-join the Concert once Mehemet Ali had submitted in early 1841. The agreement of July 1840 was superseded by the Straits Convention of 13 July 1841 that forbade the passage of foreign warships through the Bosphorus while the Ottoman Empire was at peace and ended the advantages that Russia had gained in 1833. Palmerston regarded his Near East policy as a triumph He had successfully resolved the crisis in conjunction with the Eastern Powers and had not humiliated France by involving her in the 1841 Convention. The Conservatives were willing to back him but his own party and the cabinet was divided. The press was very critical but the Conservative Lord Aberdeen persuaded *The Times* to call off its attacks.

China and opium

The assertiveness Palmerston displayed was not confined to his handling of France in the Near East and Russia in Central Asia. His approach to the Chinese question demonstrated the same approach. Trade with China had always been difficult and was, until the abolition of its monopoly in 1833, under the control of the East India Company. After 1833, the protection of British trade and British citizens fell to the British government. The result in 1839 was war, though wider issues were involved than opium. Britain was determined to open up the Chinese trade and to compel Peking to adopt normal western diplomatic conventions, but opium smuggling was the flashpoint.

There was a considerable demand for opium in China and the East India Company made good profits by growing it in India and exporting it in return for Chinese merchandise. The Chinese authorities in the 1830s hesitated between banning opium imports or regulating them. In the late 1830s, those calling for a ban won the argument. The authorities in southern China were unable to board British ships to search for opium and placed the small British trading community at Canton under virtual house arrest. They then attacked *The Arrow*, a British warship and ordered the suspension of all trade with Britain. Banning trade was one thing but the arrest of British citizens and attacks on British shipping another. Palmerston found himself in the position of having to endorse policy being made by British officials in India and China but did so wholeheartedly. The British government in India had already sent naval assistance to Canton, which had little difficulty in defeating the Chinese fleet sent against it.

Palmerston's handling of the Chinese question was criticised by contemporaries, though given the limited extent to which he determined the policy much of this criticism was partial. Gladstone raised the question of the morality of the opium trade but his attack was exceptional. To Palmerston the issue was not whether Britain could protect opium smugglers; he did not question the Chinese government's right to ban the trade. The issue was that British interests in the trading community in Canton, not implicated in the opium trade, were under attack. The Chinese maintained that the community to which criminals belonged should be held accountable for their actions and this notion of collective responsibility was alien to the British concept of individual innocence or guilt. Palmerston did not accept that this gave the Chinese the right to interfere with British subjects. The war was still in progress when the Whigs were defeated in the 1841 election but the incoming Conservative government made no significant change in policy. The war continued until the Chinese made concessions in the Treaty of Nanking of 1842. Five treaty ports were opened up to foreign trade, and not merely to the British, though they did get a special grip on China by the annexation of Hong Kong as a Crown Colony.[10]

Britain and the United States

Britain had several outstanding disputes with the United States of America especially slavery and the slave trade, the Canadian boundary, and the problem of Texas that resulted from the breakup of Spain's American empire. Britain had declared the slave trade illegal in 1807. In 1815, the Congress of Vienna, under pressure from Castlereagh also outlawed it. Enforcing the ban proved a more intractable problem. Britain had signed a number of 'right of search' treaties with the smaller nations of Europe, permitting British ships to arrest slavers flying their flags. Larger nations were more difficult to convince. Palmerston negotiated treaties of this type with France in 1831 and 1833 and in 1838 almost secured the agreement of all the great powers of Europe to one treaty that would have allowed a common right of search over all slavers. French anger at Palmerston's

---

[10] Hong Kong was under British rule from 1841 to 1997 excluding the Japanese occupation of 1941-1945. Although Hong Kong Island and Kowloon were ceded to Britain in perpetuity, the New Territories--which made up over 90 per cent of Hong Kong's land was leased for 99 years in 1898. When the lease expired in 1997, Britain transferred sovereignty of the entirety of Hong Kong to China.

handling of the Eastern question led them to withhold ratification and the treaty never became as effective intended.

The United States had consistently refused to enter any right of search agreement with Britain. This was partly the result of Britain's action against American shipping during the Napoleonic War but largely because of the powerful lobby of the slave-owning southern American states. Palmerston accepted that Britain could not in the absence of a treaty, stop and search American shipping but was concerned that slavers of other nations hoisted the American flag to escape capture. He therefore argued for a more limited 'right of visit' to check whether a suspected ship was entitled to the flag she was flying. Palmerston inflamed Americans by saying that they would not want slavers to escape simply by hoisting a 'piece of bunting'.

The most likely catalyst for war between Britain and America, however, was the failure to agree the boundary between Canada and the United States west of Rocky Mountains and in the east between the American state of Maine and Canadian New Brunswick. The 1814 Treaty of Ghent had left the matter to be settled by independent arbitration and in 1831, the disputed territory was arbitrarily divided between the two claimants. As settlers entered the disputed areas clashes were inevitable. In 1837-1838, there were rebellions in Upper and Lower Canada (present-day Ontario and Quebec) caused by local demands for greater political autonomy. This embroiled Britain and America in a series of incidents on the disputed borders. Some Americans ran guns into Canada and the defeated rebels found safe refuge in Maine and Vermont. In the north-east, British and American settlers and trappers clashed violently over the disputed border.

A major crisis was initially avoided by the overtures of the American government, despite warlike pressure from British public opinion and by Palmerston's preoccupation with the Eastern Question. However, in December 1837 a band of Canadian volunteers crossed into American territory and sank the American steamer, the *Caroline*, which had been involved in gunrunning and killed an American citizen. In November 1840, a Canadian, Alexander McLeod, was arrested and charged with the murder. Palmerston made it clear that he would regard McLeod's conviction and execution as an occasion for war. Matters were still uncertain when Lord Aberdeen became Foreign Secretary in the new Conservative government in September 1841 but matters calmed after McLeod was acquitted.

Palmerston also became involved in the problems of Texas that had broken away from Mexico and formed an independent republic in 1836. The Texans, many of whom were American immigrants, initially sought entry into the American Union. This was refused, largely because of the opposition of the northern states. In 1837, the Texans sent agents to all the leading commercial powers in Europe to obtain commercial treaties and loans. Palmerston recognised the value of an independent Texas since she was a major cotton producer and could free Britain from dependence on American cotton. British anti-slavery groups hoped that Texas would abolish slavery in return for commercial concessions. In November 1840 Palmerston signed three treaties with Texas: a commercial treaty; a treaty offering British mediation between Texas and Mexico which still claimed jurisdiction over Texas; and a mutual 'right of search' treaty.

Palmerston 1830-1841: success or failure?

Historians have generally regarded the period between 1830 and 1841 as the most consistently successful period in Palmerston's career. He believed that bluff was an essential part of diplomacy and perhaps he not only bluffed his contemporaries into believing his successes were greater than they were but also later historians. This period showed Palmerston more as an opportunist than as a man of principle. His pragmatism gave room for manoeuvre but it also meant that he embarked on policies without seeing where they could lead. He desired, like Castlereagh and Canning, peace and stability in Europe and some sort of 'balance of power', though this meant different things at different times. His achievements were modest. He did little for Poland, Germany and Italy. His plans in Spain and Portugal were of limited success. He sought to contain Russia in the Near East and Central Asia. His actions against America could have led to war and in China they did. Only in Belgium was he entirely successful.

9 The First Industrial Nation.

In the latter part of the eighteenth and the first half of the nineteenth century, Britain underwent what historians have called an 'industrial revolution' with factories pouring out goods, chimneys polluting the air, escalating exports and productivity spiralling upwards. This was an epic drama, of Telford, the Stephensons and the Darbys, Macadam, Brunel and Wedgwood, a revolution not simply of inventions and economic growth but of the spirit of enterprise within an unbridled market economy. This is, however, misleading. Industrial change was not something that occurred simply after 1780 but took place throughout the eighteenth century. There was substantial growth in a whole range of traditional industries as well as in the obviously 'revolutionary' cases of textiles, iron and coal. Technical change was not necessarily mechanisation but the wider use of hand working and the division of labour. Changes were the result of the conjunction of old and new processes. Steam power did not replace waterpower at a stroke. Work organisation varied: the 'dark satanic mills' were not all conquering. In 1850, factories coexisted with domestic production, artisan workshops, large-scale mining, and metal production. Change also varied across industries and regions.[1]

How did industrialisation occur in Britain 1780-1850?

Why did economic change occur in Britain between 1780 and 1850? Answering this question usually focuses on why industries like cotton, iron and coal expanded and what influence the spread of steam power had. These areas were important but undue emphasis on them neglects the broader economic experiences of Britain. Similarly, the question 'Why did the industrial revolution take place in Britain rather than France or Germany?' misses the crucial point that economic change did not occur in Britain as a whole. Growth was regional and industrialisation took place in particular locations like Lancashire, the Central Lowlands of Scotland and South Wales and around Belfast. Explaining the industrial revolution is a very difficult undertaking since economic change had an effect, however small, on all aspects of society. Some circumstances that were present in Britain made change possible and, in that sense, can be said to be causal. Others held back progress but change occurred despite them.

---

[1] Historians disagree on a number of issues concerning the industrial revolution. It is, however, increasingly clear that the traditional view of the revolution as dynamic and relatively short-lived provides an incomplete picture. We have to consider change 'in slow motion' as well.

Population

If it is possible to identify a single cause for the industrial revolution, then a strong case can be made for population increase. Between 1780 and 1850, the population of England and Wales increased from over seven to nearly eighteen million. This led to mounting demand for goods like food and housing. Nevertheless, the increase in demand for other goods--more manufactured goods or more efficient means of communication--did not necessarily follow from population expansion. The problem is one of timing. When did population growth occur? When did economic growth occur? Did they correspond? Although historians broadly accept population growth from the mid-eighteenth century, they do not agree when the economy began to grow.

If population growth stimulated demand, you would expect economic and population growth to coincide. However, they did not. Accelerated economic growth was concentrated in the last quarter of the eighteenth century while the maximum rate of population growth on mainland Britain was not achieved until after 1810. Population began to expand after 1750 and some historians argue that this provided the final ingredient necessary to trigger off industrialisation. Berg and Craft have shown that the origins of higher growth rates went back to the early decades of the century. In this scenario, population growth came after the beginnings of economic growth.

The impact of population growth causes problems for historians who argue for economic growth from the 1780s and those who see growth as something that began earlier in the century. It had favourable effects on economic growth in three important respects. Population growth provided Britain with an abundant and cheap supply of labour. Population growth also stimulated investment in industry and agriculture by its effects on demand for goods and services. Urbanisation made it profitable to create or improve services.[2] For instance, the building of the canal from the Bridgewater coalmines at Worsley to Manchester took advantage of the growing demand for domestic coal. The role of population growth in the origins of Britain's industrial revolution was far from straightforward. Population growth in mainland Britain stimulated an already growing economy. However, in Ireland population growth in the eighteenth

---

[2] There were 800 market towns in England and Wales in the 1780s. This reflected the intensity of production and the ability of particular areas to specialise in particular products. These products were then moved to markets across the country often using the turnpike roads. In 1767, 16,000 sheep and 14,000 cattle passed through the Birdlip Hill Turnpike in Gloucester en route from south Wales to London. Imports of coal into London from the north-east rose from one million to three million tons per year between 1720 and 1790.

century was followed by stagnation in the first half of the nineteenth century and by famine.

Investment

Britain was a relatively wealthy country in the mid-eighteenth century with a well-established system of banking. This enabled people to build up savings and provided them with capital to invest. Between 1750 and 1770, there was growing investment in roads, canals, and buildings and in enclosing land. This process continued after 1780 through to the 1850s with continued investment in transport and enclosure and in the expansion of the textile and iron industries, and after 1830 in the development of railways.

The annual rate of domestic investment rose from about £13 million in the 1780s to over £40 million by the 1830s. The ratio of gross investment to the gross national product rose from 6 per cent in the 1770s to 12 per cent by the 1790s at which level, it remained until 1850. Widespread capital investment was largely confined to a small, though important part of the economy. Capital investment rose in farming, communications and textiles, especially cotton and in iron and steel. Other areas of the economy were often undercapitalised relative to these industries.

Capital investment in farming was largely on enclosures, drainage and buildings. Landowners ploughed back about 6 per cent of their total income into the land. This rose to about 16 per cent during the French wars when high wheat prices encouraged investment in enclosure. Investment fell back after 1815 with the onset of depression and did not revive until the 1840s. In the 1780s, a third of investment was in farming. By 1850, this had fallen to an eighth. By contrast, there was a rapid growth of investment in industry and communications. Annual investment in industry and trade rose from £2 million in the 1780s to £17 million by 1850. Between 1780 and 1830, there was an annual investment of £1.5 million on canals and roads and for the improvement of docks and harbours. These figures were dwarfed by investment in railways that peaked at £15 million per year in the 1840s, some 28 per cent of all investment. The increase in the availability of capital to invest allowed economic growth to occur.

Trade

Britain was already a well-established trading nation. Colonies were important sources of raw materials as well as markets for manufactured goods. London was a major centre for the re-export trade. The slave trade played a major role in the development of Liverpool and Bristol and its profits provided an important source of capital for early industrialisation. By the 1780s, the export trade was expanding annually by 2.6 per cent. Cotton production depended on international trade and was responsible for half the increase in the value of exports between 1780 and 1830, for just over half Britain's exports by 1830 and three-quarters of all exports were associated with textiles. This represented a narrow trading base and helps to explain why the British economy underwent depression in the 1830s and early 1840s. British factories were over-producing for European and global markets already saturated with textile goods. The result was some changes in the goods exported with iron exports growing from 6 per cent in the 1810s to 20 per cent by 1850 and the growing importance of coal exports. In the 1780s, Europe was a major market for British goods and this remained the case in 1850.

However, there were important changes in the destination of British goods. The United States increasingly became a focus for exports of manufactured goods and for raw cotton. This process was helped by the opening up of the Latin American markets in the early nineteenth century. India was a huge market for cotton goods. Similar possibilities exited in the Middle East and South America. Britain increasingly shifted trade towards less developed economies that provided growing imports of tropical products to Britain and other industrialised countries like Germany and France. Overseas trade has been highlighted by some historians as a primary cause of economic growth. The growth of export industries at a faster rate than other industries was closely linked to foreign trade.

To what extent was the growth in trade between 1780 and 1850 central to Britain's economic development? It stimulated a domestic demand for the products of British industry. International trade gave access to raw materials that both widened the range and cheapened the products of British industries. It provided purchasing power for countries to buy British goods since trade is a two-way process. Profits from trade were used to finance industrial expansion and agricultural improvement. It was a major cause of the growth of large towns and industrial centres. The role of British trade must, however, be put into perspective. Changes in the pattern of British trade between 1780 and 1850--the export or re-export of manufactured goods in return for imports of foodstuffs and raw materials--were relatively small and the industrial developments from the 1780s consolidated already existing trends. Exports may have helped textiles and iron to expand but they made little impact on the unmodernised, traditional manufacturing sectors.

Transport

By 1750, Britain was already a highly mobile society. Travel may have been slow and, on occasions dangerous but it was not uncommon. Within a hundred years, the British landscape was scarred by canals and railways and traversed by improved roads and the movement of goods and people quickened dramatically. Turnpike roads and the emergence of a sophisticated coaching industry, canals with their barges carrying the raw materials and manufactured goods of the industrial revolution, new harbours and the railways were symbolic of 'progress' as much as factories and enclosed fields.

Britain's road system in the mid-eighteenth century was extensive but under-funded.[3] Just over £1 million was spent annually but this was insufficient to maintain the road system necessary to growing trade and manufactures. Turnpike roads, the first was established in 1663, grew slowly in the first half of the eighteenth century. An average of eight were established each year. From the 1750s, this went up to about forty a year and from the 1790s, to nearly sixty. By the mid-1830s, there were 1,116 turnpike trusts in England and Wales managing slightly more than a sixth of all roads, some 22,000 miles. Parallel to this, there were improvements in the quality of road building associated particularly with Thomas Telford and John Loudon Macadam. What contribution did turnpike and parish roads make to improved communication in Britain between 1780 and 1850? Spending on parish roads did not increase markedly though there was a significant growth in spending by turnpike trusts. This reached a peak of £1.5 million per year in the 1820s. The problem was that improvements to the road system were patchy and dependent on private initiatives. Despite this, there were significant reductions in journey times between the main centres of population. In the 1780s, it took ten days to travel from London to Edinburgh; by the 1830s, 45 hours. This led to a dramatic increase in the number of passengers carried by a rapidly expanding coaching industry. The road system transported all kinds of industrial material and manufactured goods. There was a significant growth of carrier firms after 1780. In London, for instance, there were 353 firms in 1790 but 735 in the mid-1820s and a five-fold increase in the number of carriers in Birmingham between 1790 and 1830. These firms were, however, unable to compete with the canals or the railways and

---

[3] From the 1550s, the parish had responsibility for maintaining roads. This may have been adequate for dealing with local roads but the major or trunk roads not maintained very well. Local people thought that the people who used these roads should pay for their upkeep. The result was the development of turnpike roads, financed by private turnpike trusts, which people were charged a toll to use.

concentrated on providing short distance carriage of goods from canals and railway stations to local communities.

The major problem facing early industrialists was the cost of carrying heavy, bulky goods like coal or iron ore. The solution was to use water, rivers, coastal transport and from the 1760s, canals. The first phase of canal development took place in the 1760s and early 1770s beginning with the construction of the Bridgewater canal. The second phase, in the 1790s, has rightly been called 'canal mania' with the completion of several important canals and the setting-up of fifty-one new schemes. By 1820, the canal network was largely completed linking all the major centres of industrial production and population.

Canals dramatically enhanced the efficiency of the whole economy by making a cheap system of transport available for goods and passengers. The price of raw materials like coal, timber, iron, wood and cotton tumbled. The needs of farming, whether for manure or for access to markets for grain, cheese and butter, were easily satisfied where farmers had access to canals. Canals were a means of overcoming the fuel crisis that threatened to limit industrial growth by making cheap, abundant coal supplies available. The building of canals created massive employment and spending power at a time when growing industries were looking for mass markets. It is difficult to exaggerate the importance of canals to Britain's industrial development between 1780 and 1830.

From 1830, railways were the epoch-making transport innovation. Between 1830 and 1850, 7,000 miles of track was laid with railway 'manias' in the 1830s and between 1844 and 1847 when investment was at its peak. Their economic importance lay in their ability to handle both major types of traffic--people and goods--that no other single mode of transport had previously been able. They offered lower costs and greater speed attracting passengers, mail and high-value goods. Mail went to new railways within six months and coaches running in direct competition lost out. However, canals were able, by cutting their rates and improving their services, to continue to carry goods for several years. In 1840, the volume of traffic carried by canal from Liverpool to Manchester was more than twice that carried by railway. The Victorians had no hesitation in assuming a direct link between railways and economic growth though historians are today far less convinced. There was increased demand for coal and iron. In the 1840s, 30 per cent of brick production went into railways and between 1830 and 1845, some 740 million bricks were used in railway construction. Towns grew up round established engineering centres at Swindon, Crewe, Rugby and Doncaster. Food could be transported more cheaply and arrived fresher. There is, however, no doubting their social and cultural impact of railways. This is clearly supported by the statistics. 64,000 passengers were in 1843 but 174,000 in 1848 with an increase in the third-class element from 19,000 to 86,000 in the same period. The Great Exhibition of 1851 reinforced this increased mobility of population.

Between 1780 and 1850, great output was achieved by the transport industry, as in manufacturing industry, by applying a rapidly increasing labour force to existing modes of production as well as using new techniques and applying steam-driven machinery. Historians have emphasised the importance of canals and railways that respectively in the eighteenth and nineteenth centuries in reducing transport costs. However, coastal and river traffic and carriage of goods and people by road remained important and the horse was the main means of transport well beyond 1850.

Social factors

British society in the eighteenth and nineteenth century was profoundly conservative. How was a society with highly traditional structures able to generate changes in so many areas of economic life? By 1780, British society was capitalist in character and organisation. Its aristocracy was remarkably 'open', allowing the newly rich and talented to 'climb'. The most successful merchants, professional and businessmen in each generation were funnelled off into landed society. Success brought wealth and the ultimate proof of success in business was the ability to leave it. In France, where social climbing was discouraged there was political and social discontent and ultimately political revolution. In Britain, where social climbing was not obstructed, there was an industrial revolution.

Britain was already a highly market-oriented society. Imports, whether smuggled or not, were quickly moved to market. Domestic goods, both agricultural and manufactured, were bought and sold directly at the network of markets or through middlemen, who acted as a channel between producer and consumer. Until 1830, the key to economic growth was growing home demand for consumer goods. Growing consumption influenced trade and economic growth. Possessing and using domestic goods enhanced social status or displayed social rank. Lower food prices after 1780 may well have stimulated a consumer boom: people had more disposable income. There was a dramatic increase in the number of permanent shops in major urban centres and many of the characteristics of modern advertising emerged with circulars, showrooms and elaborate window displays. Changing patterns of consumption created an environment in which manufacturers could exploit known and growing demand.

Finally, entrepreneurial skill and 'enterprise' played a major role in the development of the late-eighteenth and early-nineteenth century economy. British society did not prevent entrepreneurs from using their talents and motivation. Entrepreneurs organised production, brought together capital (their own or others') and labour and selected the geographical site for operations, the technologies to be used, bargained for raw materials and found markets for their products. They often combined the roles of financiers, capitalists, work managers, merchants and salesmen. Three main explanations for the place of entrepreneurs in leading economic change have been identified by historians. There was a change in the ways people viewed social status from one where it was the result of birth to one where it related to what individuals achieved. Status was based on what you did, not who you were. This was a reflection of the openness and mobility of British society. Nonconformity seems to have been a crucial experience for many of the first-generation entrepreneurs encouraging a set of values outwardly favourable to economic enterprise. Entrepreneurs were able effectively to exploit advances in technology and industrial organisation. Most entrepreneurs were not pioneers of major innovations or inventions but realised how best to utilise them. James Watt would not have been successful but for the entrepreneurial skills of Matthew Boulton. This allowed them to manufacture and market goods effectively within a highly competitive consumer society.

Conclusions

There was no blueprint for the 'industrial revolution'. Population growth stimulated demand that entrepreneurs were able to satisfy. Developments in transport led to reductions in the cost of production making manufactured goods cheaper. Investment in industry often brought good returns. The state made little attempt to control growth. Foreign trade brought raw materials and profits that could be invested in enterprise. The social structure was adaptable and relatively flexible. Each of these factors helped create an environment in which change could occur.

What was the nature and extent of change?

The view that the industrial revolution represented a dramatic watershed between an old and a new world has recently been questioned by historians. Growth was considerably slower and longer than previously believed. Few historians would go as far as Jonathan Clark, 'England was not *revolutionised*, and it was not revolutionised *by industry*'. Recent research suggests that change in the economy was two-dimensional. There were dynamic industries like cotton and iron where change occurred relatively quickly and that may be called 'revolutionary'. In other industries, change took place far more slowly. Between 1750 and 1850, the British economy experienced rapid, and by international standards, pronounced structural change. The proportion of the labour force employed in industry (extractive, manufacturing and service) increased while the proportion employed in farming fell.

Much employment in industry continued to be small-scale, handicraft activities producing for local markets. These trades were largely unaffected by mechanisation and experienced little or no increase in output per worker. Increased productivity was achieved by employing more labour. The experience of cotton textiles, though dynamic and of high profile was not typical and there was no general triumph of steam power or the factory system in the early nineteenth century. Nor was economic growth raised spectacularly by a few inventions. The overall pace of economic growth was modest. There was no great leap forward for the economy as a whole, despite the experiences of specific industries. By 1850, Britain was 'the workshop of the world'. Productivity in a few industries did enable Britain to sell around half of all world trade in manufacture. This, however, needs to be seen in the context of the characteristics of industrialisation. The 'industrial revolution' involved getting more workers into the industrial and manufacturing sectors rather than achieving higher output once they were there. The cotton and iron industries existed with other industries characterised by low productivity, low pay and low levels of exports.

Inventions and mechanisation

Between 1760 and 1800, there was a significant increase in the number of patents giving exclusive rights to inventors, what the historian T.S. Ashton called 'a wave of gadgets swept over Britain'. Certain key technical developments pre-dated 1760. Coke smelting was developed by Abraham Darby in Shropshire in 1708-1709 but it was not until the 1750s that it was widely used. Thomas Newcomen's steam-atmospheric engine was developed between 1709 and 1712 but its cost and inefficiency meant that it too was not widely used until mid-century. James Kay developed the 'flying shuttle' in 1733 increasing the productivity of weavers but it was thirty years before advances were made in spinning. Registering patents was expensive and some inventions were not patented as a result. Samuel Crompton, for instance, did not register his spinning mule. Many of the patents covered processes and products that were of little economic importance, including medical and consumer goods as well as industrial technologies. Some patents represented technological breakthroughs while others improved existing technologies. Although figures should be used with care, between 1700 and 1760, 379 patents were awarded. In the 1760s, there were 205, the 1770s, 294, the 1780s, 477 and the 1790s, 647 with growing awareness of obtaining patents and the danger of failing to do so.

Despite these reservations, there were important groupings of technological advances after 1760. In the textile industries, there were advances in spinning thread (James Hargreaves' 'jenny' 1764, Richard Arkwright's water frame 1769 and Samuel Crompton's 'mule' 1779), weaving (Edmund Cartwright's power loom 1785) and finishing (mechanised printing by Thomas Bell in 1783). James Kay's 'flying shuttle' had speeded up the process of weaving producing a shortage of hand-spun thread. The mechanisation of spinning after 1764 reversed this situation. The new jennies allowed one worker to spin at least eight and eventually eighty times the amount of thread previously produced by a single spinner. Improvements by Arkwright and especially Crompton further increased productivity. The problem was now weaving. The power loom did not initially resolve the problem and the decades between 1780 and 1810 were ones of considerable prosperity for handloom weavers.

Although the introduction of new machines for textile production, especially cotton occurred over a short timescale, their widespread use was delayed until the 1820s. There were three main reasons for this. The new technologies were costly and often unreliable and modifications were necessary before their full economic benefits were realised. It was not until the early 1820s that the power loom was improved and the self-acting mule was introduced. There was also worker resistance to the introduction of the new technologies and some employers continued to use handworkers because they were cheaper than new machines. This was particularly evident in the Yorkshire woollen industry that lagged behind cotton in applying new technology. Finally, the original spinning jennies were small enough to be used in the home but Arkwright's water frame was too large for domestic use and needed purpose-built spinning mills. These early factories used waterpower though increasingly steam engines were used. By 1800, a quarter of all cotton yarn was spun by steam. It was not until after 1815 that factories combined powered spinning and weaving. By 1850, some factories employed large numbers of workers, but many remained small. In Lancashire in the 1840s, the average firm employed 260 people and a quarter employed fewer than a 100. The mechanisation of the textile industry was a process of technological evolution rather than an immediate revolutionary process.

This was even more the case in the iron industry. In 1700, charcoal was used to smelt iron but it was expensive and Britain increasingly relied on European imports. Although Abraham Darby perfected coke smelting in 1709 it was fifty years before coke-smelted iron posed a major threat to charcoal. It was not until demand for iron rose rapidly after 1750 that coke became the fuel for smelting. The stimulus for expansion in iron making came from the wars with France and the American colonies in the 1750s and 1770s and especially between 1793 and 1815. This led technological change. Henry Cort's puddling and rolling process of 1782 was of comparable importance to Darby's earlier discovery. The new technologies led to a four-fold growth of pig iron between 1788 and 1806, a significant reduction in costs and virtually put an end to expensive imports. The 'hot-blast' of 1828 further reduced costs. Rising demand for iron stimulated developments in the coal industry. Here the major technological developments were led by the need to mine coal from deeper pits. Pumping engines, first Newcomen's and then Watt's helped in this process. Sir Humphrey Davy's safety lamp improved safety underground from inflammable methane gas (or 'firedamp') though mining remained a dangerous occupation. Increases in productivity were, however, largely the consequence of employing more miners.

Contemporaries emphasised the importance of the steam engine to the industrial revolution though this has been played down by recent writers. Wind and water remained important as sources of mechanical energy. Windmills were used for grinding corn, land-drainage and some industrial processes. Waterpower was far more important and remained so until the mid-nineteenth century. Before 1800, most textile mills were water powered and in 1830, 2,230 mills used waterpower as against 3,000 using steam. Metalwork, mining, papermaking and pottery continued to use waterpower. The development of steam power in the eighteenth century was gradual. Newcomen developed his engine in 1712. It was largely used for pumping water out of mines and though costly and inefficient was in widespread use by 1760. Watt trebled the efficiency of the Newcomen engine by adding a separate condenser in the mid-1760s. This made steam engine more cost-effective but they could still only be used for tasks involving pumping or vertical motion. The breakthrough came in 1782 with the development of 'sun and planet' gearing that enabled steam engines to generate rotary motion and power the new technologies in textiles. By 1800, about a fifth of all mechanical energy in Britain was produced by steam engines. Steam power was a highly versatile form of energy and its impact on British industry was profound. It allowed industry to move into towns often on or near to coalfields where it could be supplied by canals. Though older means of generating energy remained important, the application of steam power to mining, iron-making, the railways and especially the booming cotton industry meant that by 1850 it was the dominant form of energy.

How important was technical advance to the industrial revolution? Adam Smith in his *Wealth of Nations* published in 1776 seemed unaware that he was living in a period of technical change and mechanisation. For him, economic growth was achieved through the organisational principle of division of labour rather than the application of new technologies. Others followed Smith in assigning less importance to technical change that historians subsequently did. The effect of technological change was neither immediate nor widespread until after 1800. Cotton and iron set the pace of change but other industries, like glass and paper-making, shipbuilding and food-processing were also undergoing organisational and technological change. Change varied across industries and regions. Steam power did not replace waterpower at a stroke. Work organisation and the uses of newer technologies varied and in 1850 factories coexisted with domestic production, artisan workshops and large-scale mining and metal-producing organisations. Both revolutionary technologies and traditional techniques remained important to Britain's economic development

Geographical diversity and urbanisation

The pace of economic change and its geographical distribution after 1780 was uneven. Dynamic growth took place in specialised economic regions. Cotton was largely based in south Lancashire and parts of the joining counties of Derbyshire and Cheshire. Wool was dominant in the West Riding of Yorkshire. Iron dominated the economies of Shropshire and South Wales. Staffordshire was internationally renowned for its pottery. Birmingham and Warwickshire specialised in metal-working. Tyneside was more diverse with interests in coal, glass, iron and salt. London with its huge population and sophisticated manufacturing and service sectors-- docks, warehouses, engineering, shipbuilding, silk weaving, luxury trades, the machinery of government and the law, publishing and printing, financial centre and entertainment--was also an economic region. De-industrialisation was also regional in character. After 1780, the West Country and East Anglia textile industries declined. The iron industry disappeared from the Weald in Kent and the Cumberland coalfield declined.

Regional growth or decline depended on a range of factors. Growth depended largely on access to waterpower as an energy source or as a means of processing, easy access to coal and other raw materials, and an ample labour force. In 1780, regions and their industries retained their rural character in varying degrees. Increasingly, however, industrial growth took on an urban character and the late eighteenth and early nineteenth centuries saw the rapid expansion of towns that specialised in various industries. Around each of these urban centres clustered smaller towns and industrial villages whose artisan outworkers specialised in particular tasks. Walsall in the Black Country, for instance, specialised in buckle-making; Coventry in ribbon production; tobacco boxes at Willenhall. The concentration of specialised commercial and manufacturing industries, especially skilled labour, in and around towns was a major advantage for entrepreneurs and businessmen. They were helped by the expanding communication network of roads and canal and after 1830, railways that provided cheap supplies of raw materials and fuel as well as helping distribute finished products.

Economic change and population growth led to the rapid expansion of urban centres. Towns, especially those in the forefront of manufacturing innovation, attracted rural workers hoping for better wages. They saw towns as places free from the paternalism of the rural environment and flocked there in their thousands. For some migration brought wealth and security. For the majority life in towns was little different, and in environmental terms probably worse, from life in the country. They had exchanged rural slums for urban ones and exploitation by the landowner for exploitation by the factory master. Between 1780 and 1811, the urban component of England's population rose from a quarter to a third. This process continued throughout the century and by 1850, the rural-urban split was about even. The number of towns in England and Wales with 2,500 inhabitants increased from 104 in 1750 to 188 by 1800 and to over 220 by 1851. England was the most urbanised country in the world and the rate of urban growth had not peaked. London, with its one million inhabitants in 1801, was the largest city in Europe. The dramatic growth of the northern and Midland industrial towns after 1770 was caused largely by migration because of industry's voracious demand for labour. Regions where population growth was not accompanied by industrialisation or where deindustrialisation took place found their local economies under considerable pressure. Surplus labour led to falling wages and growing problems of poverty.

Economic growth and rates of development

What was 'economic growth' in the late-eighteenth and first half of the nineteenth centuries and what were its major characteristics? The main indicator of long-term growth is the income the country receives from goods and services or gross domestic product (GDP). During the eighteenth century, GDP grew slightly from just under one per cent per year to just over it. Between 1800 and 1850, growth remained at over two per cent per year. Growth in GDP depends on three things: an increase in labour, an increase in capital investment and an increase in productivity. Growing population accounted for the increase in labour after 1780. Labour grew at around one per cent per year between 1780 and 1800 and 1.4 per cent for the next fifty years. Increased capital investment is also evident after 1780. Between 1780 and 1800, capital investment rose by 1.2 per cent per year. This rose slightly to 1.4 per cent between 1800 and 1830 and, largely because of investment in railways rose to 2.0 per cent between 1830 and 1850. Increasing productivity is more difficult to estimate.

The debate about economic growth and rates of development is largely statistical. Historians face major problems in trying to work out precisely what rates of development were in the late-eighteenth and early-nineteenth centuries. Statistical information is far from reliable. This has led to major discrepancies in modern estimates. For instance, the production of coal in the late-eighteenth century is estimated to have grown annually at 0.64 per cent or alternatively at 1.13 per cent, twice that speed. The statistics also show only part of the picture and it is very difficult to extrapolate from specific data on specific industries to the economy as a whole. Total figures also blur the important differences between the experience of different industries and regions. It was not until the development of the railways after 1830 that the notion of a British economy, as opposed to localised economies had real meaning.

Conclusions

Historians face significant problems in examining the industrial revolution. There is the problem of what precisely the 'industrial revolution' was. In addition, its national nature has been questioned. How far was there a British industrial revolution or was economic change essentially local or regional? There is also the question of timing. When did the revolution begin? When did it end? Finally, historians increasingly recognise the diversity of economic experiences and the existence of both change and continuity of experience in the eighteenth and early nineteenth century? The 'industrial revolution' is increasingly seen as a metaphor for the changes that took place in the British economy between 1780 and 1850. While it would be perverse to refrain from using a term 'hallowed by usage', it is important to recognise that change occurred slowly in most industries and rapidly in a handful.

An industrial revolution or not?

Contemporaries were aware that they were living through a period of change. Robert Southey wrote in 1807, 'no kingdom ever experienced so great a change in so short a course of years'. Population growth, economic and social change, technological advances, changes in the organisation of work, the dynamism of cotton and iron as well as urbanisation were bunched in the last twenty years of the eighteenth century and the first thirty years of the nineteenth. This was revolutionary change. However, change was itself a process that extended across the eighteenth century. The revolution in the economy did not begin in 1780 nor was it entirely completed by 1850.

10 Responding to economic change.

Between 1780 and 1850, economic change had far-reaching effects on British society. From being an overwhelmingly rural and agricultural society, Britain was transformed into a manufacturing and urban society. This chapter examines how and why this process occurred, its effects on rural and urban society and the ways in which working people responded to these changes.

How did the rural economy change between 1780 and 1850?

In what ways did farming change between 1780 and 1850 and why? How 'revolutionary' was this? Change in farming took place far more slowly than in the dynamic manufacturing industries. Output increased by less than fifty per cent between 1700 and 1800 compared to nearly two hundred per cent in industry and commerce. However, the most significant advance was not in yield per acre but the amount of land under cultivation by about half. Total corn output rose from 15 million quarters in 1750 to 19 million by 1800 and 25 million in 1820. By 1800, the number of sheep reached 26 million and cattle numbers stood at 4 million. There were, however, imports of grain and cattle from Europe. The achievement appears even more moderate when it is remembered that the major part of the increase in grain output was the result of the expansion of cultivated.

Changes in farming techniques.

Increased productivity in farming was the result of a combination of improved techniques of farming (many of which predated 1780), mechanisation (though its impact can be overstated) and the enclosure of large areas of land.

New crops

The most important change in agriculture lay in improved techniques of farming: the introduction of new crops, greater attention to soil fertility, and improved livestock breeding. The impact of new fodder crops was widely felt.[1] They had been introduced from the Low Countries in the mid-seventeenth century and were widespread by the 1750s. Their impact was of major importance. They allowed large waste areas to be brought

---

[1] Fodder crops were used to feed animals in the winter.

into cultivation.[2] These included extensive areas of light soil on scarp land England that had previously been used only as sheep runs but also the areas, which had previously been left fallow. New rotations were introduced and spread throughout the eighteenth century. The most famous was the four courses of wheat, turnips, barley and clover introduced in Norfolk in the late-seventeenth century. A second consequence of the new crops was that they underlay the increase in livestock production in the eighteenth and early-nineteenth centuries by providing winter-feed.

Improving soil fertility

A variety of other methods was used to improve fertility. The supply of manure remained of critical importance in maintaining the fertility of the soil. Until 1850, the main source of manure was animal dung hence the importance of new root crops and legumes which made it possible to keep more animals. Dung was also brought in from outside and farmers within reach relied heavily on 'town muck'.[3] They also made use of industrial waste materials--coal ashes, soot, waste bark from tanneries, bones, pulverised slag from ironworks, and marl and lime. Guano, the dried droppings of seabirds, began to be imported in 1835 but quantities remained small until the 1840s. 'Artificial' fertilizers were introduced on a commercial scale in the 1840s.

Drainage was not a new problem in 1780. Some surface drainage was achieved by the ridges and furrows created during ploughing. The importance of effective under-drainage was not recognised until the mid-eighteenth century. Joseph Elkington had proposed the making of borings to enable water to pass through the impervious stratum to a porous one in 1764 and James Smith used shallow drains in the 1820s. However, it was not until the appearance of a tile-making machine invented by Thomas Scraggs and mole or drainage ploughs in the 1840s that the clay lands were brought into more productive farming.[4]

---

[2] Large areas of England consisted of wasteland. This land had previously not been cultivated because it would have been unprofitable to do so. The new crops ended this practice. They had the same effect on leaving land fallow for a year to restore its fertility.

[3] 'Town muck', the product of the swelling urban population, was either given to farmers willing to take it away or sold by people who collected urban sewage: a further example of recycling waste products.

[4] Britain's soils can be divided into three broad types: sandy, chalk and clay. In the late eighteenth century, sandy soil was the easiest to cultivate because it was generally fertile and porous. Chalk soils were less fertile than sandy soils. Clay soil was very fertile but suffered from major drainage problems.

Improved livestock breeding

Livestock breeding improved considerably during the eighteenth and early nineteenth centuries. Robert Bakewell emerged as Britain's foremost livestock expert by the 1770s but he extended the work of earlier breeders. His work was built on by the Culleys, the Collings and Jonas Webb. Bakewell's pre-eminence rested with his improved longhorn cattle and the 'New Leicester' sheep. Though both his sheep and cattle had defects--his longhorns were wanting in milk and fertility and his sheep fattened too quickly--he did succeed in producing animals ready speedily for the market.

Better machinery

Advances in stock, drainage, fertilizers and crops emphasised the need for improved farm tools and machinery. Before 1800, changes in implements, other than ploughs, proceeded slowly. Mass-produced tools originated in the 1780s and by the 1840s, Robert Ransome of Ipswich was producing as many as eighty-six different designs of ploughs to suit local needs. From 1786, Andrew Meikle's threshing machine began to be adopted and horse-drawn reapers appeared in the early decades of the nineteenth century.

Mechanisation in farming was primarily a mid-nineteenth-century development. The threshing machine was first adopted in Scotland and by 1815 was common both there and in northeast England. However, it was not general in the south or in Wales until after 1850. Seed-drills were increasingly advertised in newspaper after 1820. Reapers and mowing machines did not appear until the 1850s and only became common after 1870. In 1850, most of British corn was still cut and threshed by hand. The unreliability of the early machines partly accounted for this. Far more important was the cost of labour. In the north, where labour costs were higher because of competition from non-agricultural employment, the early adoption of powered threshing was economic. It was more sluggish in the south where cheap labour was plentiful.[5] Some farmers kept the

---

[5] Winter employment was often provided by farmers for their regular workforce especially in southern England. This helped keep the parish poor rate at a lower level but also reflected the widespread belief that farmers had a paternal responsibility for their 'men'. The same responsibility, however, was not applied to casual workers and there was chronic under-employment in rural England especially after 1815.

old methods to provide a major source of winter employment in order to prevent throwing their regular men on to the parish.[6]

Effects

The spread of new farming techniques altered the pattern of late-eighteenth and early-nineteenth-century agriculture. Until the 1820s, arable prosperity shifted away from the heavy clay vales to the lighter chalk land, soils. Many were close enough to London to profit from the overall rise in grain prices after 1780. Change occurred more quickly on the lighter soils, more slowly on the heavy clay soils which suffered from a shorter growing season and a higher risk of harvest failure. Important though these changes were their impact would have been lessened after 1780, without the changes in the organisation of farming.

Enclosure

Enclosure did more than any other development to alter the face of the countryside.[7] By 1780, large areas of Britain had already been enclosed or had never known open field cultivation. It was important in improving the efficiency and flexibility of the open fields and in bringing into fuller use wastelands, marshes, heaths and hill grazing. Enclosure led villages to improve their road system, dig drainage channels, rebuild farmhouses, barns and byres and plant new hedgerows to provide windbreaks and shelter for stock.

Enclosure between 1750 and 1850 was largely as the result of parliamentary acts and fell into two phases. Thirty-eight per cent of all acts were concentrated between 1750 and 1780, with 630 acts in the 1770s. The second phase of activity occurred between 1790 and the mid-1830s, though 43 per cent of all acts were passed during the French wars. The first phase was concentrated on the heavier-soiled counties of Midland clay belts, the lighter clays of much of Lincolnshire and Yorkshire. The second phase completed this process but included the lighter soils of East Anglia, Lincolnshire and the East Riding, marginal soils of the Pennine uplands and heaths of Surrey, Berkshire and Middlesex.

---

[6] In 1851, James Caird, in his study of British farming, divided the country into high and low wage areas. In northern and parts of central England, where industrialisation was widespread, farm labourers' wages were high. In southern England, where there was no alternative and attractive employment available supply exceeded demand and wages were significantly lower.

[7] Enclosure was achieved either by agreement between the local landowners or, increasingly, by getting Parliament to pass an enclosure act.

Many contemporaries were certain about increased productivity achieved in terms of both improved output and rent. Ten per cent increases in grain output occurred in Oxfordshire, Warwickshire and Northamptonshire when enclosed fields were compared with open ones and improvements of 25 per cent may well have been possible. For the landlord enclosure was a good investment. Rents were increased by 15 and 20 per cent but this was both a cause and a consequence of enclosure. From the 1770s until the end of the French wars, prices rose. This too helped landowners, who often relied on fixed rents for income, to enclose and renegotiate leases with tenants who benefited from rising prices.

There was a significant rise in prices from the 1750s to the inflationary prices during the French wars. This coincided with the growth of parliamentary enclosure. Rising wheat prices are attractive in explaining who large areas of commons and waste were enclosed after 1793 even though much of this was poor in quality and capable of only low yields. Relatively stable interest rates in the 1760s and 1770s coincided with the growth of enclosure while the higher rates during the American war of the late 1770s and early 1780s saw a significant decline. During the French wars, high interest rates and large numbers of enclosures coexisted. However, the level of prices was higher than the interest rates and in real terms, money was 'cheaper'. Farmers could borrow money to enclose their land knowing that high wheat prices would enable them to repay their loans and still make a good profit.

After 1780, population growth increased the demand for agricultural products. Price levels moved ahead more rapidly than in industry. These encouraged farmers to invest in change. British farming was highly capitalised by 1800. High-intensity arable farming was situated near the main centres of population in the band from Lancashire to London. Lower levels of investment occurred on the upland fringes where stockbreeding dominated. Rising population increased the supply of labour. In 1801, 3.3 million people or 36 per cent of the population of England and Wales were involved in agriculture, forestry and fishing. This represented an increase of about eight per cent since 1750 compared to the seventy per cent increase in total population. Although there were only slightly more people working in farming they were feeding more people. One person in 1750 fed 1.7 persons; by 1800, it was 2.5 people. The percentage of the total population employed in farming fell relative to other industries after 1800, but people employed continued to rise until 1850. Farming remained a labour-intensive industry with no dramatic breakthrough in mechanisation.

A chronology of change

Between 1750 and 1790, there was a gradual but consistent increase in all food prices paralleled by gradual but accelerating enclosure. Wheat increasingly became the staple grain food--89 per cent of Londoners were on a wheat diet by 1764. Potatoes were increasing important helping to explain demographic growth in Ireland and parts of Scotland. Homegrown food supplies were sufficient until the 1770s but after that, substantial imports were necessary. Corn prices began to rise faster than other prices and faster than wages. This stimulated further agricultural change.

Years of shortage, amounting between 1795 and 1800, in 1808 and 1812 to 'famine', became more frequent. Local shortages and food riots were often caused by failure to distribute supplies effectively. Increased demand was met largely by increased productivity. Grain output rose at the same rate as population: 14 per cent between 1793 and 1815. This was achieved by extending of the land under cultivation and the use of new crops and new breeds of livestock. The major problem facing farmers in this period was labour costs. The extent to which enclosure and new techniques required more labour is debatable but in some areas labour shortages pushed up costs further. Many farmers were forced to rely on casual workers. Yet, this did not lead to widespread mechanisation. Between 1790 and 1815, British agriculture increased its productivity by only 0.2 per cent per year. This compares adversely with the 0.3 per cent per year achieved between 1816 and 1846, a period regarded as one of 'depression'.

Prices fell dramatically after 1814 and thousands were demobilised or released from war industries. The severity of distress was greatest on the clay land arable farms and least in dairy and stock-rearing districts or in areas like Kent where hops and fruit were important crops. Depression was closely linked to the flexibility of the land under cultivation. Farmers sought legislative support in the form of protection or reductions in taxes. The Corn Law of 1815 was the result. However, by the 1830s many farmers were adjusting their costs to lower prices or moving across to mixed farming. The social cost of 'depression' was most severe in areas with falling agricultural wages. Tariffs did little to protect arable farmers and provoked a violent reaction that the Anti-Corn Law League built on the 1830s and 1840s.

By the mid-1830s, British farming had got through its 'depression'. The introduction of inexpensive drainage techniques liberated the clay lands from high production costs. Farming generally became more 'scientific', producing higher output at lower cost. From the mid-1840s until the 1870s, agricultural production rose at 0.5 per cent per year. There was a more intensive application of the techniques of mixed farming on the light soils of southern and eastern England and on the Lothian area of southeast Scotland. There was some shift on the clay soils, especially those in the north and west of England, to beef and dairy production. Railways reduced transport costs--cheap food had become both an economic and a political necessity. British farming was more productive in 1850 than it had been in 1780.[8]

The end of the French wars in 1815 saw up to a quarter of a million men demobilised. They had to be absorbed back into the labour force at a time when both farming and industry faced depression. This caused considerable distress in rural England where there was a surplus of workers. Farmers needed to reduce their costs (at a time of falling wheat prices) to repay loans they had taken out during the war when prices were higher. Rural wages fell.

Why were there so many problems in the countryside?

Agricultural labourers were rarely at the centre of protest in the eighteenth century but this situation changed after 1780. Why did this change occur and why were the protests of farm workers largely confined to southern and eastern England? The agricultural revolution, especially enclosure, upset traditional rural society. There was a decline in hiring farm servants and 'living in' disappeared. Labourers were paid by the day or week and were employed for short periods for harvesting, hedging, ditching and threshing.[9] There was little guarantee of work. The social and financial gulf between farmer and labourer widened.

There was growing rural poverty in southern England. In 1795, Berkshire magistrates introduced a system of relief to supplement the wages of labourers. Similar schemes were introduced across southern England. This was known as the 'Speenhamland system'.[10] The name gave the schemes a sense of uniformity that in practice they did not possess. Its attempt to redress low wages became part of the framework of labourers' lives instead of a safety net in hard times. The system encouraged low pay and did not fully make up the difference between high

---

[8] Historians disagree about the impact of enclosure on rural labour. Some argue that farmers who had enclosed their land needed fewer workers. Others suggest that during and immediately after enclosure more workers were needed. In the longer term, the combination of enclosure and mechanisation led to a reduction in the agricultural workforce.

[9] It had been customary for farm workers to be hired for a year receiving food, clothes, board and a small annual wage in return for work, only living out when they wished to marry.

[10] The Speenhamland system was named after the village of Speen, near Newbury where the Berkshire magistrates met in May 1795.

prices and low wages. Wartime farming transformed much of southern and eastern England into a region dominated by wheat production. Boom conditions ended abruptly in 1815, grain prices slumped while rents, fixed during wartime inflation, did not. Farmers were faced with falling profits and sought to reduce costs by cutting wages, quite possible in a labour market saturated by the demobilisation of the armed forces, or by introducing economies that technological innovations like the threshing machine offered.

The 1816 riots

Industrial workers, townsmen, cottagers and agricultural labourers were linked together in 1816 in ways not repeated in 1822 or 1830. There were three main types of protest. There were incidents in some market towns, a continuation of the tradition of food riots and collective action by textile workers. Agricultural labourers took little part in these. On the loam and clay lands of Essex, Suffolk and Norfolk, there were protests over the use of the mole plough and threshing machines and demands for a subsistence wage. The third series of disturbances was in the Fens, centred on Littleport and Ely. The diversity of rioters--one in three arrested was not an agricultural labourer and one in seven had some land--reflected the impact of enclosure and drainage and the particular effect of depression. The authorities at local level had limited resources at their disposal to stop riots spreading and, especially in the Fens, there were too few gentry to act collectively. Magistrates made concessions to stop the protest but the dramatic breakdown of law and order could not be tolerated by central government. Sidmouth ordered the military to be sent to Norfolk and Suffolk, not just in the Fens. Magistrates who had made concessions were overruled and harsh sentences were passed. Five rioters were executed and this, as much as anything, ensured that rioting spread no further.

Disturbances in 1822

Protest occurred in three areas in Norfolk in late February and early March 1822. All three involved the destruction of threshing machines and in contrast to 1816, these attacks were not simply symbolic, drawing attention to the plight of the labourer, but were a campaign to sweep the machines away. Local magistrates acted quickly to prevent widespread disturbances and the use of the military drove the rioters underground.

The Swing riots of 1830

The problem of pauperism was worst in south of a line from Norfolk to Gloucestershire. In these so-called 'Swing' counties, enclosure had taken place on a grand scale. In the 1820s, high poor rates led to increasing attempts to cut relief. Between 1815 and 1820, Poor Law spending was 12/10d per head; by 1830, it was 9/9d. Reductions were made by stopping people asking for relief. This created a hatred of the Poor Law but it is noticeable that between 1824 and 1830, rural crime rates increased by 30 per cent--mainly poaching and food thefts. Pauperism, desperation and discontent were almost universal in agricultural areas.

The Swing riots[11] lasted from August until well into December 1830 and took several forms. In some areas, there were demands for higher wages; in others, tithes were the issue; Poor Law officials and workhouses were attacked but the destruction of threshing machines was most widespread. The major difference between protests in 1816 and 1822 and those in 1830 was their scale. Although the 'Swing' riots are normally associated with southern and eastern England with over 3,000 incidents, workers across the North responded to the political and social unrest in 1830 and over 50 incidents of actions against farmers, whether threatening letters, machine-breaking or arson occurred in northern England between 1830 and 1834. Why was there such a widespread mobilisation of agricultural labourers in 1830? The aims of the rioters were remarkably similar throughout the 'Swing' counties. Men demanded a minimum wage, the end of rural unemployment and tithe and rent reductions. Farmers supported the labourers in the two latter demands.

The leaders of the riots were often craftsmen and the led were predominantly labourers, often paupers on poor relief. Rioters were usually young men, many of them married. Their concern was for a living wage. The riots began slowly and initially machine breakers were given lenient sentences. This was interpreted by many labourers as tacit approval of their actions and led to protests gathering momentum. Revolution in France in July gave rural protest a more threatening dimension than in either 1816 or 1822. The Whig government made suppressing the disturbances its first priority on achieving power in mid-November. Concerted local action, especially by the gentry of Wiltshire and Hampshire, the use of troops and unwillingness of Lord Melbourne, the Home Secretary, to tolerate weakness or compromise on the part of local magistrates gradually restored order.

After Swing

Swing did not destroy the willingness of agricultural labourers across the country to protest. There was widespread, if unsuccessful, rural action against the Poor Law Amendment Act in 1835, rural trade unionism in

---

[11] The Swing riots were called after their assumed leader, Captain Swing. There is no evidence that the riots were coordinated in this way.

the south-east and at Tolpuddle and protests in the form of arson. Labourers were experts in slacking in undetectable ways. More seriously, they could steal their employers' corn, fruit and game despite the severity of sentence if caught; transportation to Australia was widely used. Sheep and horse stealing were capital offences until 1831 and arson remained so until 1837. Poaching was endemic in rural areas. Stacks could be fired, farm buildings lit, fences pulled down, animals maimed and drainage channels breached though the systematic nature of these actions died down after the 1840s. Rural protest after 1790 can be explained by the failure to understand the nature of change by both labourers and their employers. Change imperfectly understood aroused fear. This was made worse by 'want' and 'distress' and under- or unemployment.

How did the working-class develop between 1780 and 1846?

Richard Dennis, in his study of nineteenth century industrial cities, sums up the problem of class in the following way: 'Evidently the road to class analysis crosses a minefield with a sniper behind every bush.... it may not be possible to please all the people all of the time'. What did contemporaries understand by the idea of *'class'*? How many classes were there? When did a working-class come into existence? Despite all the literature on the subject, the years since the publication of E. P. Thompson's *The Making of the English Working-class* in 1963 have done little to clarify the situation. Answers to the central questions of 'when?', 'how?' and 'why?' have been surprisingly inconclusive.

Old values under pressure

After 1780, social values that had existed, largely unaltered for several hundred years, began to be challenged. British society before the industrial revolution, and in some areas after it, was based on face-to-face, often daily, contact between individuals of different social status who recognised their 'place' in the social structure and the duties and responsibilities their 'rank' gave them. Social control was based on recognition of social status, be it political power, economic wealth or social and cultural development. Population growth, the expansion of towns and the move from a rural to urban economy shattered this ordered structure. The poet Robert Southey wrote in 1829 'The bond of attachment is broken'.

Urbanisation occurred largely outside the paternal net. People moved to towns because they perceived them as 'free' from the constraints of rural society as well as providing economic opportunities. As towns and cities expanded after 1820, they ceased to be face-to-face societies and became places where paternalist values had little place. There were important changes in religious observance with declining support for the Church of England in towns and cities. In the countryside, the challenge to the Church of England from Methodism broke the link between squire, parson and labourer. Working people, especially artisans began to group together for protection in trade unions to negotiate for better conditions with their employers. Labour became more mobile and centred in urban communities. These conditions led to many working people becoming increasing conscious of their own interests. This, in turn resulted in the development of economic and political demands for better wages and the right to vote.

How many classes?

Benjamin Disraeli wrote in 1845, that there are 'Two nations; between whom there is no intercourse and no sympathy.' Twenty years earlier, William Cobbett, the radical journalist suggested in the *Political Register* that 'You are for reducing the community to two classes: Masters and Slaves.' Disraeli[12] and Cobbett divided British society into two broad groups: the rich and the poor and exploiters and exploited respectively what today we call 'them' and 'us'. Others saw society differently. David Ricardo, the economist, identified three economic classes based on rent, capital and wages broadly 'upper', 'middle' and 'working' classes. The journalist Henry Mayhew went further dividing society in the late 1840s into 'those who will work, those who cannot work, those who will not work and those who need not work'. Contemporary attitudes have been complicated by lack of agreement among historians on when a 'class system' came into being and how far the older values survived into the Victorian period.

How was the working-class structured by the late 1840s?

Variations in standards of living, wages and working conditions were as great in towns as in the countryside. Average urban wages were higher but so were rent and food. Women's wages were well below those of men and families dependent on a sole female wage earner were among the poorest people. Jobs guaranteeing a regular weekly wage, with little cyclical unemployment, were rare and jealously guarded. Cyclical unemployment[13] was the norm for most workers and was a major factor

---

[12] Benjamin Disraeli (1805-1881) was a future Conservative Prime Minister. He also wrote novels dealing largely with social and political issues.
[13] Cyclical unemployment. Unemployment that was largely the result of the cycle of boom and slump.

in the labour market.

The urban population was organised in hierarchical terms, largely in terms of levels of skill. At the base of the urban labour hierarchy were the genuinely casual workers. Work like hawking and street trading, scavenging, street entertainment, prostitution and some casual labouring and domestic work fell into this category. Casual trades were largely concentrated in large cities, especially London. Low and irregular incomes condemned casual workers to rooms in slums.

Above the casual street traders was a whole range of unskilled often-casual occupations where workers were hired for a few hours and could be laid off for long periods without notice. These included labourers in the building trades, in factories, carters, shipyard workers and especially dockers. All towns had such workers but they were especially important in port cities such as London, Liverpool and Bristol and in industries like coal mining or clothing that had a partly seasonal market. In Liverpool over 22 per cent of the employed population in 1851 were general, dock or warehouse labourers. They needed to live close to their workplace since employment was often allocated on a first-come, first-served basis. When in work dockers earned high wages, ranging from 27s a week for quay porters to 42s for a stevedore but few maintained these earnings for any length of time and in a bad week many earned only a few shillings. Conditions changed little between 1780 and 1850. Unskilled workers were frequently in debt and regularly pawned clothes.

After 1820, factories provided regular employment, as did public services as railway companies and many commercial organisations. Skilled manual labour was relatively privileged. Lancashire skilled cotton spinners earned 27-30s per week in 1835 and iron foundry workers up to 40s. Textile towns like Manchester, Bradford and Leeds and metal and engineering centres such as Sheffield suffered less from poverty than cities like Liverpool or London. Skilled engineering trades were amongst the earliest to unionise, along with artisans and craftsmen, particularly in London and northern industrial towns. They protected their interests jealously and they commanded higher wages and regular employment. This gave many advantages. They could afford to rent a decent terraced house, sometimes in the suburbs avoiding the squalor of Victorian slums but with a long walk to work.

Three major issues can be raised about working-class women's work in this period. There was a sexual division of labour. Women's work had low pay, low skills and low status. Women were also a cheap source of labour. Finally, the Industrial Revolution brought about a decisive separation between home and work. In pre-industrial society, women were engaged in production at home. Industrialisation shifted production into the factories or workshops and many women became factory workers or 'sweated labourers'. Many women were tied to the home yet needed money to support themselves and their families. Outwork or homework, particularly exploitative forms of employment was often their only option. Single women often entered domestic service but married women were severely limited in choice. Away from the textile districts most found work as domestic cleaners, laundry workers, in sewing, dressmaking, boot and shoemaking and other trades carried on either in the home of small workshops. Wages were always low producing incomes ranging from 5s to 20s per week. Women were excluded from many areas of the economy but they dominated others. The 1851 census suggests that just over a quarter of the female population--some 2.8 million out of 10.6 million-- were at work and that women made up about thirty per cent of the country's labour force. There were very few activities where women actually made up three out of every ten workers involved. Four activities accounted for almost ninety per cent of women's work. Domestic service accounted for two out of every five working women. The textiles and clothing industries provided employment for a similar proportion. About one woman in twelve worked in agriculture. What women did depended largely on the particular economic structure of the communities in which they lived.

Class helped working people describe themselves in relation to society as a whole. It provided identity for workers no longer bound by paternalist values. It evolved in response to growing population, greater social mobility, urban growth and new patterns of work based in the factory or workshop. When a working-class came into existence is a matter of some debate. The popular radicalism and conservatism of the 1790s marked its beginnings. The radicalism between 1815 and 1821 gave class substance. However, there were significant divisions within the working-class between skilled and unskilled workers, working men and women, and rural and industrial workers that were perhaps more important. What marks the working-class in 1850 was the diversity of its lived experience rather than its unity of purpose.

How did working people respond to economic change?

Between 1780 and 1850, how working people responded to economic change was transformed. In 1780, people dissatisfied with economic conditions rioted. This was spontaneous, largely unorganised and short-lived. During the eighteenth century, there were protests about prices, enclosure, turnpike roads, the militia and against new technology. They were reactions to situations and their aims were generally limited. By 1850, working people had developed organisations that allowed them to campaign for better standards of living and for a share in government. In addition, they established co-operative associations and friendly societies to provide mutual aid. The remainder of this chapter looks at four ways in which working people sought to maintain their position in society.

Spontaneous protest: food riots

There were four major outbreaks of food riots between 1790 and 1820, all corresponding to harvest failure and high prices. The harvest of 1794 was about 25 per cent below that of 1793 and led to shortages in the spring and summer of 1795. This provides a partial explanation for the protest. Many industrial workers were laid off because of the trade depression. The French war disrupted grain imports and the authorities seemed unaware of the scale of the problem. These circumstances combined to produce a major crisis. There were a few riots in 1794 and early 1795 but major protests did not begin until March. There were 74 major disturbances. By late 1796, it was clear that, because of the poor harvest, the authorities must take measures to ease food shortages. Action was taken to increase the supply of food and to regulate prices by both local authorities and private individuals. This was sufficient to prevent major disturbances in 1796.

Good harvests between 1796 and 1798 were followed poor yields in 1799 pushing grain prices up sharply. This corresponded to the beginnings of trade depression. Major disturbances occurred in late 1799 and early 1800 in the industrial centres of Lancashire, Yorkshire and the Midlands. The crisis was ended by the government actively encouraging imports. Good weather reduced tensions and prices fell in anticipation of a good harvest in 1800. Widespread rain in August saw prices increase. This had a marked effect on consumers, who believed the harvest was good and that prices increased because of speculation in the grain market by farmers, dealers, shopkeepers and merchants. Major incidents occurred in London, unusually because government always tried to maintain the food supply of the capital. There were also incidents in southern England, the Midlands, Nottinghamshire, Derbyshire, Yorkshire and Lancashire. High prices lasted through the winter of 1800-1801 when industrial recession was at its height. The government instructed magistrates to deal quickly with any protests and this action led to fewer riots.

Food riots in 1810-1813 and 1816-1818 were caused by food shortage and high prices. There were disturbances in the southwest but the major problem was in the industrial centres of Lancashire, Cheshire and Yorkshire that were suffering from acute commercial distress. The pattern of food riots that emerged in 1799-1801 concentrated in urban and industrial centres completely separate from the countryside, continued between 1810 and 1818. There was a problem transporting food to areas with shortages. Urban growth made this worse. This helps to explain why the focus of food riots altered from rural to industrial settings. Food riots declined after 1815. They were replaced by other protests aimed at defending living standards that were more suited to the industrial environment. After 1820, food riots were confined to the remoter areas of Britain and some of the poorer urban slums.

Protest against technological change: Luddism

In 1812, there was a series of disturbances in Yorkshire woollen industry where skilled workers formed secret organisations dedicated to smashing the new machines.[14] Croppers[15] felt they must make a stand against industrial change. When a crude machine was invented on which an unskilled man and a boy could do in a day what it took a skilled cropper a week, they took direct action. The value of woollen exports had dropped from £12 million to £1 million a year because of the French wars. Poor harvests had pushed up the price of food. Distress was intense and the poor relief system was put under immense strain.

For several months through the early part of 1812, Luddites attacked mills.[16] They smashed the new cropping frames often in the presence of the terrified mill owner. Rarely was anything else damaged and other machines and property were usually left untouched. Some of the mill owners began to defend their property and when about 200 men attacked a mill at Rawfolds they were repulsed. William Horsfall, a local mill owner was murdered in April 1812 as he rode home from market. This turned popular feeling against the Luddites--smashing machines was one thing, killing a defenceless man in cold blood was something else.

The authorities saw in these attacks the threat of potential revolution.[17] The area was swamped with spies and informers and a reward of £2,000 was offered for information that would lead to convictions. Eventually, a magistrate extracted a confession from one of the Luddites. It led to the arrest of the Luddite leaders, who were brought before a special judicial commission at York Castle in January 1813. Twenty-four men were found guilty and seventeen were executed, fourteen at the same time. The others were transported for seven years. Luddism was broken. As new machines were introduced the number of

---

[14] Machine breaking was nothing new in the 1810s. Both James Hargreaves and Samuel Crompton had their machines smashed in the 1760s and 1780s. What was new was the scale of the protests and their organisation.

[15] Croppers were highly paid workers, the aristocrats of the labour market, whose skills lay in neatly cutting off the nap of the cloth, using giant iron shears that weighed up to 60lbs.

[16] Luddites were called after their leader, real or imaginary, known as King Ludd, after a probably mythical Ned Ludd.

[17] Machine breaking was made a capital offence in 1813.

skilled croppers in the Leeds area dropped from over 1,700 to barely a handful in five years.

Was Luddism a purely industrial phenomenon or did it possess a political dimension with distinctly revolutionary undertones? Luddism was not a uniform movement. In Nottinghamshire, for example, where its non-political character is not seriously in doubt, it is the role of violence in the furtherance of industrial objects which historians find contentious. In the northern counties, by contrast, there is no denying the presence of a revolutionary element. The Luddites had contacts on either side of the Pennines that was active during the disturbances of 1811-1812. The scope and importance of such seditious activity has, however, been questioned. The Luddites were neither local heroes nor the bearers of budding class-consciousness, but workers who resorted to archaic and negative forms of protest.

Seeking fair wages: trade unionism

In 1799 and 1800, Combination Acts made trade unions illegal. Contemporaries agreed that they were largely ineffective. The campaign for their repeal, led by Francis Place,[18] began in the improved economic conditions of the early 1820s. It was successful and in 1824, the Acts were repealed. The economy slumped briefly in late 1824 and there were strikes as unions came into the open demanding wage increases. Employers blamed repeal calling for the return of the Combination Acts. Place needed all his skill to prevent this. By an Act of 1825, workers could form trade unions but were not allowed to 'molest' or 'obstruct' either employers or fellow workers. Trade unions were legal again but their activities were still restricted.

Early trade unions were small, local organisations composed largely of skilled artisans. Many workers were convinced that small unions could never succeed. They were easy targets for the masters. Employers could easily bring in 'blackleg' labour and lock workers out of their workplaces. What was needed, some argued, were national or general unions representing all the workers in a particular trade from different parts of the country.

1829	John Doherty was an Irishman and leader of the Lancashire cotton spinners. He formed a Grand General Union of Spinners.
1830	For greater negotiating power, the next step was to try to unite all unions in all trades into a single union. Doherty formed the

---

[18] Francis Place (1771-1854) was a radical activist who campaigned against the Combination Acts with the support of Joseph Hume in Parliament. He also helped draft the People's Charter.

	National Association for the Protection of Labour. The National Association lasted two years, claimed over 100,000 members from textiles, mining and twenty other trades as far afield as Wales and the Midlands. It had its own newspaper, *The Voice of the People*. The NAPL collapsed when attempts to back up striking spinners in Ashton-under-Lyne failed
1831	Other workers formed the Operative Builders' Union transformed by Robert Owen into a 'National Building Guild of Brothers' in 1833. More national unions followed among potters, textile workers and others.
1834	The Grand National Consolidated Trades Union [GNCTU] established in February. By June 1834, it claimed to have over half a million members. The inspiration behind the GNCTU was Robert Owen though he did not take an active role until April. In October 1833, some forty villagers formed a branch or 'lodge' of the Friendly Society of Agricultural Labourers in the Dorset village of Tolpuddle. Six members of the lodge were charged under the Unlawful Oaths Act 1797, an act passed to deal with naval mutinies. In March 1834, they were sentenced to seven years' transportation in Australia. They became known as the 'Tolpuddle Martyrs'.

Robert Owen[19] had considerable influence on the union movement in 1833-1835. Many working-class leaders regarded him with suspicion. However, by 1833, his ideas had been sufficiently accepted for the term 'Owenite' to be used for the outburst of trade union activity between 1832 and 1834. At first Owen took little notice of trade unions. In April 1832, he sought to avoid violence by 'a rational and therefore beneficial compromise between...the producers of real wealth on the one part, and the non-producers and governors of society, on the other part.' Trade unions, he thought were selfish organisations fighting for small gains such as wage increases. Owen was surprised when in 1833 he met unionists like Doherty and realised how 'business-like and encouraging' they had become. For a time, he saw unions as a possible way of changing society but his enthusiasm was short-lived and by early 1834, he recognised that confrontation not co-operation lay behind much union activity. This judgement reflected the increasing union concern with short-term industrial gains rather than the longer-term creation of a new moral world. Strikes spread across the Midlands and the North and the employers reacted with considerable ferocity. In Derby employers forced workers to sign 'The Document': 'We, the undersigned, do hereby declare that we are not members of a trade union; that we do not and will not pay towards

---

[19] Robert Owen (1771-1858). A radical thinker who wrote his *A New View of Society* in 1813. He was a successful mill owner at New Lanark. He was leader of the trade union movement in the mid-1830s but never fully understood the working people whose cause he wanted to champion.

the support of any such association.' 1,500 Derby workers refused and were locked out. The Grand National Consolidated Trade Union emerged from a conference of trade union delegates meeting in London in early 1834 to discuss the Derby strike. It set up the Derby Fighting Fund and although help poured in, it was not enough and the workers were slowly starved into submission.

Owen watched events approvingly. In the summer of 1834, he briefly became leader of the GNCTU during the protests against the transportation of the Tolpuddle Martyrs. He led the mass demonstration at Copenhagen Fields in London but was keen to limit any trouble. Owen hoped that the GNCTU's huge membership--by June 1834 it was claimed to have 500,000 members--would give workers greater control over the running of the country. This was not the view of the trade union leaders like James Morrison and James Smith who were extremely hostile to employers. This division between Owen and trade union leaders did not bode well for the future. In May 1834, the London tailors went on strike. When employers presented them with a 'document', they left the GNCTU. The London cordwainers followed in late June. The loss of these two unions was a severe blow and the GNCTU collapsed in August.

Why did this occur? Early historians suggested that the GNCTU had half a million members. More recently, historians have concluded that the GNCTU was 'insignificant and fragmentary'. It was always a fragile organisation, a loose federation of different working-class groups. Despite its grand claims, only 16,000 members paid subscriptions. Subscriptions were hard to collect, so finances were always weak. Its size proved a problem. It was based largely on London trades with only 6,000 members outside the capital. Poor communications made local branches difficult to control and it was hard to get agreement on common policies. Some unions refused to support workers in other trades and clothiers, potters, spinners and builders never joined the GNCTU. The union was too radical. It hoped to give workers more influence and neither employers nor the Whig government could afford to stand by and watch it grow.

The high hopes of 1830-1834 had come to nothing. Trade unionists abandoned the idea of a national organisation. Some turned their energies to new causes, such as factory reform, the anti-Poor Law agitation or Chartism. Others again set out to build strong local or single craft unions. Mass national unions were not successfully revived until the 1880s. Population growth and its implications for the labour market were at the heart of workers' problems. Skilled workers were under pressure from demands for cheaper, ready-made goods produced by the 'sweated' trades. Despite the failure of general unionism, there was plenty of industrial conflict after 1835. In the National Typographical Association, for instance, there were 51 local disputes in 1845 and 90 the following year. Craft unions continued to expand their organisations with the growth of union branches in the same trades in different areas, some centralisation of funds and the emergence of national officers. The limitations of trade unions in 1850 were clear. They were largely confined to skilled workers seeking to retain their social and economic status.

Helping themselves

There were middle-class philanthropic organisations to meet every conceivable need: charities for the poor, the sick, the disabled, the unemployed, the badly-housed, charities for the reclamation of prostitutes and drunkards, for reviving drowning persons, for apprentices, shop-girls, cabbies, costermongers, soldiers, sailors and variety artistes. Often judgemental and based on the conviction that poverty was an individual failing, some in the working-classes improved their lot by mutual aid

Workers, especially artisans and skilled factory workers sought to protect themselves by setting up specifically working-class voluntary associations. Friendly societies and savings banks encouraged workers to put by money in good times to offset the effects of unemployment, sickness and to some extent old age. Co-operative societies gave workers greater control over their wages by providing good quality, cheap food. These working-class associations gave workers greater control over their lives and were without the middle-class baggage associated with charity.

By 1800, there were about 7,200 societies with 648,000 members, rising to a million by 1820. Friendly societies developed where there was at least some industry. In 1821, 17 per cent of Lancashire's population was in societies, compared to 5 per cent in rural counties. This is explained by higher industrial wages but also because industrial workers felt greater need to make provision against sickness than those who worked on the land. The main financial benefits expected by a member of a local friendly society were a weekly allowance when he was sick and a funeral payment for his widow.

Savings banks appealed to artisans and the lower sections of the middle-classes. The 1834 Poor Law Amendment Act stimulated an expansion of savings bank activity in the late 1830's, particularly in some southern agricultural areas. The Sussex Savings Bank, for example, had deposits of £43,466 in 1834 increasing to £51,409 by 1837. Savings banks were more attractive in rural than industrial areas, the reverse of the case with friendly societies. This reflected the persistence of paternalist attitudes since many banks were established by landlords, squires, parsons or other notable figures. Many of the depositors had only small accounts indicating they were probably workers. However, nationally the two largest identifiable groups were domestic servants and children. Savings banks did not meet the needs of the poorer groups in society. This led the emergence of the penny bank movement in the late 1840s and particularly the 1850s. Some temperance societies established penny to help those who could not use normal savings banks but who might otherwise have drunk it away. Considerable numbers of penny banks were established in the 1850s often centred on a church or chapel, a club or a workplace.

There were isolated attempts at co-operative societies before 1844. Some were the result of the influence of Robert Owen. The development of the Rochdale Equitable Pioneers Society and the opening of their store in Toad Lane in 1844 mark the beginnings of the modern movement. What made the Rochdale Society different was its decision that the profits from sales should be divided among all the members who made purchases. If the Society failed, members would lose nothing but if it flourished, they would obtain further shares of the profit. The strong appeal of the trade dividend kept members loyal to the store and gave them an immediate interest in its success. This led to widespread imitation and by 1850, more than 200 societies had been established, largely in northern England. The Rochdale Pioneers stressed the earlier ideas of the cooperative movement but increasingly the stores saw themselves as a way of improving the economic position of working people.

How successful were friendly societies, savings banks and co-operative societies in improving the social conditions of the working population? There is ample evidence of their appeal: friendly societies had more members than trade unions into the 1870s. However, this appeal was to those who could afford membership. For millions of people a lifetime of hard work petered out in the poverty of old age and the spectre of the workhouse. The abyss of poverty was ever-present for the working-classes.

11 The Condition of England 1832-1853

In 1839, Thomas Carlyle published his essay on *Chartism*. Written at the beginning of what historians once called the 'Hungry Forties', he posed the 'Condition-of-England' question: 'Is the condition of the English working people wrong; so wrong that rational working men cannot, will not, and even should not rest quiet under it?' Was Carlyle right?

A context in ideas

How did government in the 1830s and 1840s influence people's lives and with what effects? The widely-shared assumption was that the government's role was strictly limited. The intellectual context for a 'revolution in government' is important. This included looking at economics through the 'free market' and examining the 'utility' of existing institutions and procedures. These were popularised during the 1830s and 1840s and combined in the middle-class notion of 'respectability'.

An economic theory

Industrial capitalism was justified by the 'political economy' of a group of thinkers known collectively as the 'classical economists'. Adam Smith in his *Wealth of Nations*, published in 1776 called for the freeing of the economy from tariffs (taxes paid on imports and exports) and monopolies. He wanted the economy to function in a free market that would allow individuals to reach their full potential. This marked a significant change from seeing society as an organic whole in which people were responsible to others for their actions. He did have a positive role for the state providing public services that were not possible for the individual alone.

Later writers like Malthus and David Ricardo built on Smith's work. Malthus was concerned with the pressure on resources caused by population growth while Ricardo demonstrated the central role of capital in a society. Ricardo strengthened the case for freeing the commercial classes from the restrictions imposed by legislation like the Corn Laws. By 'freeing' the market he argued that the economy would become more competitive and that, in the long term living standards would rise.

A theory for utility

Parallel to these economic ideas was a philosophy of government associated with Jeremy Bentham. He accepted the free market economy but, like Adam Smith, recognised that the state was necessary to ensure that community interests were catered for. He and his followers applied the test of utility to all institutions. Were they economic, efficient and above all did they lead to 'the greatest happiness to the greatest number'? His supporters were consequently called Utilitarians and, though they recognised the need for intervention by the state, it was to be geared to the needs of individuals.

The issues for Bentham's disciples, especially John Stuart Mill, were what were the limits of laissez-faire and what intervention by the state was acceptable. To Mill, laissez-faire was an ideal and every intervention by the state was a step away from that ideal. In his *Principles of Political Economy,* published in 1848, J. S. Mill maintained that government intervention was only justifiable where there was an exceptional need. The crucial issue was which were exceptional cases and which were not. Eleven years later in *On Liberty,* Mill concluded that individuals should be free to behave as they wanted unless those actions caused 'harm to others' in which case the state could intervene to regulate unacceptable behaviour.

Popularising theories

By the 1850s, the ideas of the political economists and utilitarians had been absorbed into a body of attitudes and values often known as 'Victorianism'. Samuel Smiles and others crystallised this social philosophy into four elements: work, thrift,[1] self-help[2] and respectability.[3] These ideas were middle-class in origin but their impact crossed society. Service, respectability and, at least in public,

---

[1] Thrift broadly meant being careful with wages and not wasting it on vices like drinking and gambling. This led to respectability and independence

[2] Self-Help, epitomised in Samuel Smiles' best-selling book of that title in 1859, was the means through which people, especially in the working-class achieved respectability

[3] Respectability is perhaps the most difficult nineteenth century concept to define with any accuracy. Geoffrey Best sees it as 'a style of living understood to show a proper respect for morals and morality; usually it meant some degree of formal Christianity, but you could be respectable and value your respectability without being Christian.' He went on to add. 'Here was the sharpest of all lines of social division, between those who were and those who were not respectable: a sharper line by far than that between rich and poor, employer and employee, or capitalist and proletarian...The respectable man was a good man and also a pillar of society. He might be poor, he might be rich; it really made no matter which.'

stricter religious observance and a moral code spread upwards into the ranks of the landed elite. This was paralleled by important political changes in 1832, 1835 and 1846.[4] There is some disagreement about the extent of middle-class dominance. Harold Perkin argues that middle-class entrepreneurial ideas triumphed while W.L. Burns maintains that at least until the 1870s it is 'extravagant' to maintain that England was being governed by and in the interests of the middle-classes. Nevertheless, there was a linking if not fusion in politics and society of aristocratic and middle-class interests, of property and capital to form a new ruling class.

Against capitalism

There were, however, alternative anti-capitalist theories, associated with Thomas Paine, Thomas Spence and Charles Hall and, in the 1820s Robert Owen and Thomas Hodgskin, that challenged Smith's concept of equal individuals pursuing their own self-interests.[5] They were based on a co-operative rather than capitalist view of society. Many of these theories were evident in the Chartist movement. After the mid-1840s, some working people were affected by middle-class values and became concerned to get a better deal from capitalism rather than overthrow it. By 1850, the behaviour and attitudes of parts of the working population had impressed the middle-classes. 'New model' trade unionism, adult education, friendly societies and co-operatives among the working population suggested an increasingly shared value system.

A 'revolution in government'?

Britain had effective central government[6] institutions, but unlike other European countries did not develop a strong bureaucratic structure until the 1850s. The Victorian central state involved itself in the lives of its

---

[4] Political changes in 1832, 1835 and 1846: the Reform Act, the Municipal Corporation Act 1835 and the repeal of the Corn Laws in 1846.

[5] Thomas Paine, Thomas Spence and Charles Hall and, in the 1820s Robert Owen and Thomas Hodgskin. These individuals questioned the dominant capitalist way of looking at society. Thomas Paine (1737-1809) supported the Americans in their War of Independence (1775-1783) and the French Revolution. His *Rights of Man* (1791, 1792) argued for the ending of monarchy and aristocracy and its replacement with a democratic republic. Thomas Spense (1750-1814) favoured common ownership of the land. Hall, Owen and Hodgskin critically examined the existing system of manufacturing and commerce with Owen suggesting a 'new view of society' based not on competition but co-operation.

[6] Central government was based in London. It included Parliament, the government ministries like the Home Office and the agents of central government like government inspectors or Poor Law assistant commissioners.

citizens in many ways but these were often indirect and discreet. A range of institutions, official and voluntary, developed between the central state and the citizen. The belief in local responsibility for local needs was strong and jealously guarded.[7] The combination of strength and overall control by central government linked to decentralised local institutions with a strong sense of local community created a distinctive type of state.

The first half of the nineteenth century saw a 'revolution' in the role of government. In the simplified 'self-help' view of the ideal society the state had a purely negative role. A. V. Dicey and Samuel Smiles agreed that Benthamism or individualism dominated the period from 1825 to 1870. However, this is difficult to reconcile with the increased activities of the state. The age of laissez-faire and individualism saw the emergence of the centralised administrative state. How can this be explained? Derek Fraser suggests that it can be resolved in a variety of ways recognising that there was a difference between theory and practice. Laissez-faire may have been the ideal but the problems of urban and industrial society made an extension of the activities of the state necessary. A second explanation sees differences between theory and practice not in general terms but between one area of policy and another. Intervention in social matters was acceptable but laissez-faire for the economy. The line between social and economic was, however, far from clear. Poor law, public health and factory reform involved economic as much as social questions. Even in clearly economic matters, like the development of the railways and the governance of companies, the state took greater responsibility.

A third explanation considers Benthamism as a combination of laissez-faire and state intervention. Some historians go further and argue that Bentham pointed the way to increased state activity. The tension between these two ideals lay in the conflict between Smith's natural harmony of interests in the free market and the need in certain circumstances to create artificial harmony through intervention. Laissez-faire or intervention, in this explanation, could be equally Benthamite depending on the specific context.

In the fourth solution, associated with the historian Oliver MacDonagh, Benthamism has no central role. MacDonagh examined the growing involvement of government in emigration and

---

[7] Local government consisted of the newly reformed vestries and town councils but also included local bodies like Improvement Commissions and local officials like Poor Law Guardians. There was considerable tension between the powers of central and local government. For policies to be successful both needed to work together. Between 1830 and 1850, with few exceptions and then only briefly central and local government tended to pull against each other. Attempts to reduce the power of local government by telling it what to do were invariably met with cries about local democracy and traditional rights.

shipping in the first half of the nineteenth century and produced a five-stage model of government expansion. The first stage involved identifying some 'intolerable evil' that, it was believed, could be legislated out of existence by a prohibitory Act. The second stage recognised the deficiencies in this Act and it was replaced with new legislation involving inspectors for enforcement. Thirdly, the momentum created by a body of professionals, with intimate knowledge of the problem, led to growing centralisation and inspection by a central agency. Fourth, growing professional awareness led to the conclusion that the problem could not be swept away and that slow regulation and re-regulation was needed. Finally, a bureaucratic machine pursued research to produce preventive measures that passed almost unnoticed into law. MacDonagh's thesis rests on two main principles, the pressure of 'intolerable facts' and inevitable administrative momentum. Benthamism was incidental to the process and this led to a debate among historians over what was meant by the term 'Benthamite'. Are historians talking about people who had read Bentham, or his followers, or those who were influenced directly or indirectly by him or them?

The final explanation takes the MacDonagh thesis a stage further and argues that the evolving administrative state had little to do with concepts of individualism and collectivism but with a conflict between two views of the role of government, a traditional and a so-called incrementalist view. William Lubenow suggests that these two models of government conditioned the response of the state to intolerable evils. The traditional model put great faith in historic rights and customs with a particular emphasis on local self-government. Growing centralisation was seen as an attack on the traditional freedom of English institutions. The incrementalist model faced up to problems hesitantly and pragmatically without any clear-cut or pre-determined programme of action.

It is possible to highlight three aspects of the emerging administrative state. The response of the state to social and economic matters was largely practical, unplanned and pragmatic. Pressure from the real world led to intervention. The collection of 'facts' was essential to the transformation of the relationship between local and central government.[8] Commissions of inquiry increased rapidly after 1800. Between 1832 and 1846 over 100 Royal Commissions were established.[9] The relationship between central

---

[8] Select Committee. A committee consisted of MPs and/or peers established to look at a particular issue. Select Committees tended to be set up in reaction to an identified problem like the plight of handloom weavers. They have the power to call witnesses.

[9] Royal Commission. The Crown technically establishes Royal Commissions though in practice they are set up by the government of the day. They consist of a variety of different people--MPs, peers, 'experts', representatives from vested

and local government also cannot be ignored. The problem was not whether the state should act to deal with human problems like public health, but whether this should be done at central or local government. When intervention was justifiable, there was an alliance between central and local government.[10] Contemporaries saw intervention as a means for individuals to duck their responsibilities and combining voluntary and state action was the only way many felt that progress could be made. Finally, there was the vital element of administrative momentum, whether it was grounded in Benthamism or not. State inspectors--for factories from 1833, the Poor Law from 1834, prisons from 1835, and schools from 1839, for the mining population from 1842 and for mines from 1850-- were central to this process. They were the vanguard of central intervention in two important respects.[11]

The emergence of the modern state was largely the result of the demographic and economic changes that occurred in Britain in the late eighteenth and early nineteenth centuries. The reasons behind the 'revolution' in government are far less clear. Contemporary views of particular policies and the proper role of the state varied. It was possible for the same policy to be regarded simultaneously as benevolent, a solution to a practical problem, an effective bureaucratic measure, a prop to the existing social and political order, an asset to the middle-classes and yet also a response to popular demands. Social reform was rarely motivated by one thing

What had and had not been achieved by 1850?

National and local government disagreed on who should be responsible for social policies but there was recognition at both levels that they could

---

interests--and generally have a wider brief than Select Committees. Their recommendations often become the basis for reforming the law.

[10] Voluntary action. The first half of the nineteenth century was one of intense religious disagreement. The state found this a problem when it was seen to act in support of one denomination rather than another as, for instance over the 1843 Factory Bill. This was particularly the case if any form of taxation was involved. Anglicans were not prepared to be taxed to pay for Nonconformist reforms and vice versa and both objected to money being spent on Catholic institutions. Voluntary action was one way round this problem. It meant that individuals financed social initiatives out of their own pocket because it was the Christian charitable thing to do or the 'right' thing to do or because it indicated a person's social status or any combination of the three. Voluntary action played a significant role especially in education.

[11] Centralisation. The process of bringing social policy under direct state control. This generally meant policy-making, supervision and inspection. Day-to-day administration was often left in the hands of local bodies.

not be left to individuals. The division of responsibility between central and local government had been defined. Central government established national policies and then supervised their implementation. Local authorities were responsible for the day-to-day administration of these policies. There was a growing understanding that local implementation meant recognising local conditions. A system of central government inspection was created. This allowed dialogue between centre and locality as well as consideration of the effectiveness of national policies at local level.

Problems remained. Policies tended to be implemented through their own institutions. This led to overlapping roles between different local bodies. It was not until the 1870s and 1880s that all-purpose authorities were established and only then was co-ordination of social policies possible.[12] The question of who should pay for social reform was also not resolved. The middle-classes objected to paying local taxes to pay for improvements for working people who did not generally pay the rates. An obvious answer was the use of national taxation through income tax but the same concerns arose plus the addition of objections of religious grounds. Powerful vested interests opposed to reform. Factory owners saw factory reform in terms of lost profits, landlords the higher cost of maintaining their properties, private water companies in falling dividends for shareholders and voluntary agencies that believed they could do a better job than the state, central or local. This prevented rapid reform. It was not until the 1860s and 1870s that this issue was finally and not always satisfactorily resolved. Finally, the democratic principle involved in elections to bodies like the Board of Guardians led to social reform becoming a political football. What was 'right' frequently came second to what was politically expedient.

---

[12] All-purpose elected authorities. Local authorities that have responsibility for a wide range of local government functions. This allows for more effective co-ordination in implementing central government policies.

12 Children, work and education 1833-1853

In Kirkheaton churchyard near Huddersfield there is a fifteen-foot stone obelisk topped by a flame that commemorates:

> The dreadful fate of 17 children who fell unhappy victims to a raging fire at Mr Atkinson's factory at Colne Bridge, February 14th 1818.

All the dead were girls; the youngest nine, the oldest eighteen. The fire started when about 5 am a boy aged ten was sent downstairs to the ground floor card room to collect some cotton rovings. Instead of taking a lamp, he took a candle that ignited the cotton waste and the fire spread quickly through the factory that became a raging inferno. The children were trapped on the top floor when the staircase collapsed. The entire factory was destroyed in less than thirty minutes and the boy who had inadvertently started the fire was the last person to leave the building alive. It is not surprising that child labour and calls to regulate it became a national issue in the early 1830s.

Work determined two things: the ways in which workers spent most of their waking hours; and the amounts of money they had to spend. Work also shaped most other aspects of workers' lives. The standards of living they enjoyed; standards of health; the type of housing they lived in; the nature of the family and community life; the ways in which leisure time was spent and the social, political and other values that they held. Children were central to this situation. This chapter examines the problems raised by children and how effectively those problems were resolved.

Children, factories and reform 1830-1853

The industrial revolution cannot be viewed as a simple transition from an agricultural and domestic economy to one dominated by factories. Although contemporaries emphasised the development of large-scale factory production, domestic production and small workshops dominated manufacture until the mid-nineteenth century.

Children and adults

The development of factory conditions was sufficient advanced by the 1830s to justify a serious and sustained effort by the state to regulate their application. There is ample evidence of exploitation and cruelty towards children, especially paupers, by fellow workers.[1] Two examples illustrate this problem. Sarah Carpenter, interviewed for the *Ashton Chronicle* in 1849 said,

> 'The master carder's name was Thomas Birks; but he never went by any other name than Tom the Devil. He was a very bad man - he was encouraged by the master in ill-treating all the hands, but particularly the children. Everybody was frightened of him. He would not even let us speak.'

Jonathan Downe was interviewed by Michael Sadler's Parliamentary Committee on 6 June 1832 and said,

> 'When I was seven years old I went to work at Mr. Marshall's factory at Shrewsbury. If a child was drowsy, the overlooker touches the child on the shoulder and says, 'Come here'. In a corner of the room there is an iron cistern filled with water. He takes the boy by the legs and dips him in the cistern, and sends him back to work.'

Contemporaries did not agree on how widespread these practices were or how far particular cases were used as propaganda for the Ten-Hour movement.

Several influential accounts of what factory life was like in the 1830s and 1840s. Frances Trollope's fictional *Michael Armstrong, the Factory Boy* was published in 1840. There were factual or semi-factual accounts such as John Fielden, *The Curse of the Factory System* (1836), Charles Wing, *Evils of the Factory System* (1837), William Dodd, *A Narrative of William Dodd,: A Factory Cripple* (1841), Frank Forrest, *Chapters in the Life of a Dundee Factory Boy* (1850) and the widely read account by John Brown, *A Memoir of Robert Blincoe* (1828). Edward Baines, an opponent of factory reform attacked their propaganda in his *The History of the Cotton Manufacture* in 1835:

> 'It is alleged that the children who labour in factories are often cruelly beaten by the spinners or overlookers that their feeble limbs become distorted by continual standing and stooping, and they grow up cripples... But this is the exception not the rule.'

There was a wide range of experience within factories. Many late eighteenth and early nineteenth century textile mills were rural and recruited labour from the local domestic industries. Families often moved together to a new factory so that all members of a household could gain

---

[1] Paupers were often apprenticed to factory owners to give them a trade. They were frequently exploited. The 1802 Health of Apprentices Act tried unsuccessfully to give them some protection.

employment. A weaver used to the workings of a small weaving shed would be familiar with many aspects of the work environment--if not the scale--of a factory. Boys were apprenticed to weaving, power spinning or in the machine shop; girls worked in the carding room before moving to other low-technology jobs within the mill. Generally, as new technology was adopted, men took control of the new processes in spinning and weaving while women were left with the older machines and more poorly paid jobs.

Increasingly, as factories became steam-powered, workers moved from rural mills to towns. The new large urban mills offered greater opportunities and the wider range of employment in towns was some insurance against depression and unemployment. Nevertheless, factory work altered labourers' lives in a variety of ways. Most obvious was the loss of freedom and independence, especially for men who had previously been their own masters. Factory workers could no longer combine industrial work with agricultural labour or other activities. Many factory masters introduced rigid and harsh regulations to keep the workforce at their machines for long hours and to break their irregular work patterns.

The Ten Hour Movement

Concerns about the deteriorating conditions in child employment initially developed in the late eighteenth century. Early legislative efforts, however, depended on individuals. Sir Robert Peel senior was behind both the 1802 and 1819 Acts but he received considerable support from Lancashire cotton spinners and three other groups. For old labour aristocracies such as the east Midland framework-knitters, Yorkshire woollen croppers and the handloom weavers, factories threatened their social status and incomes. Some doctors drew attention to the pernicious effects of factory labour on health. Northern clergymen played important roles in successive factory campaigns. Richard Oastler wrote in 1836:

> 'his only object was to establish the principles of Christianity, the principles of the Church of England in these densely people districts.... the Factory question was indeed.... a Soul-question -- it was Souls against pounds, shillings and pence.'

The Health and Morals of Apprentices Act 1802 was extended in 1819 from pauper apprentices to cover all cotton factory children restricting them to twelve hours' daily labour. There was further agitation in the 1820s by the cotton spinners. John Cam Hobhouse[2] obtained minor improvements to existing legislation in 1825 and 1829. However,

---

[2] John Cam Hobhouse (1786-1869) a leading advocate of parliamentary reform and factory legislation in the House of Commons.

the Lancashire cotton operatives became disillusioned with the lack of enforcement of existing law. In 1828 John Doherty, leader of the Manchester Spinners' Union formed the Society for the Protection of Children Employed in Cotton Factories. Doherty's organisation tried to secure enforcement of existing legislation and the passage of new factory laws. The organisation continued until 1831 when it changed its name to the Manchester Short-Time Committee. The Factory Movement began in Lancashire.

Pressures for action

The early industrial reformers had little or no organisation. The campaign between 1825 and 1829 achieved little. After 1830, demands for reform were supported by wide range of people of differing opinions. The movement was active in the first half of the 1830s, between 1838 and 1841 and again from 1844 until the passage of the Ten Hours Act in 1847. In late 1830, Richard Oastler, a Tory land agent from Huddersfield sent his celebrated letter to the *Leeds Mercury* on 'Yorkshire Slavery' and he later followed this up with letters to the *Leeds Intelligencer* and the radical *Leeds Patriot*. He believed in paternalism in which the values of 'rural' society were used to judge the excesses of industrialism. Oastler developed a kind of 'Tory Radicalism'.[3] He spoke of the 'monstrous' nature of the factory system and the 'terrors' of child labour. He denounced political economy as 'earthly, selfish and devilish' and pointed to the abnormality of 'the tears of innocent victims [wetting] the very streets which receive the droppings of an Anti-Slavery Society'.

Substantial sections of the propertied classes--merchants, gentry and professional men--recognised that their interests and values were similar to artisans. Their views cut across the political spectrum from traditional Tories to Whigs. There was considerable support from Tories and Anglicans committed to a paternalistic model of society that if necessary, might be promoted through state intervention. Many of those who financed the movement, like Michael Sadler,[4] John Fielden[5] and John Wood, were well-established factory owners and members of the Tory

---

[3] Tory Radicalism. Something of a ragbag of attitudes that emerged in the 1820s and 1830s as a reaction to the ideas of Political Economy. Tory Radicals like Oastler took a moral view on issues like child labour and the Poor Law arguing that society had a moral responsibility to remove social evils. The state should therefore intervene passing laws to regulate these issues.

[4] Michael Sadler (1780-1835) was a banker and Tory MP who introduced a bill in Parliament in 1831 to limit the working hours of children. He lost his seat in the 1832 General Election.

[5] John Fielden (1784-1849) was a cotton manufacturer in Yorkshire. As an MP, he introduced the 1847 Factory Act.

urban elite facing a challenge locally from Dissenting entrepreneurs. Many Tory , Richards like William Ferrand of Bingley wanted to extend protection to workpeople and children. Clergymen were also prominent like the Tory Parson George Bull of Bradford and the Nonconformist minister Joseph Rayner Stephens who led the Lancashire short time movement from 1834-1835. There were the mill operatives themselves and their supporters, of whom Richard Oastler was the most prominent. Their demands for reductions in the working day exposed the hardship faced children and provided a way of seeking limitations on the working day of adults.

In the laissez-faire atmosphere of the period, any direct attempt to achieve State regulation of the hours of adult males was doomed to failure. However, because children aged 10-13 were an essential part of the workforce it was hoped that restricting their hours would filter through to the rest. The reformers did not oppose child labour but were opposed to unregulated labour. They judged legislation not by its direct effect on child labour but by its indirect effect on the position of adult workers. There were the Tory humanitarians among whom Lord Ashley was most active. They were concerned about the moral and religious deprivation of young workers and the ineffectiveness of existing protective legislation. Romantics like William Wordsworth, Robert , and William Cobbett looked back to a pre-industrial 'golden age' and blamed the industrial revolution for alienating workers from the land and forcing children to play a major role in the workforce. A final group of reformers came to the fore in the debates over amendments to the factory legislation that occurred in the 1840s. They included active supporters of laissez-faire principles, such as Thomas Babington Macaulay, but who argued for regulation on economic and moral grounds. Child labour, he suggested, damaged the health of youngsters who were later in life unable to achieve their potential productivity. Restricting child labour was a rational means of promoting investment in the country's future workforce.

Agitation and Parliament

During the winter of 1830-1831, attitudes became increasingly polarised. By early 1831, short time committees had been set up in the West Riding, Lancashire and Scotland. Oastler acted as the central organiser. He possessed considerable oratorical skills and journalistic gifts. He controlled the central funds and gave a crusading edge to the movement. He met a delegation of workers and agreed to lead the campaign for shorter hours in what has been called the 'Fixby Hall compact'. Thousands of pamphlets, petitions and tracts were issued, as 'missionaries' went throughout the textile areas of England and Scotland to highlight the horrors of child labour in the mills.

Oastler had little success with the Whig government and the Conservative opposition kept the agitation at arm's length. The extra-parliamentary activities of the Ten-Hour movement gave strong support to those who tried to get legislation through Parliament. Michael Sadler, MP for Newark took up the cause when a factory bill was rejected in 1831. A petition signed by over 130,000 people was presented to Parliament in early 1832. However, when Sadler moved a Ten-Hour Bill he was asked to chair a Select Committee to take evidence in connection with his Bill. The work was cut short by the 1832 General Election following the passage of parliamentary reform.

Sadler was defeated at Leeds and the young Evangelical Anthony Ashley Cooper replaced him as parliamentary spokesman for the campaign. Factory masters organised a vigorous lobby to resist further legislation, arguing that shorter working hours would help foreign competitors and lead to lower wages and unemployment. The publication of Select Committee report in January 1833 identified the stark realities of conditions and led Anthony Ashley Cooper to introduce a factory bill. Criticisms, largely justified, that the 1833 report was somewhat one-sided, as it had only heard the workers' views. The government felt that the employers should be consulted and this delayed the bill. In April 1833, the government set up a Royal Commission to investigate the employment of children in factories led by John Southwood Smith and Edwin Chadwick. Reform had been taken out of the hands of the Ten-Hour Movement.

Why did the Whigs take control of factory reform?

The agitation in Yorkshire convinced the Whigs that factory legislation was inevitable. Determining the composition of the Royal Commission ensured that the range of options available to them would be wider and less unpalatable to manufacturers than Ashley's proposals. The report, produced in forty-five days, looked at factory conditions far less emotionally than the Select Committee. Its conclusions were not based on humanitarian grounds--the position adopted by the Ten-Hour Movement--but on the question of efficiency. Chadwick argued that human suffering and degradation led to ineffective production and that a good working environment would lead to health, happiness and an efficient workforce. It accepted the opposition of factory owners to state intervention but argued that children were not 'free agents' and therefore needed protection. It did not extend the same argument to adults.

Within a month, Ashley's Bill was defeated but in August Althorp, the Whig Chancellor introduced his own bill that became law. The 1833 Factory Act applied to all textile mills except for lace and silk manufacture.

Children under nine were barred from all work. Children aged 9-14 were restricted to 8 hours a day and a maximum of 48 hours in a week with 2 hours at school. Young persons under 18 were restricted to 12 hours a day and a maximum of 68 hours in a week. Four Factory Inspectors were appointed to enforce the Act. They were aided by a group of resident superintendents who could start prosecutions.

The debates in 1832 and 1833 aired the issue publicly as never before. The legislation in 1833 was confined to children's work and applied only to textile mills and its effectiveness depended on the factory inspectorate enforcing the regulations. There was widespread evasion. Employers wanted to employ cheaper child labour. Parents wanted their children to work and bring in much needed income for the family budget. Deciding the age of a child was difficult and it was not until the civil registration of births (and marriages and deaths) in 1836 that this proved possible. In addition, except for Leonard Horner, the inspectors and their assistants were largely ignorant of factories and their conditions. During the first four years of operation, they sought to establish working relationships with employers. However, the inspectors soon broadened their activities, became more critical of conditions and applied the law with greater rigour. Yet, fines were low. Prosecutions in Lancashire and the West Riding of Yorkshire suggest that about three-quarters of prosecutions were successful between 1833 and 1855. Horner argued that further state intervention was necessary and was highly critical of the exclusion of silk mills from the 1833 Act. Overall, however, he argued that the Act was successful.

Oastler was disappointed. The legislation still allowed young persons to work long hours and imposed inspection and centralisation. Factory masters were little happier. They believed state regulation would restrict their ability to compete effectively. Although there were several attempts in the 1830s to get the legislation changed, they were unsuccessful. The extra-parliamentary movement may have been frustrated by what had been achieved and the 1833 Act may have not been based on any real moral principles, but it did mark an important stage in the emergence of effective factory legislation and underpinned the developments of the 1840s.

Legislation in the 1840s

The pace of the campaign of the 1840s varied considerably. Ashley Cooper failed to inject 'ten hours' into unsuccessful bills in 1838, 1839 and 1841. By 1840, the Inspectors had concluded that the law needed to be extended and the return of the Conservatives under Sir Robert Peel in 1841 raised hopes for further reform. Peel, however, opposed the Ten-Hour movement until the passage of the 1847 Factory Act. He accepted the argument of political economists that wages would fall under a ten-hour day and the cost of production would increase pushing prices up. This approach was based on a genuine concern for the welfare of workers and in 1841, this was mistaken for acceptance of the ten-hour principle. This led to widespread and misleading publicity, raising then shattering workers' hopes intensifying hostility to the government during 1842.

Peel was prepared to accept intervention when convinced that the moral case was overwhelming. He opposed Ashley over ten-hour legislation because he believed that the moral case was weaker than the economic one. However, he accepted the moral arguments in the Mines Act 1842. Working conditions in collieries were dangerous and children and women played an important part in mining coal. In 1840, a Royal Commission was established to investigate the working conditions of children in coalmines and manufactories. Its findings were horrific with children as young as five or six working as 'trappers' (operating doors to enable air coursing). There were also many comments about the poor health of the mining community. Artists were employed to go underground. They made sketches of workers and these appeared when the Commissioners' Report was published in 1842. They were graphic and had immense propaganda value. Public opinion was shocked.

Shaftesbury drafted a bill that became law at the end of 1842. It made the employment of women underground illegal. Boys under 10 could no longer work underground. Ashley had suggested that the age should be 13 but this was reduced in the House of Lords. It also said that parish apprentices between 10 and 18 could continue to work in mines. There were no clauses on hours of work and inspection could only take place to check on the 'condition of the workers'. Many women were annoyed that they could no longer earn much needed money. In 1850, a further Act widened the authority of colliery inspectors who could now check the condition of machines.

Peel's intentions were insufficient to dampen class antagonism that intensified during the industrial distress and disturbances of 1841 and 1842. The series of strikes across large swathes of the country in mid-1842, speeded government action. In March 1843, the Home Secretary Sir James Graham introduced a Factory Bill that would restrict children aged 8-13 to 6½ hours' work with three hours' daily education in improved schools largely controlled by the Church. Peel and Graham agreed on the importance of improving educational provision for the working population and making the educational clauses of the 1833 Act effective. Fear and prejudice came together in the massive campaign by Nonconformist groups. Graham's proposal for state assistance in the education of factory children--motivated by the need to raise the 'moral feeling' of the people as a counter to Chartism--was thought by

Nonconformists and Roman Catholics to favour the Church of England unfairly. Parliamentary and extra-parliamentary opposition resulted in the whole bill being withdrawn.

Oastler mounted a major campaign in the spring of 1844 but he was unable to graft a '10 hour clause' on to the revised Factory Bill, shorn of its contentious educational clauses that was reintroduced in early 1844. Ashley moved a ten-hour amendment that carried with 95 Conservatives supporting it. Peel refused to accept ten hours or compromise with eleven hours. The Bill was forced through when Peel threatened to resign unless the vote was reversed. The Factory Act 1844 effected considerable improvements. Children (8-13) became 'half-timers', working 6½ hours. Dangerous machinery was to be fenced in, the beginnings of health and safety legislation. Women shared the young persons' 12-hour restriction. It was permissible for a factory to operate for only fifteen hours in a day.

There was, however, considerable disappointment in the textile towns. A series of conferences tried to revive the Ten Hours Bill in Parliament, and after a winter campaign, Ashley Cooper tried to introduce it in January 1846. However, the debate over industrial conditions was overshadowed by the controversy over the Corn Laws. Ashley felt morally obliged to resign his seat and Fielden took his place as parliamentary leader. Fielden pushed ahead but was defeated in May. A further campaign was mounted in the autumn but gathering industrial recession weakened the case for opposition. Whig attempts to compromise on 11 hours were defeated and Fielden triumphed in May 1847 with the Ten Hours Act receiving the Royal Assent in June.

Why ten hours was achieved in 1847 is a matter of some disagreement. One explanation was that Tory protectionists wanted revenge for the repeal of the Corn Laws in 1846. By contrast, Karl Marx saw it as the first success of the working-classes. The revival of the extra-parliamentary movement supports this view though it lacked the energy and probably the support it had enjoyed in the early 1830s. A final explanation put forward by W. C. Lubenow and William Aydelotte, examined the view that the ten-hour issue divided all political parties. After repeal in 1846, protectionists, no longer restrained by party loyalties, voted according to their conscience and tipped the balance in favour of reform. There does appear to have been a shift in the Conservative Party on the ten hours' question. In 1846, only half of all Conservative MPs voted for reform but this increased to over three-quarters in 1847.

The 1847 Act was a landmark in the emergence of state intervention but northern rejoicing was premature. From 1848, there were reports of evasions in Lancashire and of masters' campaigns to repeal the Act. Several employers resorted to the relay system that meant that hours of work could not be effectively enforced. Gradually, a new campaign emerged to protect the Act but it was increasingly obvious that the Factory

Movement was divided. Ashley Cooper and a 'liberal' group were prepared to accept compromise. Oastler was not. A test case on the illegality of the relay system--*Ryder v Mills*--was heard in early 1850 and failed. The Factory Act 1850 increased weekly hours from 58 to 60 hours and in return for banning relays by establishing a working day between 6 a.m. and 6 p.m. Attempts to include adults failed. As a result, men might work 15 hours, aided by relays of children beyond the hours allowed for women and young persons. Children only received their fixed day in the 1853 Factory Act. Adults had to wait until Disraeli restored the '10 hours' in 1874.

In the 1830s, Oastler saw the regulation of factories and the protection of children as the key to remedying social distress. The factory question in the 1840s can be seen through the language of negotiation within a growing consensus in favour of further regulation. From the 1860s, the factory agitation could be recalled as part of the general progress of society. For employers, the improvements associated with the Acts became part of an image of the well-regulated factory. The factory inspectors saw themselves as agents of moral improvement among workers, as much as their protectors from unscrupulous employers. Factory reform reflected a recognition that the free market existed within a moral and legal framework.

Elementary education and children

By 1830, few people believed that the working-classes should not be educated at all. Education was a means of reducing crime and the rising cost of punishment and a way of keeping the child or the child when adult out of the workhouse. It was also a major concern in the 1830s and 1840s for those who believed in social control as a means of moulding correct public morals and social attitudes.

Child employment meant many children were denied the disciplines of schooling. New types of schools--factory schools, Sunday schools, evening schools and infant schools--were established to compensate for these factory-related developments. These new schools sought not only to teach morals but also to mould their pupils to fit in with the needs of an industrial society. Schools placed much greater emphasis on continuous and regular attendance with teachers making sure that children remained busy at their allotted tasks. It was assumed that if children knew how the world worked, they would be more ready to accept their place in society.

Types of school

From the 1780s working-class enthusiasts and middle-class reformers were concerned with extending working-class children's encounters with schooling. Among the most successful enterprises were Sunday schools. They originated in the 1780s and in 1801, there were some 2,290 schools rising to 23,135 in 1851 with over 2 million enrolled children. By then three-quarters of working-class children aged 5-15 attended. Sunday schools fitted into working-class life: Sunday was the one day when schooling did not compete with work. Chapel or church could be used as schoolroom; and teachers gave their services free, so that if fees were charged at all, they were very low. Sunday schools differed from most day schools that required some sort of building and paid teachers, as well as a regular income from fees.

The promotion of day schools led to the formation of two Religious Societies. The National Society for Promoting the Education of the Poor in the Principles of the Established Church in England and Wales[6] was formed in 1811 and three years later, the British and Foreign School Society replacing the Lancastrian Society[7] formed in 1808. The sectarian divide had been established: the Anglican National Society and the broadly Nonconformist British and Foreign School Society. The appeal of these voluntary schools was not helped by their teaching methods. Both favoured the monitorial or mutual system of teaching, by which a teacher taught the older children (or monitors) who then passed on what they had learned to groups of younger children. It was designed to enable a single teacher to cope with very large groups of children. It was mechanical in its approach relying on rote learning and memorisation but it was economical and this appealed to many contemporary adult observers. The reaction of the children who endured this approach was far less positive. These voluntary religious day schools offered an experience significantly different from the pattern of schooling familiar to the working-classes and one that many of them chose to avoid.

Historians have identified a large sector of cheap private schooling educating one in four working-class children outside the church and state system. Why did the working-class reject the new National and British

---

[6] National Society. This was an Anglican body established in 1811 in opposition to the work of the Lancastrian Society. Its origins lay in the work of Reverend Andrew Bell (1753-1832) in Madras, India in developing the monitorial (or Madras) system.

[7] Lancastrian Society. Supporters of the educational ideas of Joseph Lancaster (1778-1838) founded this in 1808. Lancaster had developed the monitorial system independently of Bell, around the same time. In 1814, it became the British and Foreign Schools Society, a change that offended Lancaster. In 1818, he emigrated to North America where he opened a number of schools.

schools and choose slightly more expensive, small dame and common day schools? They had no taint of charity or of social control, were not regarded as part of the authority system and parents could regard the teachers as their employees. They also fitted in with working-class lifestyles. The expansion of this type of education did result in the creation of a remarkably literate working-class.

Four types of school mopped up those children who, left to themselves, would have remained illiterate: the ragged, workhouse, prison and factory schools. Ragged Schools began during the 1840s and the Ragged School Union dated from 1844. They charged no fees and took the poorest children for a basic education, depending for their support on a circle of philanthropists including Lord Shaftesbury[8] and Charles Dickens. By 1852, there were 132 Ragged Schools in London with 26,000 children and 70 outside London in 42 towns. Education for children in workhouses and prisons was guaranteed by the 1834 Poor Law Amendment Act and the 1823 Prisons Act. Factory schools were created by the Factory Act of 1833 obliging factory owners to ensure that their child workers received a regular education either in a factory school or outside, before being allowed to work. This was firmly enforced. All these measures helped disadvantaged groups of children.

The voluntary societies and the schools affiliated to them had one resource that the working-class private day schools lacked: access to central government. In 1833, Lord Kerry's *Returns* on elementary education showed that 1.2 million (about a third of all children in England and Wales aged 4 to 12) attended day schools. He also found that 1.6 million attended Sunday schools (0.5 million of these also attended day schools). Yet, it was not enough. Despite the introduction of state grants, by 1855 39 per cent of children between 4 and 12 (1.5 million) were not at school.

The state and working-class education 1833-1850

Everyone agreed that education should have a religious core. Anglicans, as members of the established church, argued that any school named in law and supported by government funds should be theirs. Nonconformists and Roman Catholics hotly disputed this. It was for this reason that there were two voluntary day school societies, joined by a third, the Catholic Poor School Committee, in 1849.

Public support for elementary education began with a grant of £20,000 in 1833 in aid of school buildings. This was inevitably channelled

---

[8] Anthony Ashley Cooper, 5th earl of Shaftesbury (1801-1885) elected to Parliament as a Tory in 1826 and remained in the House of Commons until he inherited his title in 1851. He championed the factory movement and was largely responsible for the Mines Act 1842.

through the two religious societies. The 1833 Factory Act, 1842 Mines Act and 1844 Factory Act limited the hours that children could work. The idea behind this legislation was that if there were no work for children to do lawfully, they would go to school instead. The growth of grants to elementary schools increased dramatically from the original £20,000 of 1833 to £724,000 by 1860. The continuation of central grants ensured the expansion of the Her Majesty's Inspectorate. From 2 in 1840, they had become 23 with 2 Assistant Inspectors in 1852, 36 with 25 Assistants in 1861 and 62 with 14 Assistants in 1864.

Sectarian conflict made government intervention in education more difficult. Grants provided the first form of intervention but during the 1840s, other forms of central control over education were introduced largely through the work of James Kay-Shuttleworth whose period as secretary of the Committee of Council for Education lasted between 1839 and 1849. He believed that the key to better standards was properly trained teachers. He set out to attract teachers of the right class and calibre by raising salaries. The Minutes of 1846 introduced teacher apprenticeships. From the age of 13 teacher trainees would receive a grant of £10 increased annually to £20 when they were 18, were taught by the master for 90 minutes a day and had to pass the annual Inspector's examination. They were to assist the master in teaching. He would train them in class management and routine duties. Kay-Shuttleworth intended trainees should come from the upper working and lower middle-classes and should form a social link between the children of labourers in elementary schools and the school managers, who were clergy or gentry. The teacher training colleges formed the top rung of this ladder of recruitment and training. In 1839, there were four training colleges with model schools in the United Kingdom that took students through very inadequate courses of six weeks to three or four months. By 1858, there were thirty-four colleges partly financed through Queen's Scholarships.

Did this improve the standard of teaching? Much school teaching was mechanical, overloaded with 'facts' for memorisation. The Teacher Training colleges did provide some teaching material, method and possible much-needed self-confidence. They were criticised for their long hours, vast syllabuses, addiction to textbooks and the superficial nature of many of their courses. The main cause of poor teaching in elementary schools was the low wages teachers were paid. Salaries varied depending on the level of school fees. By the early 1850s, the average annual pay of a certificated schoolteacher was £90.

By 1850, attitudes were changing. Many people accepted that elementary education should be under state control. Some nonconformists, especially the Congregationalists and Unitarians continued to oppose state-funded education but they were increasingly in a minority. More than £200,000 was allocated by the state for education in 1850. Under Kay-Shuttleworth's successor Ralph Lingen (1849-1870) the work of the Education Department, as it became in 1856, steadily expanded but on more formal and bureaucratised lines. The age of creative innovation was over. The department's objective was to work the system as efficiently and economically as possible. Until the late 1850s, much of the schooling of the working-classes was still informal or semi-formal. Efforts to bring government resources to bear had so far been hampered by the 'religious problem' and it took another twenty years to cut through this knot.

13 Speenhamland to the New Poor Law 1830-1847

Many writers in the 1830s and 1840s saw poverty as part of the natural order of things. Society took the view that the 'haves' should provide support for the 'have-nots'. A distinction was made between the 'deserving poor', those for whom poverty was the result of circumstances often out of their control, and the 'undeserving poor' whose poverty was largely their own fault. After 1830, the distinction between poverty and pauperism became increasingly unclear.[1] There was a move away from seeing poverty as a natural state towards a moral definition where it was the fault of the individual. The poor, massed together in large towns seemed a social menace. This provided the impetus to Poor Law reform in 1834. Relief continued to be offered but only in the workhouse where the paupers would be made less comfortable than those who chose to stay outside and fend for themselves--this principle was known as 'less-eligibility'.[2] Those who were genuinely in need would accept the workhouse rather than starve. Most would prefer to remain independent and thus avoid contracting the morally wasting disease of pauperism.

Poverty is notoriously difficult to define. In simple terms the failure to provide the necessities of life--food, clothes and shelter--results in a state of poverty. British society in the nineteenth century was poor by modern standards. The net national income per head at 1900 prices has been estimated as £16 in 1830 rising slightly to £18 in 1855. Most members of the working-class experienced poverty at some period of their lives. The number of paupers had long been known. They were about 9 per cent of the population in the 1830s and this fell to less than 3 per cent by 1900. The common belief was that poverty was caused by idleness, drinking and other personal shortcomings, a belief that was used to justify the repressive nature of the Poor Law. The crucial point was that most poverty was not 'self-inflicted' but derived from circumstances over which the poor had little control.

Low wage rates and unemployment were both serious causes of

---

[1] A 'pauper' can simply be defined as an individual who was in receipt of benefits from the state. A labourer who was out of work was termed an able-bodied pauper, whereas the sick and elderly were called impotent paupers. Relief was given in a variety of ways. Outdoor relief occurred when the poor received help either in money or in kind. Indoor relief occurred when the poor entered a workhouse or house of correction to receive help. The Poor Law Amendment Act 1834 said that paupers should all receive indoor relief.
[2] 'Less eligibility'. For people, unable or unwilling to make provision for themselves, poor relief was to be on terms less favourable than those obtained by the lowest paid worker in employment.

poverty between 1830 and 1850. Real wages were low.[3] Men and women were engaged in declining domestic industries, in arable farming with its irregular labour requirements, and in occupations disrupted by poor weather, uncertain transport or loss of power. Few workers could afford to make provisions against unemployment. Old age was as important a cause of poverty as low wages in 1830. Rising life expectancy meant that increasing numbers of people lived into old age. In 1851, a quarter of the population was over 55 and often entered the workhouse in old age. Sickness was also an important cause of poverty in 1830. Chadwick and early public health campaigners pointed to the economic cost of preventable disease and emphasised how poor rates were swollen by the deaths of working men and by the vicious circle of sickness and reduced earnings.

Many contemporaries saw drinking as the most important cause of poverty. In 1850, up to a third of a labourer's wages were spent on drink. Heavy drinkers claimed that beer was necessary to their strength but drink was an extremely expensive way of obtaining nutrition. Wages were often paid in public houses. One sign of the importance of drink among the causes of working-class poverty was extensive temperance activity. The temperance movement[4] has been characterised as overwhelmingly middle-class imposing their values on a degenerate workforce. However, support for temperance was as much a working-class attribute as drunkenness. Low earnings, irregular employment, large families, sickness and old age were the root causes of poverty in the nineteenth century rather than intemperance or idleness.

The Old Poor Law

Reform of the Poor Laws widened the growing gulf between the middle-classes and the working population. The old Poor Law was introduced in 1598 and 1601. It remained the basis for poor relief until 1834. Any attempt to reconstruct the Poor Law would have to be bold.

---

[3] Real wages. The relationship between wages people received for their work and the price of goods they needed. When wages were higher than prices real wages rose--people could buy more with what they had. When prices were higher than wages, real wages fell.

[4] Temperance movement. A movement that began in the 1830s that aimed to reduce the level of drinking in society. How much drinking the temperance movement tolerated varied. Some reformers were concerned with reducing the level of drinking spirits like gin. Others were total abstainers who wanted the end to all drinking of alcohol.

A system in crisis: the operation of the 'old' Poor Law?

Parishes, supervised by the local magistrates,[5] were responsible for the collection of the poor rate and the distribution (by the overseer)[6] of the income to needy parishioners or to pay for paupers' medical treatment. The children of poor families could be bound out as apprentices and provision was made for orphans and foundlings. In the seventeenth and eighteenth centuries, poor relief was usually in the form of outdoor relief, the provision of money, food, clothing or other goods to paupers who continued living in their own homes. The able-bodied poor were sometimes given work. Women often nursed the sick or undertook laundry work and men might have 'parish work' repairing roads and bridges. A system of indoor relief in workhouses originated in the 1720s and early workhouses were largely intended for the sick, elderly and orphans. The 1723 Act allowed parishes to combine to establish workhouses to share costs. By 1815, there were 2,000 workhouses with between twenty and fifty inmates. They cost around a quarter of all Poor Law expenditure but dealt with only one pauper in twelve. Gilbert's Act of 1782 allowed parishes to join together in voluntary unions to administer the Poor Law and employ paid officials. There were about seventy voluntary Gilbert Unions involving over 900 parishes by 1834.

The 1601 Poor Law Act provided for relief to paupers only in their parish of legal settlement.[7] However, this allowed migrant workers and vagrants to move to a new parish and quickly obtain the right to receive relief and placed a considerable financial burden on parishes. The 1662 Settlement Act tightened these rules and came in for considerable criticism in the eighteenth century. It has been estimated that some 15,000 people were still being removed each year by the 1850s. Financial considerations played as important a role under the 'old' system as under the 'new'. The old Poor Law provided no clear answers to certain critical questions. Was unemployment regarded as an offence or a misfortune? Was relief administered as a deterrent, as a dole or as a livelihood? To those who believed in free market principles, the Settlement laws and outdoor relief threatened the operation of the market.

Nonetheless, parishes and unions developed varied ways of paying relief--pensions, dole, bread allowances, and payment in kind and other devices all came under the general term of outdoor relief. There was the

---

[5] Magistrates or Justices of the Peace were judges in the local courts but also had important administrative functions. They tended to be leading property owners.
[6] Overseer of the Poor. At least two people were appointed by the vestry each year to collect the poor rate and supervise its distribution.
[7] Legal settlement. The 1601 Act said that people were legally settled in a parish after they had been there for one month.

'roundsman system' where farmers employed the parish poor on a rota. Economic distress that led to food riots in the mid-1790s resulted in the introduction of 'allowances in aid of wages', generally known as the 'Speenhamland system'[8] after its initial application in Berkshire in 1795. The magistrates approved a minimum income for agricultural labourers by introducing a scale of credits to top wages up--paid for out of the poor rates--during a time of high inflation. The system was like many modern tax and welfare systems such as working tax credit and housing benefit. Payments were based on how many children a family had and this was linked to the price of bread. The Poor Law reformer Sir Frederick Eden gave the impression in 1797 that the 'system' was widespread over the southern rural counties but it hardly a 'system' as areas adopted their own bread scales.

Until 1834, a varied system of poor relief existed to cater to the pressing social needs of the pauper. It had been designed when England was a rural society in which work and employment were seasonal. Developing industrialisation and growing urbanisation from the mid-eighteenth century, combined with the economic and social impact of the French Wars after 1793 resulted in changing attitudes. The Poor Law, many believed, was in need of reform.

The Old Poor Law under scrutiny

The Poor Law came under attack from various quarters. The Revd T. R. Malthus[9] demanded its abolition. He argued for the need to delay marriage, the end of the Settlement laws, which distorted the free market, and of the 'Speenhamland' system, which he believed, encouraged the married poor to have children they could not afford. David Ricardo maintained that if the poor were given relief, there was less for wages. Adding to the abolitionist arguments was the growing cost of relief. Poor Law spending trebled during the French Wars and reached £8 million by 1817. The cost of relief fell in the early 1820s but began to rise again

---

[8] Speenhamland system. Berkshire magistrates meeting in the Pelican Inn at Speen in May 1795 devised a system that supplemented wages from the poor rates based on the current price of bread. The same idea was used across southern and eastern England.

[9] T. R. Malthus (1766-1834), a clergyman who published his *Essay on the Principles of Population* in 1798 with a second edition in 1803. Those who supported his ideas were known as Malthusians. Malthus argued that population rose faster than the resources necessary to sustain it. Unless population growth was limited he suggested that there would be a subsistence crisis with widespread famine and disease. This would then cut population back to its natural level. The Great Famine in Ireland in the 1840s is often cited as the classic case of a Malthusian crisis.

reaching over £7 million in 1831 and £8.3 million in 1832 and 1833. Landowners and tenant farmers bore the brunt of these higher rates though this was partly offset by being able to pay low wages knowing that the parish would make up the difference. The Swing Riots of 1830 was the final blow to the old system. If the existing expensive system could not deliver social stability then, many argued it should be reformed

By the early 1830s, opinion on the Poor Laws was broadly divided into those who wished to retain them, those who wished to modify them and those who wished to abolish them. Humanitarians, radicals and paternalistic Tories belonged to the first group. They believed that there was a strong argument based on humane social responsibility in providing a measure of social security for the labouring poor. This seemed to them to outweigh its disadvantages. The second group, which wished to modify the existing system, was to some degree motivated by the same sentiments but wished to reduce its increasing cost. The third 'progressive' group was the most influential though the least numerous. Its supporters believed that labourers must operate within a free market economy and that a 'deterrent' Poor Law was necessary to achieve this. The latter had the better of the argument. By the early 1830s it was widely accepted that the Poor Laws encouraged laziness and vice.

A Royal Commission

The Royal Commission set up in 1832 to investigate the workings of the Poor Law was weighted towards 'progressive' opinion and quickly substantiated what the Commissioners had set out to prove. Twenty-six assistant commissioners were appointed. They toured the country, submitting reports on the provinces and elicited replies from the *Town Queries* and *Rural Queries* surveys sent out in August 1832. Just how selective the assistant commissioners were in their collection of evidence is a matter of considerable debate. However, they appear to have slanted their conclusions to pander to the preconceived views of the leading commissioners, especially Edwin Chadwick[10] and the economist Nassau Senior.

The 1834 *Report* reflected contemporary opinion that the Poor Law was *the* cause of poverty. Chadwick, for instance, argued that the allowance system was demoralising and pauperised rural labourers. It removed the fear of hunger and led to idleness. If it were removed, idle paupers would be forced to seek work. From the 1960s, historians have

---

[10] Edwin Chadwick (1800-1890) was the leading social reformer of the 1830s and 1840s. An inspired administrator, he laid the foundations of reform in the Poor Law, factories, the police and public health. This did not make him popular, a problem made worse by his inability to manage people.

looked critically at this assumption. Mark Blaug showed the allowances had already been dropped in many parishes and were the result, not the cause, of low wages. G. R. Boyer noted that farmers used an allowance system from the 1790s as a form of unemployment benefit to ensure an adequate workforce in periods of intense economic activity. This research suggests that relief was largely a response to growing population, low wages and underemployment not its cause as the *Report* suggests.

The motives of those who framed the Poor Law Amendment Act were clear. Chadwick objected to the notion of the 'parish in business' and argued that the old Poor Law held down productivity. He wanted to drive the able-bodied poor into the open labour market. This would reduce levels of poor relief and provide capital for economic development and increased productivity. The *Report* reflected Chadwick's thinking and established the three main principles of the new system: the workhouse test, 'less eligibility' and administrative centralisation with uniformity of provision. The workhouse test served as the mechanism for putting less eligibility into practice and this, it was argued, would end outdoor relief. Relief would be offered at a lower rate than that of an independent worker and this would remove the attraction of the Poor Law. Chadwick accepted that the old, ill and orphaned needed support. However, he believed that the able-bodied poor did not need looking after and that this was not the intention of the old Poor Law. The *Report* was not concerned with reducing poverty but with deterring pauperism.

The 1834 Poor Law Amendment Act

The Poor Law Amendment Act closely followed the recommendations of the *Report*. It was introduced in April 1834 becoming law in August. Parishes were to be grouped together to form Poor Law unions administered by professional and salaried officials responsible to elected Boards of Guardians. Parishes continued to pay for the relief of their own poor but this would be paid into a common fund administered by the union. In the case of settlement, each parish was responsible for its own paupers. The Act dealt with paupers rather than the poor through the medium of the workhouse test.[11] Unions were subject to the control of the central Poor Law Commission, a three-man body to which Chadwick was appointed secretary.

It was not practical to abolish public relief completely. However, relief for those unwilling to fend for themselves was to be based on the principle of 'less eligibility'. Pauperism resulted from defects of character. These values made a lasting impression for the rest of the century. The

---

[11] **Workhouse test.** This meant that all relief had to be given in the workhouse ending the practice of outdoor relief.

sense of shame at the acceptance of public relief, the stigma of the workhouse and the dread of the pauper's funeral were central features of the attitudes of the working population. The 1834 Act embodied the ideas of the political economists but its opponents could present it as an abuse of the poor.

The 1834 Act was important in three respects. Unlike factory or mine reform the thinking behind the Act was rural rather than urban. This led to a system unsuitable for industrial England and this accounted for the widespread opposition in the north after 1836. The new Poor Law became intensely political, first by the anti-Poor Law agitation and then by the introduction of the electoral principle into Poor Law affairs. The Act took a moral rather than paternalist view of the poor. Finally, it created the first effective element of centralised British bureaucracy with central control and supervision with local administration. The standardising aims of Poor Law Commissioners immediately came into conflict with those who dealt with poverty in the parishes. Localities ignored or evaded the instructions of the Commissioners. In practice, outdoor relief could not be withheld in seasonal employment like agriculture or during trade depressions in industrial centres.

The Act was intended as an attack on the conditions and behaviour of the labouring poor, especially in rural areas. Can this be seen as an expression of middle-class values grounded in political economy? In simplistic terms it probably can, but the relationship between political economy and Poor Law policy was in practice far more complex. Support by the middle-classes for political economy can be easily over-exaggerated and the nature of the trade cycle resulted in their refusal to implement the full rigour of the 1834 Act in their industrial centres. The *Poor Law Report* may have been over-optimistic in believing that uniformity of practice was possible.

The new system was flawed from the outset. Chadwick's original proposals were modified in three important respects as the bill went through Parliament during 1834. Chadwick proposed that the Central Board could ban outdoor relief but the Act only gave permission to 'regulate' it. This opened the way for a retreat towards the old allowance system. He also proposed that the Board should have powers to compel local guardians of the new unions to raise rates to build new workhouses. The Act limited these powers to a maximum of £50 per year or one-tenth of the annual rate. This proved fatal to the system. If the board could not make unions build workhouses, the 'workhouse test' could not be implemented. Finally, Chadwick wanted the law of settlement to be abolished but this was rejected preventing freeing the labour market.

The government followed up its concessions to public opinion by concessions to the old idea of patronage. Patronage was at the heart of government in the 1830s and Chadwick was not appointed one of the three Central Commissioners. Chadwick did persuade the government to accept him as permanent secretary to the Commission with the vague understanding that he would be next in line for promotion. This proved an unworkable solution. Of the three Commissioners, Thomas Frankland Lewis, J.G. Shaw-Lefevre and George Nicholls only the latter sympathised with Chadwick's views. Personal hostility between Chadwick and the Lewises, father and son (George Cornwall Lewis succeeded his father as Commissioner in 1839) meant that from 1837 the Commission paid little attention to Chadwick's advice. The Poor Law administration was divided into two camps. Most of the Assistant Commissioners sided with Chadwick but were under the direction and in the power of the anti-Chadwickian Commission and this had a damaging effect on the administration of the system. Chadwick suffered most with the public holding him responsible for the Commission's policy over which he had no influence.

The Act was not implemented as Chadwick intended but he cannot escape some responsibility for this situation. Chadwick prided himself in the introduction of the 'reign of fact' yet his treatment of the problem of the rural poor was seriously flawed. On critical matters like rural wage rates, actual numbers of unemployed and regional variations, very little reliable data was collected. The *Report* was cast in universal terms but it was really based on rural poverty and even here, the issues were misunderstood. Chadwick had little understanding of the nature of urban poverty or how the old Poor Laws operated in towns and cities. The administrative aspect of his plan also suffered from important weaknesses. The first was the independent status of the Central Board. This total separation from Parliament made the Commission weak, confused and subject to political pressures. Criticism of the new Poor Law was voiced in Parliament where the Commissioners had few supporters. The second weakness was the power still left to local authorities. Chadwick did not fully implement centralisation for two reasons. He believed that a national instead of a local poor rate would be too expensive. He also expected that the self-interest of the local guardians would operate in the interests of his general plan. In fact, this was a recipe for conflict between central and local government.

The fault was not wholly Chadwick's. Central government had removed coercive powers over the local unions from the hands of the Commissioners and this left the 1834 Act far more permissive than previously believed. Despite the important changes from Chadwick's original proposals, much of his work survived and in a few instances, his gravest errors were corrected in practice. Some problems were left unresolved: the political status of the new type of central commission, its relationship to representative local institutions, and central responsibility for the actions of its subordinates. These deficiencies were largely remedied by the Poor Law Amendment Act 1847. The basis of centralisation had been established.

Opposition to the 1834 Act

The old Poor Law provided some flexibility in dealing with poverty and was regarded by many labourers as their right in times of hardship. It was not surprising that the introduction of the 1834 Act provoked widespread hostility and opposition.

Rural opposition

The Act had a relatively easy passage through Parliament but even so there was some opposition. William Cobbett saw it, in his pamphlet *The Legacy to Labourers*, as an attack on the 'right' to relief and an assault on the traditional arrangements between the propertied and the poor. Other saw it as an attack on the independence of local government. Working-class radicals saw it as part of the attack on the livelihood of the poor by a penny-pinching government.

The first reaction to the implementation of the Act came in agricultural areas. There were numerous disturbances in East Anglia and the southern counties. This situation was aggravated by a hard winter that forced many unemployed labourers to apply for relief. Announcements of the implementation of the Act were greeted with hostility. In May 1835, a crowd assembled at Ampthill (Bedfordshire) demanding 'Blood or bread', 'All money' and 'No bread' and dispersed only after the Riot Act was read. In other places, labourers occupied workhouses demanding their customary rights. Attempts to separate male and female paupers under the new regulations were seen as part of a Malthusian plot to stop the poor from breeding. There were also rumours that workhouse food was laced with an anti-fertility substance or even poisoned. The most serious disturbances took place in Suffolk. Anglican clergymen openly opposed the new law and strong local feeling was more evident than in many other parts of the country.

The position of the landed gentry was ambiguous. There was often considerable local sympathy for the rioters and many gentry and parsons petitioned against the Act. Anthony Brundage suggested in the 1970s that there was considerable continuity between the 'old' and 'new' systems. Outdoor relief continued in some rural areas because it was cheaper than the workhouse. The new guardians and Poor Law officials were often the same men who had operated the old system. He also argued that the 1834 Act strengthened the authority of the landed classes. Poor Law Unions were created quickly, despite opposition and used to maintain a largely deferential society. Peter Mandler accepts that the new Poor Law was administered in rural areas for the benefit of , Michael. However, he argues that the landed classes were active agents in the process of modernisation. Many landowners accepted the free market and new attitudes to poverty. Continuity in practice and personnel did not mean continuity of principles. Both laissez-faire and deferential attitudes played a role in the acceptance of the new arrangements in rural England.

The disturbances in southern England demonstrated how sensitive people were to changes in the customary arrangements for poor relief. Reactions varied from locality to locality but there was little serious violence other than some property being damaged and a few people assaulted. However, the disturbances did little to interrupt the implementation of the Act and by mid-1836 the new system was operating across the agricultural south. The rural movement never gained the support or the success it achieved in the North.

Urban opposition

Initially the Act was received favourably by the powerful provincial northern press because it was felt to be irrelevant to the industrial areas where poor rates were much lower than in the south. Implementation in the north from the end of 1836 aroused serious and sometimes violent opposition; much of it organised by Tory radicals such as Michael Sadler[12] and Richard Oastler[13] who attacked the Poor Law as the 'catechism of Hell' and the workhouses as 'bastilles'.[14] These middle-class Tory reformers, already prominent in campaigning for factory reform, provided an organisation against the new Act that the resistance in the south lacked. The campaign stressed the Christian duty of the rich to assist the poor and accepted Cobbett's argument that the Act denied basic rights.

The timing of implementation in the north was unfortunate. It occurred when a trade depression was beginning to affect many of the textile districts, adding to the fears of the manufacturing population, especially the increasingly vulnerable handloom workers. The arrival of the Commissioners often led to violence though the leaders of the movement tried to direct the campaign in a peaceful direction. This was

---

[12] Michael Sadler (1780-1835) was a banker and Tory MP better known for his support for factory reform.

[13] Richard Oastler (1769-1861) was a leading factory reformer and Tory Radical who supported the campaign against the new Poor Law. For him both factory and Poor Law reform were issues that demanded humanitarian solutions.

[14] Bastilles. The Bastille was the French castle in the centre of Paris that was attacked by the Parisian mob on 14 July 1789 signalling the beginnings of the French Revolution. It was seen as a symbol of royal oppression. The workhouses often surrounded by high walls looked like prisons and so acquired the name of the Bastille.

not always possible. In June 1837, a crowd of people wrecked the workhouse in Huddersfield. The sensitivity of the Assistant Commissioner to local circumstances was central to the degree of opposition. In the north-east Sir John Walsham was able to get the new system accepted. By contrast, in Lancashire and the West Riding Charles Mott was more confrontational and this encouraged widespread opposition. The *Halifax Guardian* opposed the Poor Law as 'unEnglish, pernicious and wicked' and published accounts of the ill treatment of the poor. Riots by local ratepayers at Todmorden led to the military having to keep order. The new system was not introduced into Leeds until 1844 and Liverpool was given permission to return to the former system of administering relief under its own local Act. By 1838, the violent phase of resistance had died down. In 1839, the campaign began to disintegrate as working-class resentment was appeased by the continued use of outdoor relief. Increasingly Chartism attracted the more radical supporters of the agitation. The anti-Poor Law movement in the North was a temporary alliance between working and middle-classes against what was seen as an unjust law.

Opposition to the 1834 Act did little to delay its implementation in southern England but in the north, it was more effective. It delayed effective implementation until 1838 and even then, local concessions meant that outdoor relief remained important. The northern campaign demonstrated that exerting pressure through press, pamphlets and meetings was influential. This stands in contrast to the more traditional, less organised and less effective reactions in the agricultural areas.

Operation 1834-1847

The Poor Law Amendment Act was implemented with speed and determination. Nine Assistant Commissioners were appointed rising to sixteen by 1836. By the end of 1835 2,066 parishes had combined to form 112 Unions and by December 1839 13,691 parishes out of some 15,000 had been incorporated into 583 Unions. This left 799 mostly Local Act or Gilbert Act Unions catering for around a tenth of the population of England and Wales over which the Poor Law Commission had no powers. The reduction in costs was considerable. By 1838, the Commissioners reported that the country had been relieved of some £2,300,000 'direct annual taxation'. Although after 1837 costs began to rise, they did not reach the level of 1834. This was a success for those who wanted to reduce costs. For those who saw the 1834 Act as a means of social control there were also claims of success. By 1835, the Commissioners said there was now better relief for the aged, infirm and sick, improvements in educating pauper children and industry and moral habits in the able-bodied.

The southern counties felt the impact of the new Poor Law even before the new Unions were created. Some places took the opportunity to reduce poor relief wholesale. The Uckfield Union in Sussex reduced its costs in one year from £16,643 to £8,733 of which only £5,675 was spent on the poor, the remainder being used to build a workhouse. Immediate reductions occurred in widely separated areas, even if not on the Uckfield scale. In East Yorkshire, expenditure fell by 13 per cent in 1835 and by 27 per cent between 1834 and 1837. Financing the Poor Laws proved difficult and it was not until the 1860s that the move from parish to union rates was finally achieved.

The Commissioners wanted the Unions to consist of a circle of parishes round a market town and some Unions did conform to this pattern. Many did not. Most of Anglesey formed a large Union of 53 parishes while five parishes in the east of the island were attached to Caernarfon to which they were linked by ferry and 16 more were attached to Bangor across the Menai straits. In some rural areas, Assistant Commissioners only got the support of the landed aristocracy and gentry by drawing the boundaries of Unions round their estates. There were therefore considerable differences in the size, shape, population and wealth of the Unions. Far from uniformity, the 1834 Act inaugurated a period of considerable diversity and experiment in local administrative areas.

Administrative services

The success of central policies depended on the Poor Law Union officials. The new government service included Clerks to the Boards, Relieving Officers, Workhouse Masters and Medical Officers. Some of these posts were part-time and the salaries varied according to the size and population of the Union. The leading officials were the Relieving Officer and Workhouse Master, sometimes one person holding two posts. The Relieving Officer decided the fate of applicants for relief and was also supposed to supervise outdoor relief. The Workhouse Master ran the House. He served two masters, the Commission and the Board of Guardians, who frequently issued conflicting orders. He was required to meet the demands of Medical Officers for the supply and treatment of pauper patients. He needed to be of moral character and the Commissioners hoped that the Guardians would use their powers of patronage to appoint both Relieving Officers and Workhouse Masters from the police or military. Even so, between 1835 and 1841 ninety Relieving Officers were dismissed for theft, neglect of duty, misconduct or drunkenness.

Similar problems occurred in establishing professional Poor Law medical services. Initially the Commissioners encouraged Unions to offer part-time medical posts but this led to many complaints of neglect and ill treatment before the Select Committee of 1837. After this, Unions appointed qualified doctors at reasonable wages. From 1842, when the first General Medical Order was issued, attempts were made by the Commissioners to regulate the service. Unions were divided into medical districts each with its own Medical Officer. Workhouse infirmaries did provide indoor medical treatment and increased in number but they were often overcrowded and without adequate equipment or staff. They failed to improve until 1867, when the Metropolitan Poor Law Act, began to take the London infirmaries out of Union control.

The workhouses

The well-regulated workhouse was the centrepiece of the new system. Creating the Poor Law Unions occurred with few problems, but the building of workhouses was far more contentious. The Poor Law Commission could order the extension of existing workhouses but could not insist on the building of new ones. 350 workhouses had been built largely in southern England in the 1830s. There was far more resistance in the industrial north and in parts of Wales. The Leeds Guardians, for instance, refused to build a new workhouse until 1859. The building of workhouses in North Wales was delayed with the Caernarfon Guardians putting up determined opposition.

Chadwick never intended that the deterrent workhouse test should apply to all. He intended to build new workhouses for orphans, the old and infirm while driving the able-bodied to provide for themselves and their families. Existing parish workhouses were to be included in the Unions for the separate treatment of classified paupers, the old, the young and the able-bodied. He hoped to extend this principle to the separate housing of lunatics, the blind and other special categories. This proved impractical and a single large Union workhouse was more efficient with the result that the 'deserving poor' were treated little different from the 'undeserving' able-bodied.

The Commissioners never planned that workhouses should be places of repression for the able-bodied. Nevertheless, the inmates were put to heavy work, subjected to draconian discipline including banning tobacco and alcohol and men were separated from women. The workhouses were intended to be *'prisons without crime'*. Dietaries published by the Commissioners were sufficient and took notice of local eating habits but food was stodgy and monotonous. Even so, Anne Digby argues that the six published dietaries meant that inmates were better fed than agricultural labourers in southern England. Inmates had to wear workhouse uniform but the Commissioners resisted the attempts of some

Guardians to clothe unmarried mothers in yellow as a badge of shame. The picture of a stern and uniform regime in the workhouse belies the facts. Just how cruel workhouses were is a question obscured by propaganda and myth. They were often overcrowded but their nature varied. The character of the Master and Matron, the Union boards and the regional Assistant Poor Law Commissioner was crucial. If they were insensitive, this reinforced 'cruelty' in the minds of working people. The new workhouses were less crowded and insanitary than those built before 1834. The most resented deterrent effect of the new Poor Law, and the most obvious contrast with the old system was the strict monotonous workhouse routine and the increasing stigma attached to pauper status.

The Andover Scandal

The workhouse test was the feature of the 1834 legislation that caught the attention of contemporary opinion. This was unfortunate since over 80 per cent of paupers were on outdoor relief. In 1837, 11 per cent of all paupers had been workhouse inmates; by 1844 the figure was no more than 15 per cent.

The Victorian workhouse was faced with the impossible task of providing a refuge for the impotent while deterring the scrounger. This dismal view corresponded to that of contemporary critics of the 1830s and 1840s such as *The Times* and the novelist Charles Dickens. The picture of the workhouse presented by its early opponents suggested a life of horror. For even the mildly awkward, there were savage beatings and solitary confinement in the most unsuitable of cells. For the majority, existence was endured on a starvation diet, families were ruthlessly separated, accommodation was overcrowded and unhealthy and daily life was a monotonous routine supervised by unsympathetic officials. Finally, for those who died in the workhouse, the end was a pauper burial without dignity or respect. For the modern historian, the picture is no longer entirely a study in black. Most historians accept the conclusions of David Roberts that the sensational stories of cruelties were either false or the result of survivals from the former regime. In a number of cases, such as the flogging of young girls at the Hoo Workhouse or the scandal at Andover, the local authority could be shown to have ignored the directives of the central authority. However, this did not entirely excuse the inadequacy of the supervision that allowed such things to take place.

The Andover scandal was not unique but it was highly publicised and used by those opposed to the new system. Bone crushing was used in some workhouses as a 'useful' occupation for paupers. Sir Robert Peel's Home Secretary, Sir James Graham, disapproved but Commissioner George Nicholls was a great enthusiast. Andover was regarded as a model union. Outdoor relief was stopped as soon as the workhouse was opened and it was one of the few unions not to relax this rule during the 'great freeze' of January 1838. At Andover, work was hard, discipline strict and diet scanty. This was due to the choice of ex-sergeant Colin M'Dougal, a veteran of Waterloo, as workhouse master and his wife, Mary Ann, as matron. Attempts to end bone crushing at Andover in December 1844 were voted down by the chairman of the local Guardians and his supporters. However, ugly rumours began to circulate that inmates were eating the marrow from the decomposing bones. The Guardians took no action. Hugh Mundy, a local farmer frequently at odds with his colleagues went public. He turned to the local MP Thomas Wakley, who on Friday 1 August 1845, rose to ask the Home Secretary about paupers eating bone marrow at Andover. Sir James Graham replied that he could not believe this but promised to institute an enquiry. The following day Henry Parker, the Assistant Commissioner responsible for Andover, was sent to find out the facts.

His enquiry began on Monday 4 August 1845 and by the next day, he could report back to London that the charges were true. On 14 August Parker was instructed to investigate any alleged 'neglect or misconduct on the part of the Master or officers of the workhouse'. M'Dougal offered his resignation on 29 September but when Parker, now summoned back to London, suggested consulting the Commission's solicitors about prosecution the lawyers advised against it. The Commission was left with a hostile press, a critical Parliament, a seriously alarmed public and no scapegoat. Parker now found himself cast in this role. When he drafted a letter from the Board to the Andover Guardians, he was accused of trying to throw the blame on the Commissioners. On 16 October, Parker was asked to resign. If the Commissioners felt that they had saved themselves by dismissing Parker, they were mistaken. The former Assistant Commissioner published a long pamphlet in his own defence indicting his recent superiors, and his case was rapidly taken up by a group of anti-Poor Law MPs.

The public were unhappy about Parker's dismissal and the Commission made matters worse by ordering another Assistant Commissioner, William Day, to resign because he had been ill for several weeks after falling down some steps. This provided too valuable an opportunity for Edwin Chadwick, still bitter about his treatment by the Commission, who encouraged MPs to keep the issue alive. On 8 November 1845, the Poor Law Commissioners acknowledged the justice of the attacks made on bone crushing by issuing a General Order forbidding it. This came too late. Public opinion was seriously alarmed. On 5 March 1846, a Select Committee of the House of Commons was established to investigate the Andover scandal, the conduct of the Poor Law Commissioners and the circumstances surrounding Parker's resignation. The fifteen members of the 'Andover committee'--including three well-known opponents of the workhouse, John Fielden, Thomas Wakley and Benjamin Disraeli--began work two weeks later. For the next three and a half months, they heard evidence from witnesses and their words were reported at length in the press. The New Poor Law, the Whigs who had created it and the gentry who administered it were on trial.

The *Report* was published in August 1846 and was a scathing indictment of everyone involved. The government announced that it proposed to take no action but it had privately decided that the Commission must go, partly to placate public opinion but also because it had done its work. The poor rates had been cut; outdoor relief for the able-bodied had been reduced and almost the whole country had been unionised. The time had come when 'the three kings of Somerset House', as the Poor Law Commissioners had been nicknamed by their critics, could safely be replaced by a body with fewer powers and directly responsible to Parliament. When the Act that had extended the life of the Poor Law Commission ran out in 1847 it was not renewed. Legislation set up a new body, the Poor Law Board.

Further reform

The effectiveness of the workhouse test in the north was never really tested. From 1837 to 1842, Britain lay in the grip of hunger and industrial depression and the new Poor Law was impossible to operate as Chadwick intended. Opposition to the Poor Law became a central theme of Chartism and it undertook a ceaseless campaign against the Commissioners. It was soon clear that outdoor relief could not be abolished. This was recognised in 1842 when the Commission devised the Labour Test Order allowing outdoor relief as long as some work was done. The problem was that the 1842 Order contradicted the General Order of 1841 and the Outdoor Relief Prohibitory Order of 1844 issued to end outdoor relief in the southern unions. This led to considerable confusion. Increasingly the balance moved away from unions abandoning outdoor relief and this was acknowledged in 1852. It is clear that the principles of 1834 were not widely applied. The workhouse test was generally being ignored with even the rural unions moving against it from the 1840s on the grounds of cost.

The Commission was given five more years of life in 1842 but its days were numbered. Criticism gained strength from a series of mistakes, epidemics and scandals provoking public demands for reform of the worst abuses. In 1842, the first scandal led to the withdrawal of the rule imposing silence at all meals; the bringing together of families separated into male, female and infant; and the first attempts to separate prostitutes, lunatics and infected persons from the general body of paupers. The Andover scandal of 1845-1846 was the last straw. When the Commission came up for renewal once more in 1847, it was swept aside. The 1847 Act set up a new board consisting of a president, accountable as a member of government to Parliament, and two secretaries, one of whom might be an MP. The 1847 Act had two great merits. It remedied the weakness caused by the old board's independent status. The government was now genuinely responsible and there was a proper channel between the board and Parliament. It also stilled the long agitation against the new Poor Law and mean that the new board could undertake a common-sense policy of gradual improvement in peace. It was aided in this by the improved economic situation and by the fact that the laws of settlement were also swept away in 1847.

Conclusion

It is important to distinguish between the reality and rhetoric of the New Poor Law. The principles established in the 1834 Act were applied but the Commission could not impose these principles and outdoor relief persisted. The 'new' system was essentially a compromise. On major policy issues--the ending of outdoor relief, the imposition of the workhouse test, the uniformity of organisation--central government was compelled to accept the continued existence of local practices. The reality of relief after 1834 was that it was both a deterrent and a provider of humane relief.

14 Chadwick and public health 1830-1854

William, Sproat, a keelsman from Sunderland was not well known. Yet his death on Wednesday 26 October 1831 had a dramatic impact on contemporary society. On the previous Saturday believing he was recovering from an attack of diarrhoea and, against his doctor's advice he ate a mutton chop for dinner. He then walked to his boat but returned home with violent stomach cramps. When Mr Holmes, his doctor visited him on the Sunday morning he was clearly very ill. Later that day Holmes consulted two other doctors and they agreed that Sproat had Asiatic cholera. Others may already have died that summer in Sunderland but local doctors either did not recognise the disease or were reluctant to admit that cholera had finally arrived. The numbers who died of cholera during the four epidemics of 1831-1832, 1848-1849, 1853-1854 and 1866 were small compared those killed by many other contemporary diseases. However, cholera was the shock disease of the century. The *Quarterly Review* saw it as 'one of the most terrible pestilences which have ever desolated the earth'.

Why was the urban population vulnerable to epidemic diseases?

The problem of public health was made worse by the rapid industrialisation and urbanisation of the late-eighteenth and early-nineteenth centuries. In 1801, there were only fourteen towns with more than 25,000 people but this rose to forty-one by 1841. Friedrich Engels[1] wrote in his *The Condition of the Working-class in England* (1844),

> 'What is true of London, is true of Manchester, Birmingham, and Leeds, is true of all great towns. Everywhere barbarous indifference, hard egotism on one hand and nameless misery on the other, everywhere social warfare, every man's house in a state of siege, everywhere reciprocal plundering under the protection of the law....'

Alexis de Tocqueville, the French social critic, noted a decade earlier,

> 'At Manchester a few great capitalists, thousands of poor workmen and little middle-class. At Birmingham, few large industries, many small industrialists. At

---

[1] Friedrich Engels (1820-1895) was the son of a German cotton manufacturer. He worked in the family owned cotton mill in Manchester and in 1842 met Karl Marx, forming a life-long working partnership with him. His study of the working-classes gave a highly critical account.

Manchester workmen are counted by the thousand.... At Birmingham the workers work in their own houses or in little workshops in company with the master himself.... the working people of Birmingham seem more healthy, better off, more orderly and more moral than those of Manchester [where] civilised man is turned back almost into a savage.'

How unhealthy was it to live in cities and why?

It was unhealthy to live in Victorian cities, though chances of illness and premature death varied considerably. Who you were, which social class you came from, where you lived, how much you earned and how well you were fed mattered. Contemporary opinion was most concerned about infectious diseases. Diseases like typhus and influenza killed large numbers of people in both rural and urban areas but particularly affected the young and malnourished of the urban slums. Smallpox became less important, in part because of vaccination developed by Edward Jenner in the 1790s. Typhus and typhoid fever were endemic in London and epidemics occurred in all major towns in 1817-1819, 1826-1827, 1831-1832, and 1837 and in 1846-1847 coinciding with periods of slump and high unemployment.

As towns grew, polluted water became a pressing problem and was the cause of many diseases such as infantile diarrhoea, dysentery and typhoid fever and especially cholera. Infectious diseases like tuberculosis, typhus and cholera were concentrated mainly in inner city slum districts.[2] Contaminated water and food also spread cholera. Michael Flinn commented, 'Cholera struck swiftly and sharply, raising local death rates dramatically, if ephemerally. Cholera frightened people.' It was, however, because cholera sometimes spread to middle- and upper-class areas that it was more deeply feared.

What was the impact of such high rates of infectious disease? Children were particularly vulnerable especially from the effects of diarrhoea and dysentery, diphtheria, whooping cough, scarlet fever and measles. Infant mortality remained high and by the end of the nineteenth century still accounted for a quarter of all deaths. Death rates, already high in most towns, went up in the 1830s and 1840s: from about 19 per 1,000 in 1831 to 22.4 per 1,000 by 1838 and over 25 per 1,000 in 1849, a cholera year. The figures for individual towns were starker. In 1831, the

---

[2] Typhus, spread by body lice mainly to adults. Endemic in the nineteenth century, it became epidemic during economic depressions and poverty crises and was strongly associated with poor living conditions. Spread by a bacillus through droplet infection from coughs or saliva, tuberculosis is not highly contagious but its spread is encouraged by a combination of poverty, malnutrition and overcrowded living conditions. Though not immune, the middle-classes were better able to withstand tuberculosis than the poor, malnourished working-class.

death rate for Bristol was 16.9 per 1,000 rising to 31 per 1,000 by 1841. There were also marked differences in the average age of death between professional, trade and labouring populations. In 1842, Chadwick found that in Liverpool these figures were 35, 22 and 15 years respectively compared to rural Rutland's 52, 41 and 38 years. Death was only one of the effects of disease. For a poor family struggling to pay rent and buy food, illness (whether fatal or not) imposed additional strains. There were medical bills to pay, medicines to buy, extra heating costs; and the problem of childcare if the mother was taken ill. There is little doubt that the high level and concentration of infectious disease was a significant extra burden for working-class families in the Victorian city.

Why were housing and clean water a problem?

The influx of working people into growing towns created a housing crisis. Back-to-back houses, cellar dwellings and cheap, poorly built housing of various kinds were built but supply could not keep up with demand. In Birmingham, an affluent skilled worker might live in a two or three storey houses with two rooms on each floor with an associated yard and workshop. However, few workers could afford such rents and many houses were multi-occupied by 1830. Working-class families frequently lived in a single room or cellar without proper sanitation or water supply and paid 2-3 shillings per week rent. Lodging houses were common in London, and in the poorest districts as many as 15 people would sleep in one room, each paying 1 or 2 pence for a night's shelter. Contemporaries tended to focus on the horrors of urban living but the situation was little different for the rural poor. There were rural as well as urban slums. The main difference was the density of urban living. Living literally on top of or beneath neighbours in a multi-occupied[3] house or tenement was a new experience for many requiring major adjustments in lifestyles and daily routines.

The major problem was that most new houses did not have an adequate drainage, sewage and water supply. By the late 1820s, for instance, the Thames had become highly polluted. A witness told a Royal Commission of 1828 that 'Scarcely a week passes but the carcass of one or more dead dogs is deposited within a short distance of my residence.' Despite this the water companies[4] continued to praise the state of the river. A medical spokesman for the Great Junction Company said that 'The impregnating ingredients of the Thames are as perfectly harmless as any spring-water of the purest kind used in common life: indeed, there is

---

[3] Multi-occupied houses had more than one family living in them.
[4] Water companies were private organisations that provided water to houses at a price.

probably not a spring, with the exception of Malvern, and one or two more, which are so pure as Thames water.' The problem of London's water culminated in the 'great stink' of 1858. The Duke of Newcastle had sounded the alarm a year earlier in July 1857 warning that 'the river was like a vast sewer, and unless something was done before long to purify it, it would engender some frightful plague among the two and a half million who inhabited the metropolis.' A year later there were suddenly 'strange stories flying of men struck down with the stench and of all kinds of fatal diseases, upspringing on the river's banks.' Parliament took action. The experience of London was paralleled in many industrial towns where rivers were invariably open sewers. Unpolluted water was in short supply.

What were the major constraints on public health reform?

Before 1835 many of the growing industrial towns did not have a town council. Where councils existed, they were often inefficient and unaccountable for the ways in which they used the local rates. In some towns power was in the hands of the parish vestry that was elected by property owners. Local communities in the 1830s and 1840s had little effective control over building, sewers and the piping of water. The 'improvement commissioners' appointed under a local Improvement Act undertook reform of the cleaning and lighting streets. By 1830, there were about 350 of these in around two hundred of the boroughs or municipal corporations. The problem was that each Commission dealt with a specific area of health not the whole package. Each borough remained separate and did not share joint responsibilities. There was confusion and lack of co-ordination.[5]

The rapid growth of urban population outstretched the abilities of this unreformed system. Reform began with the Municipal Corporations Act 1835. It provided for elections of town councils every three years by ratepayers but contained no specific proposals with regard to public health. It did, however, allow rates to be levied for street lighting, fresh water supply and sewage disposal but this took a local Act of Parliament. The chaotic nature of local government made effective reform difficult. Added to this was self-interest. Water companies and builders were in search of profit. Builders exploited demands for cheap housing and paid little attention to drainage, ventilation or water supply. Private landlords were reluctant to pay for sanitary improvements largely because of the cost

---

[5] Local Acts of Parliament, like the Liverpool Municipal Act of 1846 were passed by Parliament to deal with problems in a particular place. They were private pieces of legislation and were often introduced on behalf of the local urban council by a local MP.

and their reluctance to accept responsibility for the health of the working-classes.

Much as they might have wished, neither local nor national politicians could ignore urban living conditions. Whose responsibility was public health? At the local level, there were groups concerned to improve their own conditions and the outbreak of cholera was a significant spur to action. The central state was, however, reluctant to become involved in public health reform and did so only as the result of outbreaks of epidemics. The laissez-faire attitudes of the period meant that central government did little except when pressed. The outbreak of cholera in 1831 led to the creation of the Central Board of Health and 1,200 local boards. The Cholera Act 1832 allowed local boards to finance anti-cholera measures from the poor rates. Finally, the Public Health Act 1848 occurred in part as a result of the return of cholera.

There was an increasing amount of statistical and other information on the nature of urban conditions. Such evidence was, however, unlikely on its own to persuade local ratepayers to spend money improving housing and sanitation for the working-class. National politicians believed that poor living conditions could lead to mass disturbances and urban violence. The impact of cholera in 1832 and 1848 brought home, especially to the middle-classes, the fact that disease could affect all classes. The poor were blamed for the disease, but it was in the interests of the middle-classes to improve conditions and prevent it recurring. Intervention was also justified through economic self-interest. Reducing levels of disease would bring about a more efficient workforce and therefore benefit industrialists and entrepreneurs.

Why reform took so long

There were, however, important constraints. Who should be responsible for public health? Who should bear the cost of reform? What should the relationship between central policy making and local government? Public health reform was slow in coming for a variety of reasons.

There were major technical problems associated with a lack of medical understanding of disease and the need to develop correct civil engineering solutions. Understanding that germs caused disease did not become widespread until the 1870s and 1880s. People did not have to know why the cesspool and the soil-heap caused disease; they only had to establish the right connection to produce the right conclusion, namely nuisance removal. More important were the civil engineering problems involved in providing a pure water supply and removing liquid sewage. There was a tension between the politicians, who were responsible for finding local solutions to problems, and who lacked the necessary technical expertise, and the 'experts' themselves. This led to conflict not over whether reform was necessary but how reform should best be accomplished.

The problem of cost was the second reason why reform was delayed. A Leeds Councillor commented that, 'The people were more solicitous [concerned] about draining rates from their pockets than draining the streets.' Sewage was not a popular subject and resources for it were scarce. Economy was important for local government. This cut across party lines and could, as in the case of Leeds in the 1840s, limit local action. Concern about the high cost of public health was linked to the question of who should pay. This raised important ideological questions. If social amenities were paid for from the rates then there was a redistribution of wealth via local taxation. The few were funding reform for the benefit of all. Property owners objected to paying twice. They spent money for their own sanitary needs and then were asked to pay taxes to provide for the needs of their neighbours. There was also a question of how far the rights of individual property owners should be infringed in the public interest. Building regulations involved limiting individual liberty in ways many people found unacceptable.

The debate was decided on largely political grounds. At local level, there were four broad groupings: the council itself, property owners, ratepayers and vested interests like water companies. Councils were often concerned to bring public health under one administrative body. This brought conflict with existing municipal organisations like water commissioners, improvement commissioners and commissioners for sewers. Property owners saw their property rights being attacked. Ratepayers often objected to the rising cost of local taxation and commercial organisations were resistant to any change that affected their profitability. Local disagreements about who should wield power with regard to public health were dominated by the wider debate about the proper role of the central state. The different local bodies may have been unable to reach agreement on the issue but immediately united when threatened by central government. Communities would have no control over spending and they knew their own problems best. Local democracy would be threatened. The constraints affecting public health were not fully resolved until the 1860s and 1870s. By then, many of the civil engineering problems had been resolved. There was a growing recognition, locally and nationally, that public health could only be established if there was a national approach to the problem.

How was public health reformed?

Local authorities had been aware of the problems to public health posed by poor sanitation and housing from the late eighteenth century. By the 1830s there were a significant number of local surveys that identified the threat to health caused by the urban environment including James Kay's famous survey of Manchester, *The Moral and Physical Conditions of the Working-classes*, published in 1832.

It was not until the 1840s that the largest cities obtained locals act to deal with their own problems. The alternative was central government legislation. The 1842 Leeds Improvement Act arose in part from an attempt to avoid the provisions of national legislation. Manchester and all the other major cities followed suit. The 1844 Manchester Police Regulation Act strengthened the powers of the corporation over public health. Leeds needed a further act in 1848 to build a sewerage system and Manchester obtained a further ten acts before 1858. The most important advances were, however, made in the Liverpool Sanitary Act of 1846. This effectively made the corporation a health authority and allowed it to appoint an engineer, an Inspector of Nuisances and in W. H. Duncan, the country's first Medical Officer of Health. These three cities also addressed the problem of water supplies. In 1837, Leeds brought half the town's water supply under public control and the remainder in 1852. In 1847, Liverpool purchased the town's private water companies and Manchester began work on its Longdendale reservoir scheme. In 1848, the City of London followed suit and appointed Sir John Simon as its Medical Officer of Health. Control over public health was, in these cities, kept firmly in local hands.

Local authorities approached public health provision in the 1840s in the following ways. They were unwilling to accept centrally imposed legislation like the 1848 Public Health Act. They dealt with public health problems though solutions were often an uneasy combination of appeasing vested interests, keeping down costs and maintaining council control. Finally, there is little evidence of long-term planning by councils. However, the development of long-term strategies for improving the public's health demanded national policies.

Intervention at national level

During the 1840s there were two contradictory trends in public health policy. Some people wanted to extend central control. Others wished to call a halt to further change. The public health movement had to operate against the pressures produced by these opposing forces. The campaign for improving urban conditions was dominated by Chadwick who put forward sanitary policies that tried to tackle all aspects of the problem. He thought out an administrative structure at both central and local levels that was intelligently related to basic environmental and geographical factors. This comprehensive planning won him a number of enemies. Any such plan was bound to antagonise powerful vested interests especially local government, landlords and the water companies. The plans suffered from Chadwick's dogmatic style and showed his usual inability to compromise or to modify his ideas. Policy development went through several phases between the late 1830s and 1848.

Awakening political interest

The creation of the Poor Law Commission in 1834 and the office of Registrar-General in 1837-1838 resulted in national statistical evidence on the issue of public health.[6] Chadwick based his *Poor Law Report* on abuses within the old Poor Law system and assumed that by imposing the workhouse test the cost of poor relief would fall. He found, however, in his first few years as secretary to the Poor Law Commission that a significant proportion of relief was given to widows and children whose male breadwinner had died often from some disease. Chadwick concluded that needless ill-health and death had the effect of increasing the cost of relief. This led directly to his 1842 *Report.*

The first step was to produce evidence that could not be challenged. In 1838, government auditors would not allow spending by guardians in the East End of London on improving local sanitary conditions. Lord John Russell, the Home Secretary, asked the Poor Law Commission for its comments on the links between disease and environment in the worst areas of London. Following reports into the sanitary conditions in East London in 1838, in 1839 the House of Lords established an inquiry into sanitary conditions under Chadwick's chairmanship.

Chadwick sought to obtain as much information as possible. Questionnaires were sent to Poor Law assistant commissioners. About a thousand boards of guardians and relieving officers provided evidence. Prison officers, employers, rural and urban doctors added a further dimension. Chadwick himself visited the main places mentioned in the *Report.* This was the most comprehensive survey of public health to date

---

[6] The Registration of Births, Marriages and Deaths Act 1836 resulted in the introduction of civil registration for England and Wales. From 1 July 1837 copies of entries for births, marriages and deaths have been placed in the General Register Office run by the Registrar General. William Farr (1807-1883), though he never held the post of Registrar General, played a leading role in the development of public health policy until the 1870s with his work on mortality as the Compiler of Abstracts from 1839. Civil registration was not introduced in Scotland until 1855.

and the *Report on the Sanitary Conditions of the Labouring Population of Great Britain* was produced in July 1842.[7]

The 1842 Sanitary Report

The 1842 *Sanitary Report* made a deep impression on public opinion and some 100,000 copies were sold within a year. It represented a damning indictment of the sanitary condition of Britain. Several points stood out. The statistical evidence collected showed a clear link between disease and environmental conditions and established a close correlation between poor housing, poor sewerage and water supplies with high levels of disease, high death rates and low life expectancy. Chadwick demonstrated that social evils were the result of insanitary living conditions and maintained that low morals standards--prostitution, crime and drunkenness--were the result of the physical environment not the other way around.

Chadwick believed that disease was carried by impurities in the atmosphere (the miasmic theory) and that the great problem was to get rid of impurities before they could decompose.[8] He put it briefly: 'All smell is, if it be intense, immediate acute disease'. The key to the whole problem, for Chadwick, was the provision of a sufficient supply of pure water driven through pipes at high pressure. This would provide both drinking water and make it easier to cleanse houses and streets. Manure could be collected in towns and used as fertiliser in the surrounding fields.

It was the very completeness of his solution that presented problems. Many water companies provided water only on certain days a week and at certain times. They did not provide it in either the quantity or at the pressure that Chadwick desired. Many houses in poorer districts had no water supply at all and no proper means of sewage disposal. Where sewers did exist, they were often very badly designed. Chadwick wished to replace the large brick-arched constructions with smaller egg-shaped types

---

[7] A draft of the report was sent to John Stuart Mill, the leader of the Benthamites. He was very critical and Chadwick benefited from his analysis when revising the work.

[8] The Royal College of Physicians did not share this view. Though germs had not yet been isolated, many doctors in the 1850s believed they existed. They believed in the theory of contagion and concluded that dirt and smells were harmless. They regarded the views of sanitary reformers as unscientific. We now know that germs do exist and that they breed faster in dirty conditions. In the early 1850s neither theory could be proved and each appeared to exclude the other.

developed by John Roe.[9] In addition to his first two basic ideas, Chadwick maintained that central direction should be combined with efficient local organisation.

The contrast between political reaction to the *Poor Law Report* in 1834 and reaction to his 1842 *Report* was unmistakable. In 1834 legislation rapidly followed the Report with Chadwick putting into effect the widely-held views of an important cross-section of society. In 1842, his views ran ahead of public and political opinion. It was four years before the first national public health laws were passed and six to produce the comprehensive legislation Chadwick envisaged. His *Report* marked the beginning of a lengthy process.

Towards comprehensive legislation

The *Report* hit its target. Opinion was outraged. In 1843 Chadwick published a report on interments,[10] arguing for the separation of burial grounds from urban areas. Chadwick's vision of a more hygienic England impressed the House of Lords. He played an important, if unofficial role in the Royal Commission on the Sanitary State of Large Towns and Populous Districts (1844-1845). Other developments helped Chadwick to spread his public health message. Southwood Smith helped organise the Health of Towns Association, a pressure group founded in December 1844. By now the public health controversy had polarised into what contemporaries called 'The Clean Party' who favoured reform and those against it, 'The Dirty Party' or 'Muckabites'.

Sir Robert Peel's government had other problems in 1845 and 1846 over the Corn Laws. Chadwick's ambitious scheme was not a priority at this time of major political upheaval. Government action was limited apart from two minor and largely ineffective pieces of legislation in 1846--the Nuisances Removal and Diseases Prevention Act that allowed JPs to prosecute those responsible for nuisances and the Baths and Washhouses Act. Both were permissive legislation and many local authorities simply ignored them. The following year the Town Improvement Clauses Act and the Town Police Clauses Act defined the obligations of towns to lay water supplies and main drainage schemes and to control nuisances.[11] Reform proved difficult but increasingly Chadwick's vision gained support. In 1847, Lord Morpeth attempted to introduce a comprehensive public health bill but it aroused so much opposition it failed. The

---

[9] John Roe was engineer to the Holborn and Finsbury Commission of Sewers. His advice was that drains should be closed pipes not open and that sewers should be capable of being flushed with water to prevent them silting up.

[10] Interments are burials in graveyards.

[11] Nuisances were public health hazards like insanitary drains.

following year he re-introduced the bill, this time successfully. It was again attacked by vested interests and those opposed to centralisation and loss of local democracy led by Joshua Toulmin Smith. The debate was not whether action was necessary but who should take it. As a result, the scope of the 1848 legislation was reduced.

The 1848 Public Health Act

The 1848 Act established a General Board of Health limited to five years with three Commissioners (Lord Morpeth, Lord Shaftesbury and Chadwick, with Southwood Smith as Medical Officer). Local Boards of Health could be established if ten percent of ratepayers petitioned the Central Board or would be set up in towns where the death rate was higher than 23 per thousand. The Local Boards of Health would take over the powers of water companies and drainage commissioners. They were given wide powers to deal with sewage and drainage; to ensure that streets were swept, watered and repaired; to erect public conveniences and to clean and purify 'unwholesome houses'. They could levy a rate and had the power to appoint a salaried Medical Officer. They also had the power to pave streets etc. but this was not compulsory.

The implementation of the Act appeared to be straightforward. It was clear and unambiguous and had widespread public support. So what went wrong? There were several important weaknesses in the Act. The life span of the General Board was limited to five years and it was an advisory and co-ordinating body rather than an initiator of reform. It could force local authorities to act but only if there was a public petition or high mortality rates. The cholera epidemic of 1848 and 1849 reinforced the argument for central action but it caught the Board unprepared for the demands of the task. The Internment Act of 1850 that gave the General Board of Health power to construct and manage public cemeteries illustrates its problems. There was furious opposition to the legislation and there were constant battles with the Treasury over even minor items of spending. It was permissive in character and most towns did not take advantage of the Act. The large cities by-passed the legislation by obtaining private acts of Parliament and so avoided central interference. London was not affected by the legislation and by 1850 it was clear that the government was not prepared to extend the powers of the General Board to cover the capital city. This proved a major weakness of political will and represented a major setback for Chadwick's case for comprehensive reform.

The cholera epidemic of 1848-1849 led politicians, locally and nationally to take health seriously and gave the 1848 Act more significance than might otherwise have been the case. However, as the experience of Chester illustrates, the relationship between the epidemic and action is difficult to define and attitudes soon changed. Even so *The Times* commented in June 1852, 'The cholera has departed out of sight and mind and we have relapsed into indifference or something beyond. Everything we ought to have done, we have left undone.' In fact, the scale of the General Board's operations was modest. Only 182 local boards were established by 1854 and only thirteen had begun work on waterworks and sewerage schemes. In Lancashire only 26 townships took advantage of the Act and by 1858 only 400,000 of the county's 2.5 million people came under Boards of Health.

The litmus test for the new policies took place in London. A new Metropolitan Commission of Sewers was set up in December 1847. Chadwick was a leading member. From the outset, bitter rivalries in the Commission between Chadwick, the representatives of the old sewer commissions and the parish vestries prevented reform. In 1850, Chadwick changed tack and encouraged the setting up of a Royal Commission on the Sanitation in London. It considered competition between the eight water companies recommending their abolition and that the Thames should no longer act as a supply of drinking water. The government was not prepared to implement the full report such was the opposition. In 1850, the General Board was given half of the London area to control. A Water Bill in 1851 was to complete the process but the Treasury refused to advance the £250,000 necessary for the purchase of the private water companies. The Metropolitan Water Supply Act 1852 left provision entirely in the hands of water companies.

There was growing opposition to the General Board in the country as a whole. Lord Seymour, who was hostile to Chadwick, replaced Lord Morpeth on the General Board in March 1850. He had few supporters in the House of Commons and a growing number of opponents especially Sir Benjamin Hall, champion of local democracy and Thomas Wakley, the editor of *The Lancet*. *The Times* orchestrated feelings against the Board and Chadwick. The Central Board should have ended in 1853 but was given a year's extension because of the return of cholera. Chadwick knew that the 'Dirty Party' was intent on his destruction. He produced a report on what had been achieved but was critical of the various vested interests. Opposition to the General Board of Health piled up. Hostility from town councils, private cemeteries and water companies, landlords, ratepayers, in Parliament and from *The Times* and *Punch* focused on Chadwick who was seen as trying to 'bully the nation into cleanliness'. Chadwick was dismissed in 12 August 1854 and never held public office again. The General Board continued but it had ceased to have any real influence once Chadwick had gone. In 1858, it was abolished and replaced by a Medical Department of the Privy Council. This body continued the statistical work begun by the General Board of Health.

Why had Chadwick achieved so little by 1854?

The legacy of Chadwick's involvement in public health falls into two broad areas. In one he was, within limits, successful. In the other he achieved little. Chadwick had considerable success in establishing the case for involving the state, locally or nationally in sanitary reform. His 1842 *Report* conclusively established the link between filth and disease and his role as propagandist for public health reform in the 1840s was of immense importance. However, his practical achievements were minimal. This was in part because of the scale of the task and the strength of the vested interests that opposed him.

His own personality also contributed to his ultimate failure. His inflexibility and inability to persuade others of his reforms made it impossible for many to follow his ideas. Many fellow workers who shared his hatred of squalor, muddle and incompetence contributed to the development of his ideas. Chadwick believed that once the 'facts' were established and solutions revealed then opposition would evaporate. In this he was politically naïve. He had little understanding of how the political system worked or that support for public health policies needed to be of political advantage to government. Finer quotes him as saying, 'By all means have a Minister–but only as the defender of the chief permanent officers.' His determination that 'the British world should be clean and live a century' was a 'fact' others, at least in the short term, contested. Chadwick was 54 when he was dismissed and lived until he was 90 but he was, as Finer says in the nine-page chapter that covers nearly forty years of his life, 'The Spent Prophet'. In his old age, a member of the Political Economy Club commented that Chadwick babbled 'not of green fields, but of sewage'.

Public health was far more complex than the pioneers of the 1840s had envisaged. For Chadwick public health was simply a matter of better sanitation and water supply and his single-minded pursuit of these issues reflected his inability to take account of views different to his own. The problem had far wider environmental causes--pressure of population, bad housing and poor nutrition--and Chadwick consistently underestimated the importance of medical questions, especially what could be achieved by preventative medicine. The Sanitary Act of 1866 represents an appropriate epilogue to the work of the General Board of Health. It placed all the responsibilities of the 1848 Act squarely on local authorities. It was mandatory but there was no central control and no inspectorate. There was little opposition as there was a greater public awareness of public health hazards than in the early 1850s. Local control achieved what centralisation had failed to do.

15 Chartism and the Anti-Corn Law League

Parliamentary reform triumphed in 1832. The 'floodgates of democracy' that Peel said would accompany parliamentary reform in 1832 were opened. Twenty years later little had been achieved. The working-classes still did not have the vote. The middle-classes were more successful. The Corn Laws were repealed in 1846. However, power--political, social and economic--remained with the landed classes.

Chartism

The Reform Act 1832 gave the vote to the middle-classes but the working population got nothing. This 'betrayal' was felt deeply. It was made worse by factory and Poor Law reform. Increasingly many working-class radicals felt that until they were given the vote nothing in their lives could be improved. The result was the emergence of Chartism in the late 1830s.

The origins of Chartism can be traced back to the early 1830s. Workers were still excluded from Parliament and felt that they had been duped by the middle-classes. The 'six points' of the People's Charter published in the spring of 1838--annual Parliaments, equal electoral districts, payment of MPs, universal manhood suffrage, vote by ballot and the abolition of property qualifications--were demanded to secure political equality. Chartism emerged as a political movement because of the policies of the Whig government. Between 1830 and 1836, the Whigs attacked the unstamped radical press.[1] Over seven hundred sellers of radical journals were prosecuted. This resulted in widespread opposition to the government even after stamp duties were reduced in 1836. The Whigs also took a firm stand against trade unionism especially the GNCTU[2] and the Tolpuddle Martyrs in 1834. In Scotland, the alliance between middle-class radicals and trade unionists broke down. The arrest of members of the Glasgow cotton spinners' union in July 1837 on suspicion of arson and murder led to a campaign in their support throughout Scotland and northern England. Parliament provided no real improvements in working conditions, also a reason for discontent. The 1833 Factory Act though it regulated the working day of children in the textile industry, left adult hours unaltered. The frustrations of factory reformers swelled the rising Chartist tide. Many of the northern delegates to the Chartist Convention in 1839 entered politics through the ten-hour movement and the campaign against the new Poor Law. The workhouses

---

[1] Stamp duty was paid on newspapers and journals. It was seen as a 'tax on knowledge' and led to illegal unstamped newspapers being printed.
[2] GNCTU or Grand National Consolidated Trades Union was a short-lived national union formed in 1834.

became the symbol of Whig cruelty. By 1838, the campaign was beginning to decline and gradually the north turned to a wider based radicalism.

The key figure in channelling separate grievances into a general demand for parliamentary reform was Feargus O'Connor. He won support from the middle-class Birmingham Political Union and artisan London Working Men's Association. The unity of Chartism should not be exaggerated. It was fuelled by a widespread sense of resentment but at all levels of the movement, there were different emphases, tactics and organisations that gave Chartism its 'kaleidoscopic appearance'.

Who became Chartists?

Support for Chartism came from across the country and across different jobs. Its power-base lay in the textiles districts of the East Midlands, the West Riding of Yorkshire and in southern Lancashire. Chartism was stronger in industrial villages and medium-sized towns like Stockport and Bradford than in the major provincial centres of Manchester and Leeds. However, there were other areas, like South Wales, the Black Country and parts of the West Country, where there had been little organised radicalism before. In the first National Petition 19,000 signatures came from London compared to 100,000 from the West Riding and mass metropolitan support for Chartism came only in the 1840s. In other areas, support was limited. In Ireland, cities like Belfast, Cork and Dublin had Chartist organisations but general suspicion of the Catholic Church that Chartism would undermine society meant its impact was limited. Chartism was weak in largely rural areas where deference remained strong. In East Anglia, agricultural labourers were not convinced the vote would remedy their economic position. In rural Wales, Chartism was accompanied by traditional protest in the form of the Rebecca riots of 1839 and 1842.[3] Beneath this regional and local diversity of Chartism, there was a real sense of national unity in the movement, especially between 1839 and 1842 and in 1848.

A wide range of different urban and industrial workers was involved. Economic conditions, especially the widespread depression from 1837-1838 was only partially responsible for this, though they were of major importance. Of the 23 local associations who responded to a survey distributed by the 1839 Convention, only two stressed the vote as a general grievance. The majority complained of low wages, dear food, and scarcity of work and economic hardship. Considerable support came from outworkers, textile handloom weavers, linen-spinners and wool-combers who were chronically depressed. In Scotland, handloom weavers were the

---

[3] Rebecca riots took place in south Wales against the introduction of turnpike roads. People objected to paying tolls to use these roads.

major force behind Chartism. The move to demands for a political answer to their economic grievances was motivated not by the belief that the vote would benefit their conditions but that without it, there could be no solution.

Factory workers played a more active role in Chartism than in previous radical movements. Here too the initial motive was economic, springing from the widespread unemployment of the late 1830s. Contemporaries saw Chartism as a 'knife and fork question'. It was more than this. The early part of the century had seen long hours offset by relatively high levels of wages. The economic slump of the late 1830s added to their sense of frustration and despair. Factory workers and miners occupied an intermediate position between the rank-and-file outworkers and the artisans and small shopkeepers who formed most of the leadership. In Suffolk and Essex, for instance, tailors, shoemakers and building artisans looked to agricultural labourers for mass support. In Bath, artisans provided the leadership and the declining cloth trade the rank and file. In Aberdeen, there was a similar balance between handloom weavers and a small articulate artisan leadership. Craftsmen were prominent partly because of a long tradition of political radicalism. Economic considerations gave artisan leadership an added edge. In the clothing, furniture and building trades, their economic position was deteriorating or at least vulnerable. The growing market for low quality goods and falling prices compelled employers to cut costs. Only a few skilled trades, like bookbinding and watch-making, could maintain their prosperity and remained aloof from Chartism.

Women were involved in Chartism to an unprecedented extent. This strong female involvement--up to a third of those who signed the First Petition in 1839 and the petition on behalf of the transported John Frost in 1841 were women--was not motivated primarily by the question of women's suffrage. Women supported men and their communities. In the early years of the movement, there were over a hundred female radical associations and a general commitment to the inclusion of women's suffrage and the improvement of women's education was accepted by many radicals. By the mid-1840s, the growing respectability of the movement meant that radical papers mentioned women less.

Chartism: a chronology

The Chartist movement did not rise to a peak and then decline, rather it peaked on three occasions: in 1838-1840, 1842 and 1848. There were, however, important differences over how the Charter should be put into effect creating local, as well as national, divisions. George Julian Harney, a Chartist leader in 1848, said, 'faction has cut the throat of Chartism'.

Phase 1: 1838-1841

In June 1836, the London Working Men's Association was formed with William Lovett as secretary. The Charter emerged out of a tradition of London artisan radicalism, with the assistance of a small group of middle-class radicals. Thomas Attwood revived the Birmingham Political Union [BPU] in 1837, initially calling for household suffrage but soon supporting universal suffrage. The LWMA and BPU drummed up support for the Charter in Scotland and northern England. Feargus O'Connor realised that success would prove difficult for a movement exclusively based in London. During the winter of 1836-1837, he broadened the basis of his support from London-Lancashire-Yorkshire to Nottingham, Newcastle and Scotland. By mid-1838, he exercised considerable dominance over northern popular radicalism through his newspaper, *The Northern Star* founded in November 1837, and by bringing it together in the Leeds-based Great Northern Union in April 1838.

The Convention 1839

From September 1838, a series of regional meetings elected delegates to a National Convention. The Convention finally met in London in February 1839. About half its fifty-four delegates were working men, the remainder radical gentry or small employers. Divisions emerged almost immediately: should the Convention regard itself simply as a means of managing the petition or should it set itself up as 'the People's Parliament'? As the language of militants became more extreme many of its moderate members, principally those from Scotland and Birmingham, returned home. It was the issue of violence and the closely connected issue of co-operation with the middle-classes that did most to divide the Convention delegates. When Melbourne's government resigned in May 1839, the national petition could not be presented and the remaining thirty-five delegates to the Convention moved to Birmingham. Various strategies were discussed. No agreement was reached and decisions were left to local associations. This was, in part, a response to the hardening of government policy. Initially Lord John Russell, the Home Secretary, resisted those demanding repression. By mid-1839 drilling was banned, Lord Lieutenants were given powers to raise and arm special constables and six thousand troops were stationed in the Northern District. The Metropolitan Police put down rioting Chartists at Llanidloes in Montgomeryshire in May. Leading figures in the London and Lancashire movement were arrested and the tempo of arrests increased after a riot in the Birmingham Bull Ring in July.

The Convention, reduced in size by resignation, differences of opinion and now arrests, moved back to London. On 12 July, the House of Commons rejected the petition by 235 votes to 46. The Convention had finally to face up to the issue of violence and resistance. On 17 July it voted, by 13 to 6, to hold a 'sacred month', despite letters from local associations questioning the wisdom of calling a general strike during a severe trade depression. On 24 July, following consultations with 63 Welsh, Scottish and English associations which showed support from only nine, the decision was reversed. The Convention was dissolved in September and the initiative moved to the local associations.

The Newport Rising 1839

Meetings were held in the early autumn to co-ordinate a national rising but this only occurred in South Wales. On the night of 3-4 November 7,000 miners and ironworkers marched in three columns to Newport to release Henry Vincent from prison. There is also evidence that they were launching a massive uprising to create a people's republic in the Welsh valleys that might spread to other parts of Britain. Troops opened fire, killing at least twenty-two and wounding about fifty. The rest fled in confusion and many, including leaders like John Frost, were arrested in succeeding days. Over 250 people were tried in the last mass treason trial in British history. Death sentences were handed down on the three leaders, though these were later commuted to transportation for life to Australia. The Newport Rising was not a small-scale affair or the work of Whig agents provocateurs or simply a 'monster demonstration', as earlier historians concluded, but was the product of a radical political culture in an area when class divisions were clear. Further risings were planned after Newport. Abortive insurrections took place in Sheffield, Dewsbury and Bradford in January 1840.

The authorities had successfully defused the situation. The Chartists assumed that the government would adopt repressive policies and that this would result in violent protest. However, it did not act as expected. Initially Russell used conciliatory tones giving the Chartists time to alienate moderate supporters by their militant language. The initiative quickly moved to the government and the Chartists found themselves on the defensive caught between defeat or revolution. By late 1839, it was clear they could not defeat the state by force. At local level, sympathetic handling defused potentially explosive situations. General Napier, for example, met Lancashire Chartist leaders and promised to keep troops and police away from a major rally at Kersal Moor as long as it was peaceful and was frequently angered by the over-reaction of magistrates.

By the summer of 1840, Chartism was in disarray. Divisions began to emerge. The Chartist Church movement that began in Scotland spread southwards, flourishing in the Birmingham area and in the West Country. Lovett launched the National Association for Promoting the

Improvement of the People, stressing education and self-help. Henry Vincent toured the country after his release from prison in early 1841 on behalf of teetotal Chartism and other leaders like Hetherington, Hill and Cleave shared his enthusiasm. In Leeds and other provincial cities, Chartists turned to local government. In Nottingham, Chartists took up the Poor Law issue again. A degree of unity and national organisation was provided by the National Charter Association (NCA) formed in July 1840 largely at O'Connor's instigation.

The NCA remained the major national organisation for the next decade. Some historians see it as the first independent working-class political party. It was very much O'Connor's organisation and this led to significant personal opposition. Many Chartists, including Lovett, refused to join. By the end of 1840, fewer than 70 local associations had affiliated. These were concentrated in Lancashire and Yorkshire, the Nottinghamshire-Derby area and in London. During 1841, O'Connor claimed 50,000 members from 401 localities. He feared Chartism would fragment. Lovett's association had considerable middle-class backing. Chartists became local councillors in Leeds. O'Connor took the view that the Anti-Corn Law League offered working people little but during the winter of 1841-1842 agreements were reached in several cities between Chartists and Corn Law Repealers.

Phase 2: 1842-1847

Chartism and the Complete Suffrage Union 1842

Some Chartists turned to the Complete Suffrage Union (CSU), launched by Joseph Sturge in Birmingham in April 1842. Sturge wanted to reconcile the middle- and working-classes through the repeal of class-based laws declaring that denying the vote to most people was unconstitutional and unchristian. This attracted the middle-classes and those Chartists like Lovett and Francis Place alienated by the violence of 1839-1840. At its first meeting, the moderate nature of the CSU was emphasised by excluding O'Connor's supporters. By late April 1842, there were fifty local associations and the CSU presented a rival parliamentary petition to that of the NCA.

O'Connor initially attacked the CSU but recognised the tactical advantage of a brief alliance with middle-class radicals and came out in favour of class collaboration in July 1842. By the autumn, under pressure from Chartist hard-liners, he reversed his position. At a CSU conference in December, packed with Chartist delegates, the middle-class radicals insisted on the use of a 'New Bill of Rights' for universal suffrage instead of the emotive 'Charter'. Lovett was not prepared to accept this and joined with O'Connor in substituting 'Charter' for 'Bill'. This led to the immediate secession of the majority of the middle-class delegates. Class collaboration ended and O'Connor's grip of the movement tightened.

The Plug Plot 1842

The experiment of class collaboration in 1842 took place in a climate of widespread industrial unrest and Chartist activity. The second national petition and Convention were launched the previous September. It met in Birmingham in April 1842 and was limited to 24 delegates from English constituencies and 25 from Welsh and Scottish ones. The petition was better-organised and contained three million signatures. The result was the same: rejection by the House of Commons by 287 to 46 votes on 1 May. This created much bitterness, a situation made worse by the worst economic recession of the century.

Up to half a million workers were involved in the series of strikes that swept across many of the industrial districts of the north and Midlands in July and August 1842. Miners on the North Staffordshire coalfields struck in July followed by a rash of strikes in the Lancashire textile industry in response to wage cuts. Strikers travelled through the county often drawing out the plugs of factory boilers. Hence the 'Plug Plot'. Within days, the strikes had spread across the Pennines into Yorkshire and north into Scotland. By September 15 English and Welsh and eight Scottish counties were affected. What was the extent of Chartist involvement? It is clear that many of those who spoke at strike meetings were Chartists who had no connection with the textile trades. Chartist leaders were caught unaware but soon exploited the strikes for their own ends. The series of regional trade conferences in August gave an opportunity for Chartist intervention and there was a widespread adoption of the Charter as one of the strike's main aims. In Manchester, Glasgow and London there was some convergence of Chartist and trade union activity. The extent to which Chartists were involved varied regionally. In Yorkshire, for instance, where trade unions were weaker and less widespread than in Lancashire, local Chartists exercised strong influence over tactics but generally Chartist leaders were too divided to take full advantage of the situation.

The unions had problems co-ordinating the strikes and the different attitudes of Chartists prevented the NCA from taking on this role. Tension eased in September because of improving economic conditions. The 1842 harvest was good, trade revived and employers agreed to cancel wage reductions. However, the strike movement had two adverse effects on the Chartists. Peel and his Home Secretary, Sir James Graham blamed the Chartists for the strikes. There was a wave of arrests in September. Harsh sentences were handed out. In Staffordshire, for example, of 274 cases tried, 154 men were imprisoned and five men transported for life. By early 1843, there was less need for harsh treatment. Peel and Graham recognised as Russell had done in 1839-1840, that pushing repression too far would alienate public opinion and create public sympathy. In addition, trade union disappointment with Chartism increased. To unionists the issue was economic rather than political and, for them, the strikes were partially successful. Wage cuts were restored and in some places increased to the 1840 levels and in the cotton districts trade unionism emerged on a more organised and confident basis

Confrontational tactics had failed in 1839-1840 and in 1842. Mass arrests and imprisonment sapped the strength of the movement and the relative economic prosperity of the years between 1842 and 1848 helped to dampen the enthusiasm of the rank and file. The agreement between Lovett and O'Connor in late 1842 over the CSU proposals was short-lived. Lovett had no intention of working with O'Connor and gradually he and others withdrew to pursue their objectives by peaceful means. O'Connor emerged firmly in control of the formal Chartist movement, which he promptly led off in entirely new directions.

Different directions 1842-1847

Lovett placed increasing emphasis on educating the working population. Henry Vincent and Robert Lowery continued their work on temperance. Other diversions took the form of increased trade union activity, support for the Anti-Corn Law League and for European republicanism. These represented attempts by radicals to find alternative solutions, though they generally failed to gain mass support. In Leeds, Chartists were elected to the Board of Surveyors for Highways and as Poor Law Guardians. In Sheffield, there were 22 Chartists on the council. In Rochdale, Chartists took control of the Board of Guardians from 1844, ensuring that the new Poor Law was not fully applied before the 1870s. Skilled and prosperous workers, organised in strong trade societies, distanced themselves from Chartism but improved trade after 1842 saw a temporary revival of national unions among workers in cotton and mining.

The Land Plan

Increasingly O'Connor turned his attention to the land question. The Land Plan provided a major outlet for frustrated Chartists, proved a highly attractive proposition as well as an opportunity for further ridicule from their opponents. It offered a means of restoring artisan independence and self-reliance. The idea was to raise capital for a land company from the purchase of shares at 3d or more a week. With the cash, land would be purchased, made into smallholdings complete with the necessary buildings and rented to shareholders chosen by ballot. Much initial support came from the industrial north and Midlands but enthusiasm soon spread south.

Momentum gathered once O'Connor purchased his first site near Watford and on May Day 1847 the first tenants moved into O'Connorville. Subscriptions soared and the re-named National Co-operative Land Company bought further estates at Lowbands, Snigs End, Minster Lovell and Great Dodford. Over £100,000 was collected from some 70,000 subscribers, though only 250 ever settled on the two-acre allotments. However, the Company and its associated Land Bank were plagued by legal difficulties. In May 1848, Parliament appointed a Select Committee to investigate the Land Company. Though there was no evidence of fraud, the accounts were confused and inaccurate and this further weakened confidence in the scheme. O'Connor found that the flow of share capital was drying up and, after exploring alternative means of saving the scheme, he finally took the route recommended by the select committee and wound the company up in 1851.

Phase 3: 1848

For contemporaries and for later historians 1848 was a watershed in the history of the Chartist movement. It is certainly true that after 1848 Chartism lost whatever unity it had, with even O'Connor willing to accept household suffrage while leaders such as Ernest Jones and Harney moved towards socialism. The winter of 1847-1848 was a severe one. Commercial crisis and growing economic distress led to increasing Chartist activity. The authorities were uneasy at the Chartist plans to present a third petition. There were fears that the revolutions sweeping across Europe would infect Britain, especially since some Chartists had been in contact with European radicals. There were also fears that the measures proposed by the Convention which assembled in London in early April would tie down the army at a time when Irish radicals threatened rebellion.

In March 1848, a middle-class radical meeting in London, demanding the abolition of income tax, was highjacked by Chartists. Attempts by police to break up the demonstration led to three days of rioting. Similar disturbances took place in Glasgow and Manchester. In each case, though there was a Chartist presence, disorder and crime were largely by non-Chartists but Chartists were guilty by association in the eyes of property-owners. Forty-nine delegates were elected to the third Convention that first met in London on 4 April. It planned a peaceful demonstration on Kennington Common on 10 April to be followed by a procession to present the petition to Parliament. Being elected MP for Nottingham in 1847 had considerably strengthened O'Connor's personal position and he hoped that the petition would contain five million signatures.

Strong precautionary measures were taken by the authorities. Eight thousand troops were drafted into the capital to support thousands of special constables. The procession was banned but the meeting went ahead. The firmness of government frightened O'Connor into asking his supporters to disperse peacefully. The petition was conveyed to Parliament in three cabs and the crisis was over. The meeting was ridiculed by many as a 'fiasco' and two days later O'Connor faced further disapproval when his petition was found to contain less than two million genuine signatures. The Convention continued to sit undaunted by the rejection of the petition. Internal disagreement, mutual suspicion and recriminations increasingly paralysed the Convention and dissolution quickly followed. On 2 June, *The Times* concluded, 'Chartism is neither dead nor sleeping. The snake was scotched not killed on the 10th of April. The advancing spring has brought with it warmth, vigour and renovation.' The summer of 1848 saw further Chartist activity, arrests and trials and several riots, against the background of events in Ireland. The focal points of government concern were Bradford in May and London between June and August. Police broke up meetings in the East End on 4 June and the provisional executive of the National Assembly called a day of protest on 12 June. The government responded with a heavy display of force at the mass meeting on Bishop Bonner's Field.

Was the Chartist threat real in 1848? To those in authority it certainly was. They saw the daily meetings and riots. They received reports of drilling and military style marches from the country. Prompt action put O'Connor in the position of having to back down. On 10 April, his hold over the movement was broken and other leaders simply did not have his authority. Just as in 1838 and 1842, Chartism was contained from without and critically weakened from within. Yet, Kennington Common and the June riots are only 'fiascos' in retrospect. Chartism's failure in 1848 was not one of ideas but of will. The united 'mass platform', already weakened, disintegrated.

R. C. Gammage, one of Chartism's first historians, may have been a little premature when travelling round the country in the 1850's lecturing on the movement's failure. Chartism lingered on for a further decade, displaying vigour in some areas like Halifax but it had ceased to be a mass movement. In 1852, Marx observed that the Chartists were 'so completely disorganised and scattered, and at the same time so short of useful people, that they must either fall completely to pieces and degenerate into cliques...or they must be reconstituted.' Nevertheless, its journals still flourished and Ernest Jones achieved some following among craftsmen especially in London resentful at the growing influence of trade unionism. Chartists continued to be active in local politics but by 1860 organised Chartism was dead. The last Convention gathered in 1858. Two years later, the NCA was formally wound up.

Why did Chartism fail?

Repeated failure sapped the momentum of Chartism. To sustain its support, the movement needed to maintain widespread belief that success was possible. The events of 1839 seriously damaged its capacity to do this. The defeat of the general strike in 1842 and the crushing failure of 1848 completed the process. The authorities inflicted the most damaging psychological defeat on any popular reform movement of the century.

In part, this was a result of the organisational weakness of the movement. Lack of administrative experience was clearly exposed by the ways in which the Conventions were organised and financed. Rejection of the three petitions showed how little parliamentary support the Chartists had. The reforming movement of 1830-1832 and the activities of the Anti-Corn Law League, both of which used similar tactics to Chartism to gain support, were successful because they had parliamentary allies. With little parliamentary backing or solid middle-class support, the Chartist movement found itself either having to give up or raise and maintain public support or opt for less peaceful methods. This divided leadership and rank and file, creating bitterness and lack of tactical direction. Chartists could agree on the Charter but on little else. To Lancashire cotton workers, Chartism held out the prospect of economic improvement and factory reform. To the London artisan, it pointed the way to political equality. The Chartist leaders also had different objectives. For Lovett, the vote was part of a general programme of social improvement; for Ernest Jones, Chartism was equated with socialism; and, for O'Connor, the franchise was the political counterpart of his schemes at land reform. Loss of momentum within the movement meant that Chartism could not maintain a unity of purpose.

Economic conditions played an important role in failure to maintain unity of purpose. Though there has been a reaction against the simple economic explanations, the fundamental importance of the trade cycle cannot be neglected. The difficulty of maintaining unity, except during economic slumps, was universally recognised by contemporaries. The changes that occurred in the policies and attitudes of government, in part the result of Chartism can be seen as evidence of its partial success. The movement drew attention to social problems and the need to tackle them. There was some liberalisation of state policies in the 1840s. This weakened the Chartist case that only a reformed Parliament would improve the conditions of the working population. A final explanation for the demise of Chartism lies in the consolidation of industrial capitalism that had occurred by 1850. In the previous fifty years, industrial change had created militancy among the working population who believed that political reform alone could arrest or reverse this process. By 1850, this battle had more or less been lost and Chartism remained relevant only in places like Halifax and Bradford where the woollen and worsted trades still fought rearguard actions against mechanisation. Militancy was associated with the traumas of early stages of industrialisation. Chartism was crucial in the shift from older forms of popular protest to the development of new ones, like the general strike and pressure group activity, more effective in a mature industrial urban society.

Chartism was the first organised, mass movement of the working population in British history in terms of its geographical and occupational breadth and the unprecedented involvement of women. But it did not draw on trade unionism in any formal way or bridge the gulf between rural and urban workers. It did not mark a vital stage in the inevitable progress of organised labour. Chartism was motivated by 'knife and fork' issues but was also concerned with the dignity of the individual and the 'rights of man'. It looked back to the campaigns of the 1790s and forward to the emergence of socialism as a political force from the 1880s.

The Anti-Corn Law League

In September 1838, the Manchester Anti-Corn Law Association was formed by a group of local businessmen. Their aim was the total abolition of the Corn Laws. Lecture tours in the north of England encouraged the formation of other local associations. Links were established with London free traders and in February 1839 a delegate meeting of all the Anti-Corn Law associations was held in London. It was not particularly successful. Few delegates attended. London radicals were indifferent. When the House of Commons rejected a motion against the Corn Laws in March 1839, the delegates set up the Anti-Corn Law League as a national organisation with its headquarters in Manchester.

The ACLL was an economic pressure group with a very specific objective. Richard Cobden[4] attacked the Corn Laws as the symbol of aristocratic privilege. The League based its appeal on the economic advantages of free trade--cheaper food, more employment, higher exports and greater prosperity--and the first phase of its work aimed to persuade the public of the case against the Corn Law. Cobden believed that repeal was as much in the interests of the working population as of the manufacturers. If he could persuade popular opinion of this he could then maintain that the ACLL was advocating a 'national' as opposed to 'sectional' cause. In this, he was less successful. Chartist leaders were either unimpressed by his case or opposed to it. Whatever the merits of free trade they believed that only the Charter could safeguard the interests of the working population. The movement looked to the anti-slavery

---

[4] Richard Cobden (1804-1865). A manufacturer of calico in Manchester who, with John Bright led the Anti-Corn Law League after 1839

movement of the 1820s and 1830s as a model for action. Cobden in 1841 claimed that protection was 'opposed to the laws of God' and was 'anti-scriptural and anti-religious'. This alarmed the more conservative among the middle-classes.

Russell had hinted in 1839 that the Whigs might support repeal. Peel remained silent on the issue. Cobden saw that repeal would only be achieved through electoral activity. This marked the beginning of the second phase of the League's activities. Success in the Walsall by-election showed the potential of the League as a third force in politics. In the General Election later in 1841, eight Leaguers, including Cobden, were elected and this gave the League the important parliamentary base that the Chartists lacked. However, the outstanding victory in 1841 lay with Peel and the protectionist Conservatives.

This put the ACLL in an awkward position. Peel's majority meant an electoral rebuff for the arguments of the League. This led to a crisis of confidence for Cobden, John Bright[5] and the other leaders of the ACLL, a crisis heightened by deepening distress in the northern manufacturing districts during the winter of 1841-1842. Peel's 1842 budget made matters worse as he had, to some extent, stolen the thunder of the free traders. The League was at its lowest ebb in the summer of 1842 with few policies and increasing lack of confidence. Cobden took the dangerous step of trying to shake public confidence in Parliament by comparing the immorality and sectionalism of the Commons with the moral righteousness of the League. A 'lock-out' of workers was seriously considered but workers pre-empted this in the series of strikes in mid-1842. Moderation, however, prevailed and by the end of 1842, the League emerged stronger and more confident than before.

The ACLL's capacity for intensive agitation was increased by an overhaul of its organisation. In March 1842, the League Council divided the country up into twelve areas each with its own organisation, improving both the collection of money and the enrolment of new members. The League's propaganda machine was expanded. From December 1842, its newspaper *The Circular* began to appear weekly. *The Economist* was founded in 1843 acting as the medium for free-trade ideas. Cobden and Bright undertook widespread lecture tours and anti-corn law tracts were sent to every elector using the new 'Penny Post' system. From 1842 to 1845, the League directed its energies towards preparing for a decisive struggle at the expected 1848 General Election. Attempts were made to win over tenant farmers. This direct assault on the shires failed because many tenant farmers supported protection and may even have influenced their landlords into a Protectionist stance rather than the other way round. The League also used indirect methods. It organised extensive postal

---

[5] John Bright (1811-1889). A cotton manufacturer from Rochdale in Lancashire.

objections to hostile county votes. It tried to create new free trade votes by buying up freeholds in key constituencies, with some success in south Lancashire and the West Riding. By the summer of 1846, only a small number of seats had been made safe in this way. Peel was not scared into repealing the Corn Laws to avoid an anti-Tory landslide in the counties.

The stimulus for repeal came from inside the Cabinet and Parliament because of the Irish crisis of 1845-1846. The League can perhaps take credit for the conversion of Lord John Russell, the Whig leader in his 'Edinburgh Letter' of November 1845. The same cannot be said of Peel's decision. He had concluded that the Corn Laws could not be defended long before the Irish crisis. He saw the Corn Laws as divisive and that retreat by the aristocracy was a necessity. Nevertheless, repeal in 1846 was an ordered retreat keeping intact the main strongholds of aristocratic power, made by a Prime Minister and Parliament and not as the result of an electoral contest or 'pressure from without'.

What was the significance of the ACLL in middle-class Radicalism in this period? Both the economic and political consequences of repeal have been exaggerated. Neither proved immediately disastrous to the landed interest and aristocratic government easily survived the crisis of 1846. The realities of political power remained unaltered and further organic reforms waited until after 1865. Repeal did mean that the gospel of free trade became a central tenet of policy and thinking and an increasing recognition of the aims and interests of the urban middle-classes in legislation. These processes were already well underway in the 1830s. The League claimed to act as the spokesman for the middle-classes but, though it received strong support from northern manufacturers, not all members of the business community were prepared to give it total support and some, like the financial elite in London, were actively hostile to free trade. The League fought a national campaign yet the strength of the middle-classes lay in local not national politics, in their business interests and the status acquired through local office. The difficulty in forming a new united Radical party in the late 1840s and 1850s was a reflection of the League's success in achieving its economic objective. In terms of its organisational structure, its use of propaganda and its tactics the ACLL looked forward to the radical politics of the second half of the nineteenth century.

Further Reading

General texts

Callum G. Brown and W. Hamish Fraser *Britain since 1707*, London, 2010, covers the subject in depth from a 'British' perspective. E. J. Evans *The Shaping of Modern Britain: Identity, Industry and Empire 1780-1914*, London, 2011, N. McCord *British History 1815-1906*, Oxford, 2nd ed., 1998, Frank O'Gorman *The Long Eighteenth Century: British political and social history 1688-1832*, London, 2016 and Michael Turner *British politics in an age of reform*, Manchester, 1999 are good introductions. J. Langton and R.J. Morris *Atlas of Industrializing Britain 1780-1914*, London, 1986 and R. Pope (ed.) *Atlas of British Social and Economic History since c.1700*, London, 1989 provide a valuable visual dimension.

2: William Pitt

J. W. Derry *Politics in the Age of Fox, Pitt and Liverpool: Continuity and Transformation*, London, 1990 and covers the period from the 1780s through to the late 1820s. Eric J. Evans *William Pitt the Younger*, London, 1999 is brief and L.G. Mitchell *Charles James Fox*, Oxford, 1992 examines his major protagonist. H. T. Dickinson (ed.) *British Society and the French Revolution 1793-1815*, London, 1989 and C. Emsley *British Society and the French Wars*, London, 1979 provide all students will need.

3: Tory dominance and decline 1815-1830

On the question of political parties, see E.J. Evans *Political Parties in Britain 1783-1867*, London, 1985. E.J. Evans *Britain Before the Reform Act 1815-1832*, London, 1989 contains text and documents. John Plowright *Regency England. The Age of Lord Liverpool*, London, 1996 is eminently accessible. Norman Gash *Lord Liverpool*, London, 1984, 2016 and P.J.V. Rolo *George Canning*, London, 1965 are good biographies.

4: The Whigs 1830-1841

E. J. Evans *The Great Reform Act of 1832*, London, 2nd. ed., 1995 is an accessible starting-point. G. Finlayson *England in the Eighteen Thirties*, London, is a useful summary of developments. There are valuable biographies of the key Whig politicians: E.A. Smith *Lord Grey, 1764-*

1845, Oxford, 1990, L. G. Mitchell *Lord Melbourne 1779-1848*, Oxford, 1996 and Paul Scherer *Lord John Russell: A Biography*, London, 1999.

5: Redefining Toryism

Paul Adelman *Peel and the Conservative Party 1830-1850*, London, 1989 contains text and documents. Richard Gaunt *Sir Robert Peel: The Life and Legacy*, London, 2010, Eric J. Evans *Sir Robert Peel: Statesmanship, Power and Party*, London, 1991 and T. A. Jenkins *Sir Robert Peel* London, 1998 are good short reassessments of Peel's career.

6: Pitt, Peel and Ireland 1789-1846

Roy Foster *Modern Ireland 1600-1922*, London, 1987 and K.T. Hoppen *Ireland since 1800. Conflict and Conformity*, London, 2nd ed., 1999 are good studies. Paul Adelman *Great Britain and the Irish Question 1800-1922*, London, 1996 is designed with the beginner in mind. On the Famine, see Christine Kinealy *This Great Calamity: The Irish Famine, 1845-52*, Dublin 1994 and *A Death-Dealing Famine: The Great Hunger in Ireland*, London, 1997. John Crowley, William J. Smyth and Mike Murphy, (eds.), *Atlas of the Great Irish Famine*, Cork, 2012 is simply superb

7: Britain at war 1793-1815

Three chapters in H.T. Dickinson (ed.) *Britain and the French Revolution 1789-1815*, London, 1989 consider diplomacy, strategy and public finance. Jenny Uglow *In These Times: Living in Britain through Napoleon's Wars, 1793-1815*, London, 2014 is very readable account.

8: Foreign Policy 1815-1841

Muriel Chamberlain *Pax Britannica?: British foreign policy 1789-1914*, London, 1988 and John Lowe *Britain and Foreign Affairs 1815-1885: Europe and Overseas*, London, 1998 provide an overview. John Bew *Castlereagh: From Enlightenment to Tyranny*, London, 2011 and Muriel Chamberlain *Lord Aberdeen*, London, 1983 are valuable on the 1810s and 1820s. Muriel Chamberlain *Lord Palmerston*, Cardiff, 1987 is readable and short. David Brown *Palmerston*, London, 2012 is longer.

9: The First Industrial Nation

M.J Daunton, *Progress and Poverty: An Economic and Social History of Britain 1700-1850*, Oxford, 1995 and *Wealth and welfare: an economic and social history of Britain, 1851-1951*, Oxford, 2007, Joel Mokyr *The Enlightened Economy: An Economic History of Britain 1700-1850*, London, 2009, Emma Griffin *A Short History of the British Industrial Revolution*, Basingstoke, 2010 and Emma Griffin *Liberty's Dawn: A People's History of the Industrial Revolution*, London, 2013.

10: Responding to Economic Change

John Stevenson *Popular Disturbances in England 1700-1832*, London 1991 is the best introduction. P. Adelman *Victorian Radicalism: The Middle-class Experience 1830-1914*, London, 1984 and D.G. Wright *Popular Radicalism: The Working-class Experience 1780-1880*, London, 1988 look at different responses to change. E.P. Thompson *The Making of the English Working-class*, London, 1963, 1968 is a controversial, classic.

11: The Condition of England 1832-1853

General studies of social reform include U. Henriques *Before the Welfare State*, London, 1979, D. Fraser *The Evolution of the British Welfare State,* London, 5th. ed., 2017 and Keith Laybourn *The Evolution of British Social Policy and the Welfare State*, Keele, 1995. E. Evans *Social Reform 1830-1914*, London, 1978 is a useful collection of documents. Philip Harling *The Modern British State: An Historical Introduction*, London, 2001, is good overview.

12: Children, work and education 1832-1853

J. T. Ward *The Factory Movement 1830-1850*, London, 1962 is the most detailed study but should be supplemented by Robert Gray *The Factory Question and Industrial England 1830-1860*, Cambridge, 1996. Peter Kirby *Child labour in Britain, 1750-1870*, London, 2003 and Pamela Horn *Children's Work and Welfare 1780-1880s*, London, 1994 provide valuable insights into children's work and how and why it changed. W.B. Stephens *Education in England 1760-1914*, London, 1998 is the best introduction to the subject. M. Sanderson *Education, Economic Change and Society in England 1780-1870*, London, 2nd. ed., 1991 is a briefer bibliographical study.

13: From Speenhamland to the New Poor Law 1830-1847

Paul A. Fideler *Social welfare in pre-industrial England: the old Poor Law tradition*, Basingstoke, 2006 and Anthony Brundage *The English Poor Laws, 1700-1930*, Basingstoke, 2012 provide convenient overview Alan

Kidd *State, Society and the Poor in Nineteenth-Century* England, London, 1999 is broader. Derek Fraser (ed.) *The New Poor Law in the Nineteenth Century*, London, 1976 and M.E. Rose *The Relief of Poverty 1834-1914*, London, 2nd. ed., 1985 are useful. The workhouse is discussed in N. Longmate *The Workhouse*, London, 1974 and M. Crowther *The Workhouse System 1834-1929: The History of an English Social Institution*, London, 1984.

14: Chadwick and public health

The development of town and city can be approached through A. Briggs *Victorian Cities*, London, 1968 and H.J. Dyos and M. Wolff (eds.) *The Victorian City: Images and Realities*, London, 1973. R. Rodger (eds.) *The Victorian City: A Reader in British Urban History 1820-1914*, London, 1994 collects together important papers.

On urban conditions and the problems of public health see A.S. Wohl *Endangered Lives: Public Health in Victorian Britain*, London, 1985. Derek Fraser (ed.) *Municipal reform and the Industrial City*, Leicester, 1982 contains useful case studies. S.E. Finer *The Life and Times of Sir Edwin Chadwick*, London, 1952. These should now be supplemented with A. Brundage *England's "Prussian Minister": Edwin Chadwick and the Politics of Government Growth 1832-1854*, Pennsylvania, l988. On cholera see N. Longmate *King Cholera*, London, 1966 and R.J. Morris Cholera, 1832, London, 1976 Christopher Hamlin *Cholera: The Biography*, Oxford, 2009 is a valuable global study.

15: Chartism and the Anti-Corn Law League

E. Royle *Chartism*, 3rd ed., London, 1996, R. Brown *Chartism*, Cambridge, 1998, 1999 and John Walton *Chartism*, 1999 are good places to begin. Dorothy Thompson *The Chartists: Popular Politics in the Industrial Revolution*, Aldershot, 1984 and Malcolm Chase *Chartism: A New History*, Manchester, 2007 are more detailed. Norman McCord *The Anti-Corn Law League*, London, 1968 and Paul Pickering and Alex Tyrell *The People's Bread. A History of the Anti-Corn Law League*, London, 2000.

Index

Aberdeen, Lord, 110, 112, 113, 119, 121, 210
Adam Smith, 157
Addington, Henry Lord Sidmouth, 21, 22, 35, 44, 45, 47, 48, 99, 100, 144
Afghanistan, 117
Agriculture. *See* Farming
Aix-la-Chapelle, 104, 107, 108
Alexander I, Tsar, 107, 108, 111, 112, 121
Althorp, John Spencer, Lord, 58, 169
Andover scandal, 191, 192, 193
Anti-Corn Law League, ii, 74, 142, 208, 213, 215, 218, 219, 220, 221
Arkwright, Richard, 132
Artisans, 2, 5, 7, 123, 134, 209, 210, 211, 215, 218
Ashley Cooper, Lord Anthony, 72, 168, 169, 170, 171, 172, 173, 175
Assistant Commissioners, 185, 188
Austria, 36, 91, 93, 94, 95, 97, 98, 99, 100, 102, 104, 105, 106, 107, 108, 109, 111, 115, 116
Baltic, the, 97, 98, 101
Bank Charter Act 1844, 63, 70
Bank of England, 9, 35, 39, 70, 98
Banking, 70, 125
Bedchamber crisis 1839, 62, 63, 64
Belfast, 78, 85, 89, 123, 209
Belgium, 92, 93, 95, 98, 104, 106, 113, 114, 115, 116, 118, 122
Bentham, Jeremy, 8, 158, 160
Benthamism, 160, 161, 162
Birmingham, 55, 57, 127, 134, 195, 197, 209, 211, 212, 213, 214
Blanketeers, 1817, 35, 43, 44
Board of Trade, 35, 41, 42, 47, 52, 71, 82
Boroughs, 10, 11, 22, 29, 50, 55, 56, 57, 68, 198
Bradford, 148, 168, 209, 212, 217, 219
Bright, John, 219, 220

British and Foreign School Society, 174
Budget, 40, 41, 63, 69, 70, 93, 170, 220
Burke, Edmund, 18, 19, 27, 28, 29, 93, 94
Canada, 25, 26, 90, 101, 121, 235
Canning, George, ii, iii, 12, 21, 22, 34, 35, 38, 47, 48, 49, 52, 61, 80, 81, 82, 91, 92, 99, 104, 106, 109, 110, 111, 112, 113, 115, 116, 122
Caribbean, the, 90, 93, 95, 96, 106
Carlyle, Thomas, 1, 9, 157
Castlereagh, Robert Stewart Lord, 22, 35, 36, 47, 48, 79, 91, 92, 102, 103, 104, 105, 106, 107, 108, 109, 110, 111, 116, 120, 122
Catholic Association, 51, 52, 80, 81, 82
Catholic Emancipation, i, 20, 34, 35, 47, 48, 49, 51, 52, 54, 63, 64, 78, 79, 80, 81, 82, 83, 84, 85
Cato Street, 1820, 35, 43, 45
Chadwick, Edwin, 169, 179, 182, 183, 184, 185, 190, 192, 193, 195, 197, 202, 203, 204, 205, 206, 207
Chartism, 61, 154, 157, 171, 188, 193, 208, 209, 210, 212, 213, 215, 216, 217, 218, 219, 235
Cheshire, 3, 44, 134, 150
Children, ii, 6, 9, 13, 42, 59, 63, 71, 72, 155, 164, 165, 166, 167, 168, 169, 170, 171, 173, 174, 175, 176, 180, 181, 188, 202, 208
China, 90, 119, 120, 122
Cholera, 89, 195, 196, 199, 205, 206
Church of England, 8, 13, 52, 59, 60, 66, 72, 147, 166, 172
Coal industry, 5, 6, 9, 23, 41, 70, 123, 124, 126, 128, 133, 134, 136, 138, 148, 171
Cobbett, William, 11, 44, 45, 147, 168, 186, 187

226

Cobden, Richard, 219, 220
Combination Acts, 33, 42, 46, 152
Commercial policies, 15, 22, 25, 26, 27, 40, 41, 42, 48, 64, 66, 73, 74, 79, 93, 99, 104, 105, 106, 110, 115, 122, 134, 138, 148, 150, 157, 200
Complete Suffrage Union, 213
Concert of Europe, 91
Congress of Vienna, 36, 91, 92, 103, 104, 105, 120
Conservatives, 4, 12, 31, 34, 61, 62, 63, 65, 67, 68, 69, 72, 75, 83, 84, 85, 91, 119, 120, 121, 147, 169, 172
Constantinople, 116, 117, 118
Co-operative movement, 149, 156, 159
Corn Laws, 3, 4, 9, 35, 37, 38, 41, 42, 46, 48, 49, 54, 61, 63, 64, 65, 68, 72, 73, 74, 86, 88, 157, 159, 172, 204, 208, 219, 221
Counties, 6, 9, 10, 11, 22, 32, 51, 55, 60, 68, 79, 87, 89, 134, 144, 145, 152, 155, 181, 186, 214, 221
Crompton, Samuel, 7, 131, 132, 151
Darby, Abraham, 131, 132, 133
Demand, 2, 6, 31, 36, 39, 44, 69, 81, 87, 119, 124, 126, 128, 129, 130, 132, 133, 135, 140, 141, 142, 197, 209
Disease, 89, 96, 178, 179, 181, 195, 196, 199, 202, 203, 207
Disraeli, Benjamin, 4, 34, 110, 147, 173, 193
Distress, 4, 29, 37, 38, 44, 45, 68, 87, 142, 143, 146, 150, 171, 173, 181, 216, 220
Doherty, John, 152, 153, 167
Dublin, 77, 78, 79, 81, 85, 209
Dundas, Henry, 16, 19, 26, 93, 94, 98
East Anglia, 134, 140, 186, 209
East India Company, 15, 23, 96, 119
Eastern Question, 92, 111, 116, 118, 121

Economic growth, 1, 6, 40, 70, 71, 74, 123, 124, 125, 126, 128, 129, 131, 133, 135
Education, 159, 173, 174, 175, 176
Egypt, 96, 116, 118, 119
Elementary education, 59, 175, 177
Engels, Friedrich, 195
Factories, 135, 166, 167, 168, 169, 171, 172, 173, 184, 187
Factory Act 1833, 61, 169, 176, 208
Factory Act 1844, 69, 72, 172, 176
Factory Act 1847, 167, 170
Famine, Irish, i, 64, 73, 74, 81, 84, 86, 87, 88, 89, 125, 181, 235
Farmers, 9, 143, 192
Farming, 3, 4, 5, 36, 37, 38, 68, 69, 73, 87, 89, 125, 128, 131, 137, 138, 139, 140, 141, 142, 143, 144, 179
  arable farming, 3, 4, 89, 140, 141, 142, 179
  crops, 73, 74, 87
  drainage, 4, 125, 133, 138, 139, 140, 142, 144, 146, 197, 204, 205
  enclosure, 3, 140
  pastoral faming, 4
Fielden, John, 165, 167, 172, 193
Finance, 40, 70, 98, 126, 199
Fox, Charles James, 14, 15, 16, 17, 18, 19, 20, 21, 26, 100
France, 3, 10, 15, 18, 19, 25, 26, 27, 28, 29, 30, 31, 34, 35, 36, 46, 54, 78, 80, 90, 91, 93, 94, 95, 96, 97, 98, 100, 101, 102, 104, 105, 106, 107, 108, 110, 113, 114, 115, 116, 117, 118, 119, 120, 123, 126, 129, 132, 145
Free trade, 4, 27, 41, 42, 73, 74, 77, 86, 219, 221
French Revolution, i, 15, 18, 19, 27, 29, 31, 77, 90, 92, 93, 105, 159, 187
French Wars 1793-1815, iii, 3, 36, 181
Friendly societies, 155
Frost, John, 210, 212
General Board of Health, 205, 206, 207

General Elections, 10, 19, 58, 59, 67, 80
George III, 14, 15, 16, 17, 19, 20, 21, 35, 45, 79
George IV, 35, 45, 49, 52, 54, 64
Germany, 106, 114, 115, 116, 122, 123, 126
Gladstone, William, 64, 71, 84, 85, 110, 120
Glasgow, 43, 208, 214, 216
GNCTU, 153, 154, 208
Gold Standard, 39, 40, 70
Graham, Sir James, 61, 63, 71, 171, 191, 192, 214
Greece, 109, 111, 112, 113, 116
Grenville, Lord, 19, 21, 93, 97, 98, 99
Grey, Charles Earl, 18, 19, 20, 30, 53, 54, 56, 58, 62, 113, 117
Habeas Corpus, 33, 35, 44, 45, 78
Hampden Clubs, 43, 44
Handloom weavers, 7, 132, 161, 166, 187, 209, 210
Holland, 90, 94, 95, 97, 104, 114
Holy Alliance, 107
Home Office, 32, 46, 47, 50, 61, 159
Hong Kong, 120
House of Commons, 10, 12, 15, 19, 26, 34, 35, 48, 53, 54, 58, 61, 62, 63, 64, 79, 82, 84, 99, 109, 113, 166, 175, 192, 206, 212, 214, 219
House of Lords, 9, 10, 13, 15, 19, 41, 53, 61, 64, 79, 80, 171, 202, 204
Housing, 9, 124, 164, 181, 190, 197, 198, 199, 201, 203, 207
Hunt, Henry, 44, 45, 56
Huskisson, William, 35, 38, 41, 42, 47, 48, 49, 52, 54, 69, 73, 112
Iberian Peninsula, 102, 104, 115, 116
Income tax, 39, 41, 63, 64, 69, 70, 98, 99, 100, 163, 216
India, 15, 23, 26, 90, 95, 96, 97, 106, 117, 118, 119, 126
Industrial revolution, 5, 7, 46, 123, 124, 127, 129, 130, 131, 133, 136, 146, 164, 168

Industrialisation, ii, 1, 26, 40, 87, 123, 124, 126, 131, 134, 135, 140, 181, 195, 219
Interest rates, 17, 23, 38, 39, 40, 51, 56, 65, 68, 73, 74, 90, 105, 106, 111, 141, 156, 198, 199, 202, 221
Investment, 7, 8, 70, 71, 87, 124, 125, 128, 135, 141, 168
Ireland, 2, 4, 6, 9, 10, 13, 16, 20, 21, 22, 51, 52, 55, 59, 61, 73, 74, 76, 77, 78, 79, 80, 81, 82, 83, 84, 85, 86, 87, 88, 89, 96, 100, 124, 142, 181, 209, 217, 235
Irish Parliament, 76, 77
Irish Rising 1798, 78, 79
Irish Union 1801, 10, 20, 51, 79, 80, 81, 83, 84, 88, 108, 121, 152, 153, 154, 167, 191, 208, 213
Iron industry, 3, 5, 6, 36, 41, 123, 125, 126, 128, 130, 131, 132, 133, 134, 136, 148, 151, 165
Italy, 45, 92, 106, 114, 115, 116, 122
Joint-stock companies, 70
Kennington Common 1848, 216, 217
Laibach, 104, 107, 108
Lancashire, 3, 5, 7, 36, 44, 46, 123, 132, 134, 141, 148, 150, 152, 155, 166, 167, 168, 170, 172, 188, 206, 209, 211, 212, 213, 214, 218, 220, 221
Land Plan, 215
Landed gentry, 9, 77, 80, 144, 145, 167, 176, 186, 189, 193, 211
Landed society, 8, 9, 129
Landowners, 9, 37, 38, 40, 56, 64, 68, 74, 75, 76, 77, 78, 80, 87, 135, 140, 141, 187
Leeds, 12, 55, 148, 152, 167, 169, 188, 190, 195, 200, 201, 209, 211, 213, 215
Legal system, 47, 48, 49, 50, 51, 59
Liberal Toryism, 47
Liberalism, 70, 105, 107, 109, 115
Litchfield House, 62
Liverpool Sanitary Act 1846, 201
Liverpool, Lord, 12, 20, 22, 34, 35, 36, 48, 69, 80, 81, 99

INDEX

London, 2, 6, 7, 8, 10, 15, 22, 23, 26, 29, 30, 32, 38, 40, 42, 43, 44, 45, 55, 59, 60, 66, 80, 81, 111, 112, 114, 119, 124, 125, 127, 134, 135, 140, 141, 148, 150, 154, 159, 175, 190, 192, 195, 196, 197, 198, 201, 202, 205, 206, 209, 211, 213, 214, 216, 217, 218, 219, 221, 222, 223
London Corresponding Society, 29, 30, 33
Lovett, William, 211, 212, 213, 215, 218
Low Countries, 26, 90, 93, 94, 98, 102, 104, 106, 114, 115, 116, 137
Loyalism, 28, 31, 32
Luddites, 36, 151, 152
Magistrates, 32, 33, 45, 46, 50, 57, 60, 143, 144, 145, 150, 180, 181, 212
Malthus, Thomas, 41, 157, 181
Manchester, 30, 42, 43, 44, 45, 55, 57, 124, 128, 148, 167, 195, 201, 209, 214, 216, 219
Manufacturing industry, 4, 5, 6, 7, 22, 36, 38, 43, 59, 69, 126, 129, 131, 134, 135, 137, 159, 187, 220
Markets, 4, 5, 8, 9, 25, 26, 38, 40, 44, 70, 71, 72, 73, 101, 123, 124, 126, 129, 130, 139, 144, 148, 150, 151, 154, 157, 158, 160, 173, 180, 181, 182, 183, 184, 187, 210
Maynooth, 64, 85, 86
Mediterranean Sea, 36, 96, 105, 106, 111, 112, 116, 118
Mehemet Ali, 116, 118, 119
Melbourne, William Lamb, Lord, 50, 58, 59, 60, 61, 62, 63, 64, 65, 113, 117, 145, 211
Metropolitan Police, 48, 50, 51, 211
Middle-classes, 8, 30, 31, 43, 44, 56, 66, 74, 78, 84, 86, 90, 155, 157, 158, 159, 162, 174, 179, 184, 187, 195, 208, 209, 211, 213, 214, 216, 218, 221
Midlands, the, 6, 32, 43, 150, 153, 209, 214, 215, 235
Mill, John Stuart, 158, 203

Mines Act 1842, 63, 71, 171, 175, 176
Ministry of all the Talents, 101
Minutes of 1846, 176
Monitorial system, 174
Monroe Doctrine, 104, 110
Moral economy, 9
Mule, spinning, 7, 131, 132
Municipal Corporations Act 1835, 56, 59, 198
Nanking 1842, 104, 120
Napoleon Bonaparte, 3, 34, 35, 36, 96, 97, 100, 101, 102, 103, 104, 105, 108
National Charter Association, 213, 214, 217
National Debt, 23, 39, 40
National Society, 174
Nationalism, 1, 78, 81, 91, 107, 109
Navarino 1827, 104, 112
Nelson, Horatio Lord, 96, 97, 98
Newcomen, Thomas, 131, 133
Newport Rising 1839, 212
Nonconformity, 8, 51, 52, 57, 60, 63, 72, 85, 162, 168, 171, 172, 176
North, Frederick Lord, 14
Norwich, 19, 30
Nottingham, 28, 53, 211, 213, 216
O'Connell, Daniel, 51, 52, 62, 80, 81, 82, 83, 84, 86, 89
O'Connor, Feargus, 209, 211, 213, 214, 215, 216, 217, 218
Oastler, Richard, 166, 167, 168, 169, 170, 172, 173, 187
Ottoman Empire, 26, 97, 104, 106, 111, 116, 118, 119
Owen, Robert, 153, 154, 156, 159
Paine, Thomas, 28, 159
Palmerston, Henry Temple Lord, 91, 92, 104, 106, 110, 112, 113, 114, 115, 116, 117, 118, 119, 120, 121, 122
Parliament, 9, 10, 11, 12, 13, 14, 15, 17, 18, 20, 24, 27, 32, 34, 38, 43, 49, 53, 54, 56, 58, 63, 64, 65, 69, 72, 73, 74, 76, 77, 79, 80, 82, 83, 85, 90, 99, 110, 112, 113, 114, 115, 140, 152, 159, 167, 168,

169, 172, 175, 184, 185, 186, 192, 193, 194, 198, 205, 206, 208, 211, 216, 217, 218, 220, 221
Paternalism, 10, 27, 135, 147, 149, 155, 167, 184
Peel, Sir Robert, i, iii, 12, 34, 35, 39, 40, 47, 48, 49, 50, 51, 52, 58, 59, 61, 62, 63, 64, 65, 66, 67, 68, 69, 70, 71, 72, 73, 74, 75, 76, 80, 81, 82, 83, 84, 85, 86, 88, 170, 171, 172, 191, 204, 208, 214, 220, 221
Pentrich, 35, 44
Perceval, Spencer, 22, 34, 35, 101
Persia, 117
Peterloo Massacre 1819, 35, 45
Pitt, William, i, iii, 14, 15, 16, 17, 18, 19, 20, 21, 22, 23, 24, 25, 26, 27, 31, 32, 33, 39, 41, 51, 69, 76, 77, 78, 79, 90, 92, 93, 94, 96, 97, 98, 99, 100, 222
Poland, 95, 98, 106, 114, 115, 116, 122
Political Economy, 8, 158, 167, 207
Poor Law, ii, 9, 58, 59, 60, 65, 71, 72, 89, 145, 154, 155, 159, 160, 162, 167, 178, 179, 180, 181, 182, 183, 184, 185, 186, 187, 188, 192, 193, 202, 208, 213, 224
Poor Law Amendment Act 1834, 59, 61, 71, 145, 155, 175, 183, 188
Poor Law Amendment Act 1847, 186
Poor Law Commission, 183, 188, 190, 193, 202
Poor Law Commissioners, 184, 192, 193
Population, ii, iii, 1, 2, 3, 7, 10, 13, 25, 28, 29, 30, 31, 32, 56, 57, 65, 73, 76, 77, 88, 89, 90, 106, 124, 127, 128, 129, 134, 135, 138, 141, 142, 148, 149, 155, 156, 157, 159, 171, 178, 179, 181, 183, 184, 187, 188, 189, 195, 198, 207, 208, 215, 218, 219
birth rate, 2, 88
death rate, 2, 197, 205
life expectancy, 2, 179, 203
migration, 2, 25, 87

Portland, Lord William, 16, 17, 18, 19, 20, 21, 22, 32, 101
Portugal, 95, 101, 102, 104, 106, 108, 110, 112, 113, 115, 122
Potatoes, 73, 74, 86, 87, 88, 89
Poverty, 29, 76, 135, 143, 148, 155, 156, 178, 182, 183, 184, 186, 187
Prices, 3, 4, 9, 29, 37, 38, 39, 40, 44, 60, 89, 96, 125, 129, 140, 141, 142, 143, 144, 149, 150, 171, 178, 179, 210
Prisons, 49, 50, 162, 175, 187
Protectionists, 4, 68, 69, 72, 73, 74, 220
Prussia, 26, 36, 91, 93, 94, 95, 97, 98, 100, 102, 104, 105, 106, 107, 108, 111, 112, 115
Public health, ii, 89, 160, 162, 179, 182, 195, 198, 199, 200, 201, 202, 204, 207
Public Health Act 1848, 199, 201, 205
Quadruple Alliance, 107, 108, 115
Queen Caroline, 35, 45
Ragged Schools, 175
Reform Act 1832, 11, 12, 43, 53, 54, 55, 56, 59, 61, 66, 67, 68, 116, 159, 208
Regency crisis 1788-1789, 17, 18
Religious societies, 174, 176
Rent, 8, 55, 60, 88, 141, 145, 147, 148, 197
Respectability, 157, 158, 210
Ricardo, David, 41, 147, 157, 181
Robinson, Frederick, Lord Goderich, 34, 35, 41, 47, 48, 49
Rochdale, 156, 215, 220
Rockingham, Charles Marquesss of, 14, 18
Roman Catholics, 17, 64, 76, 80, 82, 83, 85
Russell, Lord John, 50, 51, 58, 61, 62, 74, 75, 88, 202, 211, 212, 215, 220, 221
Russia, 26, 36, 91, 95, 97, 100, 102, 104, 105, 106, 107, 108, 109, 111, 112, 115, 116, 117, 118, 119, 122
Sadler, Michael, 165, 167, 169, 187

Sanitary Report 1842, 203
Savings banks, 155
Scotland, 2, 3, 4, 6, 7, 9, 10, 13, 55, 123, 139, 142, 143, 168, 202, 208, 209, 211, 212, 214, 235
Self-help, 158, 160, 213
Service sector, 2, 6
Settlement laws, 180, 181
Sheffield, 30, 31, 55, 57, 148, 212, 215
Shelburne, William Earl of, 14
Shropshire, 131, 134
Shuttleworth, James Kay, 176, 177
Six Acts, 35, 45, 47
Slave trade, 59, 105, 120, 121, 125
Slums, 2, 135, 148, 151, 196, 197
Smiles, Samuel, 158, 160
Smuggling, 23, 26, 119
Southey, Robert, 136, 146, 168
Southwood Smith, 169, 204, 205
Spain, 26, 36, 92, 94, 95, 97, 102, 104, 105, 106, 108, 109, 110, 111, 115, 120, 122
Speenhamland system, 143, 178, 181
Standards of living, 7, 147, 149, 164
Stanley, Edward Lord Derby, 61, 74, 84, 85
Steam power, 5, 123, 133, 134
Strikes 1842, 214
Sunday schools, 173, 174, 175
Sweated trades, 7, 148, 154
Swing riots 1830, 9, 54, 60, 144, 145, 182
Tamworth Manifesto 1834, 63, 66
Tariffs, 4, 25, 39, 40, 42, 63, 64, 70, 157
Taxation, 22, 23, 26, 29, 37, 39, 40, 46, 70, 97, 162, 163, 188, 200
Technology, 5, 7, 130, 132, 149, 166
Temperance, 156, 179, 215
Ten Hours Act 1847, 167, 172
Tenant farmers, 3, 8, 9, 38, 55, 74, 84, 89, 182, 220
Ten-Hour movement, 165, 169, 170
Test and Corporation Acts, 27, 29, 32, 34, 35, 48, 52, 82

Textiles, 2, 5, 36, 37, 44, 123, 125, 126, 131, 133, 149, 153, 209
Cotton, 2, 5, 7, 23, 25, 70, 90, 95, 101, 122, 123, 125, 126, 128, 130, 131, 132, 133, 136, 148, 152, 166, 167, 195, 208, 215, 218, 220
Woollen industry, 5, 43, 77, 132, 151, 166, 219
Tolpuddle Martyrs, 61, 153, 154, 208
Tories, i, 4, 11, 12, 18, 20, 21, 30, 34, 37, 47, 48, 49, 50, 52, 54, 57, 61, 63, 64, 65, 66, 67, 68, 69, 71, 72, 73, 75, 82, 115, 117, 167, 168, 172, 175, 182, 187, 221, 222
Tory Radicalism, 167
Trade
  exports, 42, 69, 70, 93, 101, 125, 126
  imports, 3, 37, 64, 69, 70, 73
Trade unions, 42, 46, 61, 147, 152, 153, 155, 156, 214
Transport
  canals, 5, 9, 87, 124, 128, 134
  railways, 6, 42, 70, 71, 87, 88, 125, 127, 128, 129, 133, 134, 135, 136, 148, 160
  roads, 87, 127, 129, 140, 146
Troppau, 104, 107, 108
Unemployment, 7, 29, 37, 42, 44, 145, 146, 147, 155, 166, 169, 178, 179, 180, 183, 196, 210
United Irishmen, 78
United Provinces, 26, 93, 106
United States, 16, 25, 42, 74, 101, 110, 120, 121, 126
Unkiar Skelessi, Treaty of, 104, 117
Urban poverty, 185
Vansittart, Nicholas, 39, 40, 41, 47, 48
Verona, 104, 107, 109
Victoria, Queen, 62, 64
Wages, 6, 7, 9, 29, 37, 44, 46, 135, 140, 142, 143, 144, 145, 147, 148, 152, 155, 158, 169, 171, 177, 179, 181, 182, 183, 190, 209, 210

Wales, 2, 3, 4, 6, 9, 10, 13, 18, 50, 53, 56, 123, 124, 127, 134, 135, 139, 141, 153, 174, 175, 188, 190, 202, 209, 212, 235

Water, 5, 71, 90, 93, 111, 128, 132, 133, 138, 163, 165, 196, 197, 198, 199, 200, 201, 202, 203, 204, 205, 206, 207

Waterloo 1815, i, 34, 35, 36, 92, 99, 103, 105, 192

Waterpower, 5, 123, 132, 133, 134

Watt, James, 130, 133

Wellington, Arthur Wellesley, Duke of, 34, 35, 36, 41, 48, 49, 52, 53, 54, 63, 64, 80, 81, 82, 84, 96, 102, 104, 109, 110, 112, 113, 114, 117

West Country, 134, 209, 212

West Indies, 70, 95, 97, 99

West Riding, 43, 134, 168, 170, 188, 209, 221

Wheat, 3, 4, 36, 37, 38, 63, 73, 88, 101, 125, 138, 141, 142, 143, 144

Whigs, i, 12, 14, 15, 18, 19, 20, 21, 22, 29, 34, 45, 50, 53, 54, 56, 57, 58, 59, 60, 61, 62, 63, 64, 65, 66, 67, 71, 112, 145, 154, 169, 172, 208, 209, 212, 221

William IV, 35, 53, 54, 58, 62, 63, 67

Women, 2, 7, 28, 49, 63, 71, 72, 115, 149, 166, 171, 172, 173, 179, 190, 210, 219

Work organisation
domestic production, 2, 5, 7, 38, 73, 84, 93, 97, 123, 124, 126, 129, 132, 134, 148, 149, 155, 164, 165, 179
mining, 5, 123, 133, 134, 148, 153, 162, 171, 215
workshops, 131, 149, 197

Workhouse, 178, 184, 186, 188, 189, 190, 191, 192, 193

Working-classes, ii, iii, 7, 13, 30, 32, 36, 38, 42, 43, 46, 56, 60, 146, 147, 148, 149, 153, 154, 155, 158, 174, 175, 176, 178, 179, 188, 196, 197, 199, 208, 213

Yorkshire, 3, 5, 11, 36, 132, 134, 140, 150, 151, 166, 167, 169, 170, 189, 209, 211, 213, 214

About the Author

Richard Brown has published fifty-three print and Kindle books and over 60 articles and papers on nineteenth century history. He is the author of a successful blog, The History Zone, which has a wide audience among pupils, students and researchers. He is also a Fellow of both the Royal Historical Society and the Historical Association.

Recent publications

Disrupting the British World, 1600-1980, (Authoring History), 2017
Famine, Fenians and Freedom, 1830-1882, (Authoring History), 2017
Three Rebellions: Canada, South Wales and Australia, (Authoring History), 2016.
Roger of Sicily: Portrait of a Ruler, (Authoring History), 2016.
Robert Guiscard: Portrait of a Warlord, (Authoring History), 2016.
Suger: The Life of Louis VI 'the Fat', (Authoring History), 2016.
The Chartists, Regions and Economies, (Authoring History), 2016. Also available in a Kindle version.
Chartism: Localities, Spaces and Places, The North, Scotland, Wales and Ireland, (Authoring History), 2015. Also available in a Kindle version.
Chartism: Localities, Spaces and Places, The Midlands and the South, (Authoring History), 2015. Also available in a Kindle version.
Sex, Work and Politics: Women in Britain, 1780-1945, (Authoring History), 2014.
Chartism: Rise and Demise, (*Reconsidering Chartism,* Authoring History), 2014. Also available in a Kindle version.
Before Chartism: Exclusion and Resistance, (*Reconsidering Chartism,* Authoring History), 2014. Also available in a Kindle version.
'A Peaceable Kingdom': Essays on Nineteenth Century Canada, (Authoring History), 2013. Also available in a Kindle version.
Settler Australia, 1780-1880, Vol. 1: Settlement, Protest and Control, Vol. 2: Eureka and Democracy, (Authoring History), 2013. Also available in a Kindle version.
Rebellion in Canada, 1837-1885, Vol. 1: Autocracy, Rebellion and Liberty, Vol. 2: The Irish, the Fenians and the Métis, (Authoring History), 2012. Also available in a Kindle version.

Printed in Great Britain
by Amazon